End

When I was growing up, God used Andy in a powerful way to help me become a more developed worship leader, and a more devoted worshipper. A few years on he's still pouring out the insights and encouragements. This wonderful new book will instruct and inspire many a worshipper of Jesus.

— MattRedman
Worship Leader, Songwriter and Author

Many readers will know and love Andy Park as a worship leader. In "The Worship Journey" you will come to appreciate the thinking Andy has done at the intersection of worship, spiritual formation and mission. Andy has the qualities and being and intellect to be a guiding voice in these matters.

— Todd Hunter
Founder: Churches for the Sake of Others, Anglican Bishop
Author: Giving Church Another Chance

The Worship Journey is much, much more than a text on worship. It is a literal treasure house of wisdom for living. Drawing honestly from his own life experience alongside the wisdom of both ancient and contemporary fellow travelers, Andy enticingly calls us into a life truly worth living!

— Gary Best
National Team Leader, Vineyard Churches Canada

This book came to me at just the right time. I needed to read it, and re-read it. Andy skillfully gets to the heart of worship — the heart of living — and unearths all the essential roots to inspire the soul towards a more authentic walk with God. I felt as if I was being mentored by a wise, experienced, and humble journeyman. You shouldn't just read this book. You should ponder it, digest it, and live it."

— **Paul Baloche**
Worship Leader and Songwriter

The Worship Journey places worship of the triune God right where it should be — in the center of our lives. Worship for Andy is not just what we do when we sing songs of praise. It is something we do in all of our lives. I strongly recommend this wonderfully warm and thoughtful reflection on life's supreme activity — worship of God.

— **Bert Waggoner**
National Director, Vineyard Churches USA

Andy is a man of integrity and humility. He lives a life of worship that is inspiring and infectious to anyone around him. In this wonderful devotional book we catch key insights and words of wisdom that will cultivate in us worshipping hearts.

— **Tim Hughes**
Worship Leader and Songwriter

Once again, Andy Park has unpacked for us a vital vision of worship (and its embodiment in ordinary lives) that is both astounding and practical. He is truly one of today's greatest gifts to contemporary worship thinkers and those who care deeply about an incarnational worship spirituality. Always articulate and careful to turn over each stone, Andy delivers penetrating insights that will change us if we let them. If we are willing to invest our lives in the timeless approach to the life of worship that this book unearths, and do so in a way that exposes our culture to the compelling way of Jesus, we will have all come a very long way as worshipers of the living God. Thank you, Andy, for always tending to the soul as you both challenge and encourage — we are stronger because of it. I highly commend this work of art to every spiritual leader, and to every follower of Jesus.

— **Dan Wilt**, M.Min.
Learning Community Director, The Worship And Arts
Institute, worshiptraining.com

It has been said that worship is so much more than the songs we sing. In *"The Worship Journey"*, veteran pastor, worship leader, and songwriter Andy Park does a masterful job of calling us back to the heart of what it really means to worship God. This is important reading for anyone seeking to go deeper in their *"worship journey"* with our Lord and God.

— **Casey Corum**
Worship leader, songwriter, and Executive Producer for
Vineyard Music

I've been affected by Andy's songs and leadership for many years now and this book portrays what I've seen him live out in every day life. I love that he included Linda's stories - they were very moving for me. After over thirty years of leading worship, I found this book challenged and encouraged me to continue on in my journey as a leader and to finish the race well, even if I end up mostly plodding along! This is not a book to be read only by worship leaders and those who serve in worship - it will inspire all worshippers! And, I will absolutely be contacting him to lead a retreat for the community I lead!

— Cindy Rethmeier
Songwriter and Worship Leader, Holy Trinity Church, Costa Mesa, California

I believe that the greatest sermon we'll ever preach is the life that we live. This is a characteristic strongly evident in Andy Park's life. He doesn't just talk or write about worship, nor does he just lead worship; he lives a life of worship. His desire for a deeper more intimate relationship with the Lord compels him to his knees. It is out of these passionate times with God that many of his songs have been birthed as has his newest book, *The Worship Journey: A Quest of Heart, Mind and Strength.* This book is a must read for anyone longing for a deeper understanding of the true heart of worship.

— Rauna L. May
Pastor, New Hope Christian Fellowship, O'ahu

Andy's heart to pass on pearls of wisdom comes through richly in this book. Andy was one of first people to mentor me as a worship leader and songwriter, and through this book, he is encouraging and mentoring many more. I'm really thankful that he took the time to document his journey!

— **Brian Doerksen**
Worship Leader, Songwriter and Author

It seems to me that this is vintage Andy Park. Having worked for years with his earlier work (used in education and training), I can see the same author, but also an author who has moved on in the journey of discipleship.

Worship is related more deliberately to real life stories and encounters. It's beginning, centre and life is Christ-centeredness, and the grace that comes from him. This is the foundation of all intimacy with God. With this foundation we walk the journey of discipleship, one that often includes the kind of worship that articulates the "lament" of suffering. This is not cheap grace. Once it begins it's way in us, deep inner transformation follows, probing into the depths of our inherent weakness for idolatry and greed. Then, if we engage in true worship that flows from grace, mission and mercy must be the inevitable outcome.

This content is richly embellished with a use of biblical texts that shows years of reading and reflection, along with ancient Christian classics and contemporary authors of spirituality. Quite a mix! This book will call the reader to Christ, to worship, and to mission.

— **Derek Morphew**
Architect and developer of Vineyard Bible Institute academic and online, a Vineyard Churches theologian

THE
WORSHIP
JOURNEY

A Quest of Heart, Mind, and Strength

ANDY PARK

FOREWORD BY: MARK D. ROBERTS

AUGUSTUS INK BOOKS

The Worship Journey: A Quest of Heart, Mind, and Strength
by Andy Park

AUGUSTUS INK BOOKS

Published by:
AUGUSTUS INK BOOKS
Woodinville, WA 98077
http://www.harmonpress.com/augustusinkbooks

ISBN: 978-1-935959-03-8

Library of Congress Control Number: 2010917213

Dedication

I dedicate this book to every traveler who chooses the road of worshiping Jesus. Whether you are just beginning your journey or you are several decades into it, may God continue to reveal his marvelous love to you. May you continue to know him as your closest and most trustworthy Companion. May he give you faith for today's stretch of road, and vision for the rest of the journey. May your latter years be as exciting and full of surprises from God as the first year. May you hear his voice in a thousand different ways, filling you with joy and helping you make the right turns along the way. May you never grow tired of doing good and bearing fruit in his kingdom. May your life be like a love song to the Lord.

Acknowledgements

Thanks to my wife and best friend, Linda, who has been my companion and greatest encourager along this journey of life and worship. Thank you for generously giving me the freedom to follow the path I've seen open up before me, and for joining me on this wild and wonderful journey for the last thirty years. Thank you for your close reading of the *Journey* manuscript and for adding some great examples from your own life of what it means to love and worship God.

Thanks to Gary Best for many years of friendship and great teaching. As I look through the pages of this book I realize that many of these themes have been deeply rooted in me because of your influence.

Thanks to the many authors I quote in this book who have been my mentors from afar, shaping my understanding of God and helping me to articulate these truths. Among the most influential are Richard Foster, Dallas Willard, Philip Yancey, Eugene Peterson, John Eldredge, Erwin McManus, Gary Beebe, Don Williams and Todd Hunter. Thanks to Peter Davids and Mark Roberts for being very helpful theological advisors.

Thanks to Mark Anderson for faithfully delivering the word from the Lord in 2003 to me about someday "writing another book". Thanks to the many friends who have shown me what worship is, especially Bill Bower and Mac and Louise Jardine.

Acknowledgements

Thanks to my friends who read portions of the manuscript and gave me helpful input: John McLeod, Darcy White, Ryan Flanigan and Ken Redekop.

Contents

Foreword by Mark D. Roberts

What is worship? If you were to ask that question of the average Westerner fifty years ago, it's likely that you would have heard about going to church on Sunday morning, sitting uprightly in sanctuary pews, singing hymns accompanied by an organ, listening to a sermon, and, perhaps, receiving Communion. Worship was an activity characterized by reverence, rationality, and regularity. It may not have been much fun, but it was required of faithful Christians and expected of patriotic citizens.

Then, something happened. As the Sixties upset the familiar structures of Western society, the church and her worship were not immune. I will never forget the first "8:19 Service" at my home church, the First Presbyterian Church of Hollywood. In a sanctuary that normally featured one of the finest choirs in America, we were led in worship by long-haired young men and women who played guitars and sang about Jesus in a folk-rock genre. This was bold, edgy, and controversial in 1969, when guitars were almost never to be found in church sanctuaries.

What I experienced on that watershed morning at Hollywood Pres caught on like wildfire, especially in Southern California. Soon, Calvary Chapel sponsored standing-room-only concerts with Christian bands and founded Maranatha! Music, which popularized Christian folk-rock through records and cassette tapes. Meanwhile, the Vineyard was born in the homes of popular

Christian rock stars. By the early eighties, the Vineyard's version of folk-rock, music-saturated worship began to impact not just new churches in Southern California, but also thousands of traditional churches throughout the country. That impact has grown by leaps and bounds in the last three decades, touching believers throughout the world.

Thus, if you were to ask the "What is worship?" question today, odds are that you might hear about music and singing, especially if you're asking someone under forty. In many segments of the church today, "Let's worship" means "Let's sing worship songs." These compositions, which promote intimacy with God, incorporate mind, body, and emotions. For many worshipers, the emotions matter most of all. Real worship happens when one feels peace, joy, love or some other manifestation of God's presence while singing to him.

Andy Park has been a major leader in the transformation of worship during the last half-century. As a pastor and worship leader for the Vineyard, he has been in the center of the action, with extensive experience leading people into God's presence through contemporary music. Several of the songs written by Andy have become international favorites, most notably, "In the Secret," which expresses the worshiper's desire for deeper, more intimate knowledge of God. Andy's pervasive influence on contemporary worship has also been felt through his mentoring of other prominent worship leaders and songwriters.

Thus, it comes as no surprise that Andy has written a new book on worship: *The Worship Journey: A Quest of Heart, Mind and Strength*. This is especially true if you're familiar with his first book: *To Know You More: Cultivating the Heart of the Worship Leader* (InterVarsity Press, 2004). This book, which I've used when teaching graduate level courses on worship, testifies to Andy's skill as a writer of prose, as well as his wisdom in the facets of worship.

We might expect someone with Andy's skill, experience, and vision to write a book about worship.

But we might not expect some of the things Andy has to say about worship in *The Worship Journey*. For example, he writes: "Just as we can erroneously think that believing the right doctrine makes us good Christians regardless of how we're behaving, we can be duped into thinking that singing is the main course in a menu of worship."

Then there are Andy's reflections on the role of feelings in worship: "The truth is this: when we behold Jesus on the cross, and all it means for us, we don't have to feel anything else to have a valid worship experience." He explains how this challenges our cultural assumptions about worship: "We have many songs these days about being in the Father's warm embrace and being filled with His comforting Spirit. I love those songs. But in our culture of narcissism, we could be led to believe that intimacy with God is all about *feeling* loved. It's as if we believe that if *we can get a warm, fuzzy experience in worship then we have been intimate with God.* I really enjoy every *feeling* that comes from worshiping Jesus, but friendship with God is bigger than that." In fact, according to Andy, "respect, reverence, and obedience" are central to a truly intimate, worshipful relationship with God.

You might not be surprised if I, as a Reformed Presbyterian, were to make such observations about worship, music, and feelings. But given Andy's leadership in a worldwide worship movement that has emphasized singing and helped millions of people to feel God's presence as they sing, you might wonder where he's getting this stuff in *The Worship Journey*.

He solves this puzzle throughout the book. First, Andy's understanding of worship is grounded on clear, careful reading of Scripture. The claims in this book are drawn from God's Word, which is Andy's chief authority for faith and practice. Second, Andy has been instructed by some of the greatest Christian thinkers, including both classic and contemporary spiritual writers. Third, he has learned from the experiences of Christians throughout the world as they seek to worship God with integrity.

Last, but surely not least, Andy has drawn freely from his own experience as a Christian on a worship journey with Jesus. Throughout the pages of this book, Andy shares his discoveries, joys, prayers, sorrows, and struggles. His candor and authenticity invite us to come along with him on his pilgrimage into deeper, truer, and fuller worship of the living God.

Andy surely believes that songs and emotions are central to worship. But, he knows that, in biblical perspective, worship includes far more. "If we become focused on music to the neglect of a life of worship, we're missing God's heart. If we step off the path, we become ingrown, narrow sighted and imbalanced. Because worship is all encompassing, and not limited to singing songs, I wanted to write a book about the *life of worship* instead of the *music of worship*." This is an apt description of *The Worship Journey*, a book about living a worshipful life every moment of every day.

Andy explains that "to honor Jesus in every activity is to worship him." Thus he urges us to ask: "How is a heart of worship worked out as you mow the lawn, drive on the freeway, surf the Internet, watch TV, teach school, hammer nails, and relate to your family members?" According to Andy, true worship also has to do with how we spend our time and money, how we confront our addictions and seek justice for the oppressed, how we work in the world and how we rest in God's grace.

Though worship is something we do for the Lord with all that we are, Andy continually reminds us that worship is not something we do on our own. It is our response to the grace of God in Jesus Christ. As Andy writes, "Trying to live a life of worship is an unbearable burden without the foundation of grace resounding in our hearts." Moreover, Andy's teaching and example remind us that we worship in the power of the Holy Spirit who regularly guides us, helping us to know the heart of God. The Spirit joins us to other Christians who encourage and challenge us to offer whole life worship to the Lord.

I could say so much more about this book and why I find it compelling. But, rather than read what I have to say about *The Worship Journey*, you'd be much better off actually reading the book for yourself. So I'll sign off now with a prayer: May God use this book to renew you in his love and refresh you in his grace, so that you might indeed offer to him all that you are in a life of worship. In the name of Jesus, our Lord, Savior, and Friend. Amen.

— Mark D. Roberts
Senior Director and Scholar-in-Residence for Laity Lodge
www.laitylodge.org
http://blog.beliefnet.com/markdroberts/

Chapter 1
A New Life

*Christianity is the "good news" that beauty, truth,
and goodness are found in a person.*
— Leonard Sweet and Frank Viola

I didn't have many close friends in high school, so I suppose you could say that by the time I entered university in 1975 I was ready for a friend who would accept me no matter what. And that's what I got. But this friend of mine was unlike any friend I'd ever had. He was the most beautiful, attractive, captivating personality I had ever met, and I didn't have to wait until the weekend or the next Wednesday night to see him.

It was about this time that I visited a Vineyard church for the first time. I was instantly mesmerized by the transcendence of the worship experience. It wasn't just singing; I saw people engaged in a dance of adoration of God, swimming in a sea of God's love. I was captivated by the realness of it and left with my appetite fully alive to the prospect of pressing in to knowing God for myself.

The windows of heaven opened up to me that year. Until then I didn't know that God spoke to people, and I certainly had no idea that he would make himself real to me. Yet from this point on everything was different. I had encountered the loving God and nothing would ever be the same again.

The official start of my journey with God was in 1975. It was the time when, — to borrow a phrase from *The Chronicles of Narnia* — I entered "through the wardrobe" into another world. It was the beginning of a wonderful adventure, an adventure made up of countless smaller ones, a journey made up of many voyages.

I found "goodness in a person" when I met the Lord. I found someone I could talk to, who would listen to me. I found someone who loved me no matter what. As a freshman Christian, I could be found sitting in my room of the fraternity at UCLA. (A fraternity led by Christians who are now pastors). Reading the Bible felt more like listening to someone who was right there in the room talking to me, and day-by-day, I could feel my life's story being re-written. Up until then, my "story" consisted of sports, guitars and studies, with an aim of getting a good job in the near future. Then I became part of God's story, growing to know him day by day. The most exciting adventure of all was just beginning.

Playing the guitar used to be just another form of recreation, but from this point on it became truly re-*creational*. The Holy Spirit was renewing me through the creative act of making music. It was like going from black and white TV to a hi-def color screen with surround-sound; a fourth dimension opened up. Finally, I had something to sing about, someone to sing to. Through the gift of music, the Holy Spirit opened the eyes of my heart to see Jesus.

As this books starts out it's essential that we do a little tuning up, to ensure that we are going to move on from here without too much disharmony. And so this is our bottom-E string; the worship life is all about *knowing a Person*.

> The characteristic of Christianity lies in the fact that its source, depth, and riches are involved with the knowledge of God's Son. It matters not how much we know of methods or doctrines or power. What really matters is the knowledge of the Son of God.[1]

Christianity is more than a philosophy or an ideology. It

is more than a form of morality, social ethic or worldview. We don't follow a doctrine of Christ, we follow Christ Himself. We don't worship a book, we worship a Person. Knowing doctrine is secondary, knowing Jesus is primary. The gospel reminds us of this continually with the Son of God walking among people, talking, healing, helping, making Himself know-able in the clearest possible form. "We can never let our life with Jesus turn into a depersonalized set of principles. Being yoked with Jesus is a new way of living a new story — the story of God."[2]

The idea that we are on a journey with God is nothing new, and I am sure that other writers have used similar words to describe their own experience of worship. Yet I am not interested in coming up with a brand new way to present an ancient truth. For me, as I have already pointed out, this is about faith; this is personal. This story is as old as it gets.

I want to tell you what I know about worship. I want to share what I've begun to understand about it over the years. Across the following pages you might end up surprised, challenged or intrigued. Some of it you will agree with, some you might not. But at the end what matters most is not whether I have convinced you to see the world exactly as I see it. No, what matters most is the journey: your journey, my journey, our journeys. What matters most is that you close this book for the last time determined, inspired and a little better equipped to travel the coming stages of your own journey of worship of God.

A New Creation, A New Identity

So, yes, worship of God is not worship of a static object, concept or thing. When we talk about worship, we are talking about our relationship with our heavenly Father. And just as real worship flows out of "aha" moments of encountering Jesus, it also flows out of our new identity as children of God who are born of the Spirit.

Now, I've led musical worship in many countries, including Hong Kong. I don't speak Chinese, but I've led worship in Chinese by mimicking the sounds of the words. People tell me I'm pretty good at it, but I get busted whenever someone comes up after the worship set and tries to actually have a conversation with me. While I know the gist of each line I've sung in Chinese, the basic truth is that I'm faking it.

Unless we have been reborn and transformed by the Holy Spirit, singing worship songs is a foreign activity. It's gibberish. It doesn't mean anything. It is only at the point of our conversion that God gives us a *new heart* — an enlightened *worshiping heart*. It is from that heart that our new native language flows.

When we are born of God and become citizens of heaven, we receive his implanted Holy Spirit and it causes our hearts to be in tune with Jesus. He writes his laws on our hearts. As citizens of heaven and members of a spiritual family, we understand and speak a common language of worship. We become sensitive to the ways of the indwelling Holy Spirit and we learn to quickly respond to his urgings "for his Spirit joins with our spirit to affirm that we are God's children" (Rom 8:16 NLT).

My wife Linda describes her conversion like this:

> Meeting Jesus was like coming to life; I was dead then I was alive, I was totally blind and not *aware* of being blind and suddenly I could see. Like a baby being born, moving from one world into another. I love singing about this transformation.

Each of us, when we are born anew in Christ, find the essence of our hearts changed. The old man dies and we are raised to life, leaving us spiritually joined to Jesus. "But he who unites himself with the Lord is one with him in spirit" (1 Cor 6:17). We actually become new people: "Therefore, if anyone is in Christ, he is a new creation; the old has gone, the new has come!" (2 Cor 5:17). Amazingly, in our new state of being "alive in Christ," we have the capacity to discern or understand things that were previously hidden from us: "The man without the Spirit does not accept the things that come from the Spirit of God, for they are foolishness to him, and he cannot understand them, because they are spiritually discerned" (1 Cor. 2:14).

This changes the whole ballgame. The fact that we can communicate with God is foundational in the life and language of a worshipper. It was a reality that hit me hard as a young Christian; suddenly my mind was illumined by the light of Christ as I had a new language of prayer that sprang from an enlivened spirit. I experienced a new access to God that I had never known was possible. As a member of God's household, I could hear his voice ringing throughout the house. All that I had to do was respond, as "Worship is our responding to the overtures of love from the heart of the Father."[3]

Like I said, this changes everything.

Even after almost three decades of marriage, spending time with Linda never gets old. Why? Because we're on an adventure together and we're in love. And so it is with God when we understand that his offer to us is to spend time with him in relationship, rather than just as consumers of sterile information. Get this right and we can experience an amazing sense of fulfillment and completeness as we worship, we can become " … *complete through [our] union with Christ*, who is the head over every ruler and authority" (Col 2:10 NLT, emphasis added). Words can't describe this sense of being *complete* in Christ. It can only be experienced. Even if we don't "feel" anything, it remains a fixed reality.

In *Jesus Manifesto*, Leonard Sweet and Frank Viola talk about the "Great Dance," a term the Cappadocian Fathers used to define the communion among the members of the Trinity. The word is *perichoresis*, which means to "move about" or "dance around." Just as the Father, Son and Holy Spirit share their lives in a divine "dance," we are invited into a "dance" with the Trinity, which leads to entering into our true God-given identity.

"Christians have a *perichoretic* relationship with Christ. That relationship makes you more fully yourself than you could have ever been apart from him. The gospel is not the eradication of you; it is not self-negation. Rather, the gospel is the radical reconfiguration of the "self" within a relational context. The old self has been put to death, and the new self in Christ has taken its place. And your new self is the real "you."[4]

In this age of diminishing oil reserves and increasing global demands for petroleum, it's fascinating to read about new types of fuels and engines being developed. One of the world's leading hydrogen cell companies is located where I reside in Vancouver. They're developing an engine unlike the old internal combustion type that runs most of the cars on the road today. The new engine requires a different kind of fuel — it runs on oxygen instead of petroleum.

When I was born again, it was like God put a new type of engine in me. The new "me" was thirsty for the fuel that God gives, not the old stuff my previous engine craved. When his disciples were worrying about what fuel they were going to take on board, Jesus said " … I have food to eat that you know nothing about" (John 4:32). We need the fuel of God's living words, supplied by his indwelling Spirit.

In the Royal Family

I wasn't looking for Jesus when he found me. Before I woke up to God, I was a wandering teenager. I had no plans to make Jesus the center of my life, but he chose me. He showed me who I was created to be. To quote Annie Dillard: "I had been my whole life a bell, and never knew it until at that moment I was lifted and struck."[5]

When the Lord caught my attention I gained a radically new self-image, all tied up in being his child. His revealed love prompted me to call out to him, just as it did for Paul: "For you did not receive a spirit that makes you a slave again to fear, but you received the Spirit of sonship. And by him we cry, "Abba, Father." The Spirit himself testifies with our spirit that we are God's children" (Rom 8:15-16).

Worship is a means of understanding our own identity. Tim Keller says:

> A sign of real worship is that you feel like a priest and a king. Worship of the true God makes you feel as glorious as he is ... you feel as royal and as powerful as a king and as pure and acceptable as a priest.[6]

I don't always get these feelings when I pray or sing, but it happens consistently. These moments serve as markers of eternal reality, or " ... as a deposit, guaranteeing what is to come" (2 Cor 5:5).

No matter what your station in life — banker, landscaper or shopkeeper — you see the *real you* when you draw near to God: "We are, all of us, never-ceasing spiritual beings with a unique eternal calling to count for good in God's great universe."[7] You have an earthly occupation, but that's just a piece of you. In worship you take a journey back to your true identity, your true home. You become aware once again at the deepest level of your being, you are a child of God. You've sensed him making his home in your heart, and you know that is only a foretaste of heaven.

I remember playing the song *I Have Found*[8] while leading worship in Hong Kong several years ago:

> I have found such joy in my salvation since I gave my heart to you.
>
> I have found *the reason I'm living*, so in love, so near to You ... (emphasis added)

Though I had discovered my "reason for living" many years before then, I needed to see it again. As I sang these words, fresh revelation came to me about just how God felt about me. The lines of communication between Creator and Created opened up little wider and I could see my eternal destiny with a little more clarity.

Paul The Worshipper

If there's one man in the Bible who saw his eternal destiny clearly — a man who embodies a life of worship — it is Paul. Paul knew Jesus firsthand despite never meeting him. Freed from a law-based religion, he was consumed with knowing a glorious person. Knowing and serving Jesus was his life's sole purpose and his life was all about embracing Christ and being embraced by Him. His words to the church in Philippi are clear: "Compared to the high privilege of knowing Christ Jesus as my Master, firsthand, everything I once thought I had going for me is insignificant — dog dung. I've dumped it all in the trash so that I could embrace Christ and be embraced by him" (Phil 3:8 *The Message*).

There seems to be no duplicity in Paul's life — he walks out his worship in every facet of life. He's one of the great heroes of the Bible yet we see his human weakness and everyday struggles as well. We see him viciously attacked for spreading the gospel, yet he finds a way to rejoice through it all. As he follows Jesus, giving himself as a "living sacrifice," we see his sacrificial love for the people he pastors. We see him working harder than all the rest of the apostles by the grace of God, both in tent-making and pastoral ministry. In all he does, he endeavors to please the Lord. In looking at Paul's life, we see a model of all-pervasive worship.

A High Class Jewish Boy

I'll be referring to the Apostle Paul many times throughout

this book, picturing childhood neighbor Kenny in my mind as I do so. I think of Kenny when I think of Paul because Kenny came from a good, middle class Jewish family that lived out in the suburbs, and that's kind of what I think Paul was like. But instead of Los Angeles, Paul was born in Tarsus, an ancient city on par with today's New York City or London, England. It had all the reputation, all the education and all the culture you could wish for, and there's no surprise that when the Roman soldiers were about to put Paul in chains in Jerusalem, he said to them: " ... I am a Jew, from Tarsus in Cilicia, a citizen of no ordinary city" (Acts 21:39).

Paul's family ran their own tent-making business and had the means to send their boy to the homeland Jerusalem to study. Anyone who had the means to pay for their son to be educated in another country would have been wealthy. Paul was *born* a citizen of Rome (Acts 22:27), so his father must have been a Roman citizen. For a Jewish man in Tarsus to be a Roman citizen was an exceptional distinction; the few Roman citizens who were inhabitants of Tarsus would have been considered a social elite.[9]

We know that Paul's family was very devout in the Jewish faith. Though he was born in Tarsus, his parents made sure that he received an orthodox education in Jerusalem, studying at the feet of Gamaliel, the leading Pharisee of his day. In his appeal to King Agrippa in Jerusalem, Paul says, " ... according to the strictest sect of our religion, I lived as a Pharisee" (Acts 26:5). The term "Pharisee" makes us think of legalism and hypocrisy because of Jesus' sharp confrontation of this group. But we should remember that before Jesus introduced a new covenant, this was the best option available for a Jewish family who truly wanted to serve God. Beneath the layers of legalism that had accumulated through the generations, there was likely a genuine desire to love and honor God.

In his religious zeal as a Pharisee, Paul " ... intensely ...

persecuted the church of God and tried to destroy it" (Gal 1:13). Paul helped round up Christians to be brought to trial, "… breathing out murderous threats against the Lord's disciples …" (Acts 9:1). He even went beyond the borders of Judea to find Christians and bring them to trial and punishment (Acts 26:11). "When the chief priests and their associates launched their attack on the disciples, Paul came forward as their eager lieutenant."[10]

Years later, after his conversion, Paul sorely regretted his vicious attacks against Christians: "For I am the least of the apostles and do not even deserve to be called an apostle, because I persecuted the church of God." But that big mistake set up an incredible opportunity for a much bigger experience of the grace of God.

Jesus is the Center

When I got a glimpse of God's unfathomable beauty, wisdom and riches of glory, I became a worshiper. It is an eternal truth that seeing leads to worshiping. Day by day we all need to think about his incomparable worth. How true it is that:

> … both the center and the circumference of the Christian life is none other than the person of Christ. All other things, including those related to Him, are eclipsed by the sight of His peerless worth.[11]

Paul understood this and his writings continually point the way to Christ-centered living, the sort where Jesus is the beginning, middle and end of a worshipful life. He understands that preoccupation with Jesus is the starting place — and the only way to sustain — a worship-life.

It is one of the greatest lessons to learn that meditating on the profound truth about Jesus will move us towards profound worship: "Worship isn't merely sentiment or emotion, worship keys off the exposition of truth. It ignites out of truth, it launches out of truth; it explodes off of truth. Worship is logic on fire."[12]

Paul's whole life was a pursuit of Jesus — to know Jesus and reflect Jesus' life to the world. "Paul was consumed with his crucified, risen and reigning Lord."[13] Even the number of times Paul refers to Christ in his letters is astounding (Col 1, Eph 1, Phil 1), and yet he remains aware of the fact that the love and unfathomable riches of Christ can be known and yet are "unsearchable."

"Jesus Christ is like a vast ocean. He is too immense to fully explore, and too rich to fathom. You are like a bottle. *The wonder of the gospel is that the bottle is in the ocean, and the ocean is in the bottle*" (emphasis added).[14] The Lord of glory is in me, and I am surrounded by His omnipresence. I could spend weeks thinking about that concept and still be amazed, particularly when adding in the fact that he fills the universe yet he has chosen to live in me!

We see in Paul's life that "knowing" Jesus is not just head-knowledge or sound doctrine, it is intimate knowledge of the mystery of Christ: " ... God has chosen to *make known* among the Gentiles the *glorious riches of this mystery, which is Christ in you, the hope of glory*" (Col 1:27, emphasis added). The mystery of the ages is living inside us, his Spirit co-mingling with ours.

In *The Jesus Manifesto*, Sweet and Viola point to Paul's letter to the Colossians in which we see:

> ... a stunningly elegant vision of Christ — exalted, glorious, high and lifted up ... .Paul's goal was to strip away every distraction that was being held before their eyes and leave them with nothing but Christ. He dared to displace all rules, regulations, laws, and everything else that religion offers, with a person — the Lord Jesus Himself .... He presented a panoramic vision of Jesus that exhausts the minds of mortal men.[15]

Sweet and Viola go on to say, "The need today is for the scales to fall from our eyes so that we may see the infinite greatness of our Lord."[16] I say "Amen" to that.

Behold the Lamb of God

> The Hebrew word for "behold" is used over one thousand times in the Old Testament. Why? It's simple — we have a hard time listening! The Hebrew word translated "behold" is "an interjection demanding attention, "look!" …. The term emphasizes the immediacy, the here-and-now-ness, of the situation.[17]

Jesus is the here-and-now God. He said to his disciples "the kingdom of heaven is near. (Matt 4:17). We need to stop and take note.

One day John the Baptist saw his cousin Jesus walking towards him and said "*Behold*! The Lamb of God who takes away the sin of the world!" (John 1:29 NKJV, emphasis added). He didn't see his cousin, though John was the son of his aunt Elizabeth. He wasn't seeing with *natural eyes*, but with spiritual sight. He saw the sacrificial Lamb. John *saw* with enlightened eyes.

The next day, John was with Andrew and another of his disciples. "And looking at Jesus as He walked, he said, "… Behold the Lamb of God!" (John 1:36 NKJV) Jesus invited the disciples to come to the place he was staying. *After spending the day with Jesus*, "The first thing Andrew did was to find his brother Simon and tell him, 'We have found the Messiah'" (John 1:41, emphasis added).

After *spending the day with Jesus*, Andrew knew he had found the Messiah.

The story of their visit with Jesus takes me back to my university room in 1975. I was over the moon at meeting God. But finding Jesus once isn't enough. I have to keep finding Jesus over and over again. Unless I look for him and spend time with him I don't continue to marvel at the Son of God. And unless I marvel, my eyes will grow dim.

As blood-bought, Spirit-filled Christians, we have a new identity, new eyes, a new heart and a new spiritual "engine". When we kick-start our engine with worship, God gives us the fuel to really get moving. Whether we are in the habit of spending entire days in prayer or not (and I have to admit that I'm not) we can be sure that when we put time aside to pursue God, "the kingdom is near us." We discover that this promise is true: "You will seek me and find me when you seek me with all your heart."

This chapter started with a reminder of the fact that this good news at the heart of Christianity is entirely personal. Not only does that mean we find Jesus, but the spirit of the glorious Lord has been implanted in us, enabling us to see "the mystery that has been kept hidden for ages and generations, but is now disclosed to the saints ... the glorious riches of this mystery, *which is Christ in you*, the hope of glory" (Col 1:26-27, emphasis added).

The very presence of Christ in us energizes and inspires, firing us up as we set out on a journey unlike any other. We've got some ground to cover in the coming chapters. First, we will start with the other essential — grace. We will look at what our worship really is before thinking about the notion of being a child again. Friendship and partnership with God will both get looked at, and then we jump into the idea of prayer — after all, isn't that the way it works? We start as children, become friends with God, then move into partnership, and because of all three, prayer is far less intimidating.

After that, we look at the character of the worshipper. Gratitude, our reaction to suffering, contentment and humility all get explored. And after that we move onto lifestyle. What should our relationship with God do to our attitude to work and rest? What about our approach to risk? Should we be more sensitive to issues of justice because of our devotion to God? And what about these resources we find at our disposal — how should the worshipper use them? Finally, endings; how do we end well?

It's a long journey ahead. We'd better get going. Are you coming?

Chapter 2
It's All by Grace

The grace of our Lord Jesus Christ be with your spirit (Gal. 6:18).
— The Apostle Paul

Don't run! You might fall!

This is what Linda and I heard a few months ago as we visited our son, Zachary in Montreal. We were having lunch in a park and the only thing challenging the beauty of the day were these five words that were being yelled out by a nearby mother to her child. There among the wide-open spaces, the immaculately tended grass and the early afternoon sunshine was the bellowed warning of an over-anxious parent. "Don't run! You might fall!" It was just about the most ridiculous thing anyone could have said in such a place.

If we're afraid of making mistakes, we won't run. We won't jump over rocks and creeks. We won't climb trees. We won't know how to experience a life filled with joy. Instead, ours will be soaked in fear. To be an adventurous worshipper, we can't live with our hearts being told "Don't run, you might fall!"

By nature I was a conscientious kid. Most of the time I tried hard to do everything right. When I met Jesus, I thought I should try much harder to be good. Here's what I wrote in my book *To Know You More* about my growth in grace:

It took me a long time to get a grasp on God's grace. In

my first ten years of following the Lord, I received much teaching about his unconditional love. Through wonderful encounters with God in worship and prayer, I experienced his grace. I came to the realization that I had done nothing to earn the gift of God's love and revelation. God sought me out, not the other way around. I was no different than anyone I judged as being less spiritual — we're all in need of God's mercy.

But I had much more to learn. In 1985 I began working as a staff worship pastor at the Langley Vineyard in British Columbia. Because of my "type A" hard-driving nature, I put a lot of pressure on myself to perform as a spiritual leader. I was being crushed under the weight of my own desire to succeed in the ministry. One Saturday night in 1985 as I was preparing for a worship service, the Lord's love broke through to me in a new song about his grace:

Precious Child

Show me, dear Lord, how you see me through your eyes

So that I can realize your great love for me

Teach me, oh Lord, that I am precious in your sight

That as a father loves his child, so you love me

I am yours because you have chosen me

I'm your child because you've called my name

And your steadfast love will never change

And I will always be your precious child.

Show me, dear Lord, that I can never earn your love

That a gift cannot be earned, only given

Teach me, oh Lord, that your love will never fade

That I can never drive away your great mercy[1]

As I sang that song, the revelation of God's unconditional love flooded my heart. It was one of the moments when God's grace becomes real and tangible. Through the tears, I could taste God's grace. It was one of those moments when God was redefining my view of Him. Instead of worshipping a God of my own imagination, he wanted me to see and *know* him as the loving God he really is. To know and worship anything else would be idolatry. He was dismantling my distorted view of him.[2]

I'll share one more story with you from my first book that portrays our great need for our Father's grace. This one is about a song I wrote for my second son, David. He was six years old at the time.

> I wanted him [David] to know that it didn't matter what career he chose, or how his path in life compared to the other children. His personality is very different from Zachary, my first son. Zac is the typical first-born (like me) — responsible, organized, and hard-working. Zac is successful at lots of things: school, music, and sports.

Sometimes I could see David feeling like an underachiever in his older brother's shadow. I wanted David to know I love him just as he is. It didn't matter what he would become as an adult — I would love him no matter what.

> … I wanted David to know that if his achievements weren't as impressive as some of the other kids, it wouldn't matter. I wanted him to be confident that no matter how he 'performed' in life, I would still love him. So I wrote this song for him and sang it to him in the presence of the whole family:

> My son David, I love you; my son David
>
> There are so many things that I like about you;
>
> You have a sensitive heart and a bright mind and a keen imagination;
>
> You make me laugh with the things that you say and do.
>
> My son David, I love you; my son David,
>
> There are so many things that I like about you;
>
> But no matter what you become in this life,
>
> No matter what you do, there's one thing that will always be true;

I will always, always, always love you.

When David was about six years old, I sang this song to him in the gathered circle of our whole family. As I looked into his eyes and sang these words, I could see his eyes fill up with tears. It was a powerful affirmation of my love for him, given in front of his siblings.

This picture reminds me of looking into the eyes of Father God and hearing his song of love over me. In worship, this is a place we can go.

This is what can happen in worship when we're looking into the Father's face. All of a sudden, he lets us *see him*. It's the presence of the Father in the room with us that makes the difference. It's not just a one-way recitation of song lyrics. It's a dialogue with the most loving Person in the universe. In worship we can experience God's delight in us, and have the false images of God erased in our hearts.[3]

Seeing Jesus brings life and joy. When I lose sight of Jesus, I quickly gravitate towards obligatory duty and a sense of not measuring up. I become stingy and inward and grumpy. As soon as the person of Jesus is marginalized in my life, my worship dries up. But when I know I am loved, I naturally want to yield to the Holy Spirit. When my eyes are open and focused, life is transformed.

It's All By Grace

Paul's life is a picture of the sort of extravagant devotion that results from receiving God's unmerited favor. He was an eager persecutor of the church, yet Christ set him apart before he was born to preach the gospel. God knew that underneath Paul's violent attitude towards the church was a heart that truly sought righteousness. On that fateful ride to Damascus, Jesus mercifully blinded Paul with a light of revelation and spoke the shocking words: "I am Jesus, whom you are persecuting" (Acts 26:15).

Imagine the thoughts going through Paul's head at that moment

... "I'm in big trouble now. Boy, did I ever miss it." Slowly, over the next three blind days of receiving his calling to preach the gospel, he knew he was unutterably and undeservedly blessed. This encounter changed him forever.

He writes to Timothy: "The grace of our Lord was poured out on me abundantly ... Christ Jesus came into the world to save sinners — of whom I am the worst" (1 Tim 1:14-15). Formerly proud of his religious accomplishments, now all he could talk about was God's mercy. Paul sees his life as a demonstration of God's mercy to humankind: "I was shown mercy so that in me, the worst of sinners, Christ Jesus might display his unlimited patience as an example" (1 Tim. 1:16).

I'm the Worst

Do you ever have days (or at least moments) when you feel like "I am the worst"? Join the club. Some days I have the worst attitude towards life. Then I feel like a jerk when I realize how ungrateful I've been. That's when I jump in the pool of God's unchanging grace, right next to Paul.

The feeling "I'm the worst" leads directly to the prayer, "God, you're the best. I'm amazed that you love me despite all my mistakes." This failure of humankind and contrasting victory of Jesus is exactly how God arranged the course of human history! And it all leads to worship.

When Paul thinks about the amazing mercy of God, he explodes in worship. In his letter to the Romans he writes about an amazing fact: "For God has imprisoned everyone in disobedience so he could have mercy on everyone" (Rom 11:32 NLT). That thought is jut too much for Paul and it launches him off into a glorious doxology of praise:

> For God has bound all men over to disobedience so that he may have mercy on them all.

Oh, the depth of the riches of the wisdom and knowledge of God!

How unsearchable his judgments, and his paths beyond tracing out!

… Who has ever given to God, that God should repay him?

For from him and through him and to him are all things.

To him be the glory forever! Amen (Rom 11:32-33; 35-36).

In the very next line of Paul's letter he appeals to his readers to worship *because of this mercy*: "Therefore, I urge you, brothers, *in view of God's mercy*, to offer your bodies as living sacrifices, holy and pleasing to God — this is your spiritual act of worship" (Rom. 12:1, emphasis added). The *mercy* of God is the basis for our worship.

The simple truth is that we *can't* repay God. He set up creation so that we couldn't be good enough on our own, and then he showed us the mercy we could never earn. That truth alone is enough to make you leap and dance with joy for the rest of your life. When Paul writes to the Corinthians about God's 'surpassing grace', he explodes with thanks: "Thanks be to God for his indescribable gift" (2 Cor 9:15)!

Trying to live a life of worship is an unbearable burden without the foundation of grace resounding in our hearts. Paul knew a little about burdens. He spent so much of his life trying to keep the whole law, growing up around the "experts in the law" who Jesus warned not to " … load people down with burdens they can hardly carry … " (Luke 11:46). Imagine the incredible relief for Paul — who was taught that to be comprehensively set free, he had to obey not only the Old Testament law, but all the extra rules and regulations of the Talmud — to be comprehensively set free. Little wonder his words were so clear: "Now the Lord is the Spirit, and where the Spirit of the Lord is, there is freedom" (2 Cor 3:17).

Paul knew the agony of making mistake after mistake, but he drew on the power of God's rescuing grace even in the midst of his stumbling:

> So I find this law at work: When I want to do good, evil is right there with me ... waging war against the law of my mind and making me a prisoner of the law of sin ... What a wretched man I am! Who will rescue me from this body of death? Thanks be to God — through Jesus Christ our Lord!" (Rom 7:21-24).

Pondering God's love in the face of my inability to do the right thing makes me say everyday "Thanks be to God — through Jesus Christ our Lord!"

After his conversion Paul was energized to serve the Lord, not from a sense of duty, not spiked by guilt or shame, but because of God's empowering touch: "But by the grace of God I am what I am, and his grace to me was not without effect. No, I worked harder than all of them — yet not I, but the grace of God that was with me"(1 Cor 15:10). When our hearts are set free and we are compelled by love, we serve with joy:

> Where love is the compelling power, there is no sense of strain or conflict or bondage in doing what is right: the man or woman who is compelled by Jesus' love and empowered by his Spirit does the will of God from the heart.[4]

Christ is the mediator of our worship. We can't add to his once-for-all victory over sin and death. Salvation and favor from God is a gift, not something we can earn. Worshiping God everyday is a *joyful* thing when I keep God's mercy in view.

The Centrality of the Cross

In worship, we remember the story of Jesus. The story of Jesus remains constant, fixed and permanent. This message is timeless and relevant for all peoples of all cultures. And in post-modern, post-Christian society, it is a story that is needed more than ever.

The divinity and life of Jesus defines history for us. Christ's greatest victory — and ours — is the cross and resurrection. Robert Webber said, "The story of the gospel of Jesus Christ is ... the thing that defines us, tests us, and judges us."

In current philosophical thought, everything is negotiable when it to comes to God and spirituality. The rule of the day is to make your own rules — you choose which narrative you want to live by, you "write your own story." There is no fixed vision of eternity that creates a context for daily living.

Amidst a spiritual climate devoid of a commitment to absolute truth, the simple message of Jesus and his cross is as relevant as ever. This makes it even more important to meditate on the story of the cross, giving us the right frame of reference for our lives.

Our Worship Is Based on an Unchanging Historical Fact

In today's climate of contemporary worship, we're in danger of putting too much focus on how we feel in worship. This applies equally to the church's gathered worship experience and to our daily lives. Maybe someone has asked you this question after a worship service: "Was worship good for you?" There's a dangerous implication in this question that your *feelings* during worship indicate whether or not worship was "good."

We could repeat the mistakes of history and focus on spiritual phenomena instead of Christ himself. This was an issue that Jonathan Edwards, the revivalist of the 1800s, dealt with in his ministry. In Edwards' time, many people became so enamored with their ecstatic spiritual experiences that they lost sight of the beauty and worth of Christ.

The mindset that our feelings during worship are an indication of our spirituality leads to feelings of failure and self-condemnation. The truth is this: when we behold Jesus on the cross, and all that his death and resurrection means for us, we don't have to *feel* anything else to have a valid worship experience. We are remembering a once-for-all act of unparalleled love and sacrifice that changes everything. It changes the way God sees us. The work of the cross can never be diminished — not by words, not by feelings, not by anything we could do.

It means that I can *always* be full of gratitude and wonder at God's love for me, no matter what I feel. There are other implications — we are called to follow Christ's example, to take up our cross and follow him. We are called to die daily, as Paul says. Suffering is part of life in Christ. There is a way to worship through the suffering.

I love to feel God's presence, but my feelings aren't the focal point of my worship. When Christ is the focal point, we find security in the unchangeable historical event of the cross. The benefits for us are permanent, continual, and eternal.

Impressed with God or Ourselves?

Prior to his revelation of Jesus, Paul was proud of his religious accomplishments. He describes himself as the ultimate Pharisee — a Hebrew of Hebrews with all the right pedigree. After encountering God, he considered his good reputation to be worth less than garbage compared to knowing Christ.

It's impossible to be full of adoration for Jesus if we are also busy congratulating ourselves for our own righteousness. At the beginning of my walk with Christ, I didn't have this figured out. I was zealous but not very wise. I was proud of my spiritual discipline and commitment to Jesus and it took me a while to figure out that I was putting myself up on a pedestal, admiring my own good works.

But when I saw the *free gift* of God's love I was freed from self-consciousness to really worship. It wasn't about my accomplishments; it was about Jesus' work on the cross. Without Jesus' deliverance I would be enslaved to sin and going to hell.

God doesn't want us to be worried about how "good" we are. Instead he wants us to be impressed with how *great* he is — something that (unlike our wavering feelings) never changes. When we think about his greatness, we don't have time for moping around and feeling sorry for ourselves. My self-confidence rests on the unchanging merit of Jesus' righteousness, nothing else.

In remembering Jesus' death, we see the depth of his love for us. "This is how we know what love is: Jesus Christ laid down his life for us" (1 John 3:16). If we fail to meditate on the depth of Jesus' suffering and the price he paid for us, we won't see the depth of his love.

If Jesus was willing to suffer the cross for us, it means we are of infinite value. It means that our shame and poor self-image are swallowed up in God's amazing love. The message of the cross is that *we are his passion*, and it is a unique message. It allows us to feel good about ourselves; you can love and accept yourself because God does. Even if people reject us, we know that God still loves us. Jesus' sacrifice for us makes us acceptable, even if we feel rejected.

This good news must be at the center of our worship, day-by-day and week-by-week. Putting Jesus and his cross at the center of our worship means we'll never lose sight of God's amazing grace. Through celebrating the life, death and resurrection of Jesus, the historical event of Christ becomes alive for today.

At the Foot of the Cross

When I meditate on Christ and his cross, I picture myself laying prostrate in front of the cross, absolutely surrendered and dependent on Jesus. The cross towers over me as I make myself as low as I can, facedown on the ground. I am full of thankfulness for the unrivaled love of Jesus as expressed in his supreme sacrifice. I realize that everything makes sense because of the cross. Because of the cross, I know I'm loved. Even if my life falls apart, the historical fact of God's cross is unchanged. Nothing that happens to me, no mistake I make can undo the steadfast love of God for me.

We lose control to whatever we worship. If I lose control to drugs or sex or money or power, I am worshiping or giving myself to those things. What sweet peace there is in losing control to our gracious and compassionate Father God. What joy there is in knowing I don't have to figure out the rest of my life because God is in control. What peace there is in knowing I've been bought with a price, the precious blood of Jesus Christ. What relief there is in knowing that I am not my own, that I belong to him. I find great security in belonging to him who made the planets and stars and farthest galaxies yet he became small and suffered death for our sake.

As I lay before Jesus, I meditate on his suffering and realize that I am called not just to know " ... the power of his resurrection ..." but also to " ... share in his sufferings ... " (Phil 3:10); suffering leads to greater intimacy in knowing God. Dying daily is part of the Christian journey, and only in dying do we experience new life; only in letting go do we receive the generous gifts of God. At the foot of the cross is the place where grace and suffering meet, a place where, in times of despair and discouragement, God's grace profoundly lifts us; we connect to Jesus more fully, identifying with his suffering.

At the cross, we trade our ashes for a crown of beauty (Isaiah 61:3). We trade in the ashes of disappointment, failed projects, shattered dreams and broken relationships to find contentment in the love of God. Where death has been at work, new life will spring up as I wait patiently before the cross.

At the cross, we can forget about our tasks and accomplishments and wear forgiveness like a crown — a crown of belonging instead of a crown of power. Not only that, but the cross is the place where we are made complete. My possessions don't complete me. My gifts and achievements can't complete me. Even my family can't complete me. What a relief it is to jettison the world's false definition of being complete and fulfilled. It's all about knowing God and abiding in his love; it's about experiencing the spirit of adoption. Every good act and ambition proceeds from the rest of faith, from my completeness in Christ.

At the foot of the cross, we lay every burden down. When you're lying flat on the ground, you can't carry anything. That picture helps me too. When I think about the finished work of Christ's cross, I know I can't add anything to what he has done. I don't have to be perfect because he is the Perfect One. I lay down the burden of living up to other people's expectations, and even my own unreasonable expectations of myself.

Gazing on the cross, I see not only the suffering Servant, but also the gloriously empty cross. I see the resurrection — a demonstration of the almighty power of God. I can lay every burden down because the same power that raised Jesus from the dead is at work in me, helping me to get through every day.

The cross is not just a theological concept. It's a historical reality that we experience in prayer, song and partaking in the Lord's Supper. As we worship him, laying before his cross, we soak in the reality of the unmatched, unquenchable love of God.

Worship Flows Out of a Sense of Privilege

When I found out that this omnipotent God isn't just powerful and creative and the smartest Person in the history of the universe, but a loving Father who gave His only Son for me, I wanted nothing other than to love him and live my life according to his wise design.

I still feel the same way. I feel overwhelmed by the privilege of knowing and even being *related* to this Person. I'm thunderstruck with the realization that I am His beloved child and that I've found my true Home, my permanent place of belonging.

I'm bowled over with the fact that " … there is but one God, the Father, from whom all things came and for whom we live; and there is but one Lord, Jesus Christ, through whom all things came and through whom we live"(1 Cor 8:6). I know there is no other logical choice but to worship him and take my cues for living from him.

What an amazing truth that I actually get to participate in His master plan by representing him on the earth and doing my part to spread the bounty of his goodness. There's no reason for futility or boredom; I have a reason to live. I'm affiliated with the King of the universe! I'm in the Royal family! I've hit the jackpot!

What a privilege it is to be created, chosen, forgiven and redeemed. Through the cross, Jesus conquered sin and death. By his power, he literally holds the universe together. Without him we wouldn't be able to breathe, stand or speak. Everyday is a gift. From this place of gratitude, we live our life as an offering to him.

Chapter 3
Treasure Seekers

To worship is to quicken the conscience by the holiness of God, to feed the mind with the truth of God, to purge the imagination by the beauty of God, to open the heart to the love of God, to devote the will to the purpose of God."[1]
— William Temple, Archbishop of Canterbury

I do not know an awful lot of English men named Terry, particularly not the sort who spent considerable quantities of their free time standing in fields waving metal detectors at the earth, but since reading about Terry Herbert I think I would like to get to know a few more of them. In July of 2009, this amateur treasure hunter unearthed more than 1,600 Anglo-Saxon objects of gold and silver from around A.D. 650. He found fittings from the hilts of swords, parts of a helmet and three crosses, and it was the largest Anglo-Saxon treasure hoard ever found. The value? A staggering $5.3 million, which was split equally between the farmer who owns the field and our man Terry.[2]

Here's what he said about the hunt:

> I'd been on the field before with another metal detector and hardly found anything. It had thrown up old furniture fittings, bits of clocks, pieces of brass and I just thought: "Oh, it's another useless field." But I decided to carry on anyway and switch machines to the one I call my 'old faithful.' His tenacity paid off. Within 15 minutes, just before noon, Terry's machine began to indicate that it had found something.[3]

Terry, a retired wood machinist who worked in a coffin factory, was suddenly rich. A simple walk through a farmer's field had changed everything, blowing away his assumptions and expectations in a single moment. Any of his previous finds were instantly put into context.

You can probably tell where we are going with this. For all Terry's immense increase in wealth, his treasure is a pittance compared with the value of meeting Jesus. Jesus is the treasure of the ages, the pearl of great price and when we stumble upon the treasure of knowing him, everything changes.

Worship and Revelation

"When I saw him, I fell at his feet as though dead …" (Rev 1:17). This was John's reaction to seeing the glorious vision of the Lord whose " … face was like the sun shining in all its brilliance" (Rev 1:16). He (almost) spontaneously ceased to exist. This from the man who had already spent around three years with Jesus in Galilee, walking, talking and generally being with him. But when he saw the risen, glorious Lord, he was dumbfounded by this staggering sight.

At this point you may be thinking "yeah, that's what happened to people in Bible times. They get all 'in the spirit' and strange things happen." I want to dare you to believe that Jesus might want to reveal himself to you as the glorious, risen Lord today. Why not? After all, the New Testament presents these kinds of experiences as part of normal Christianity.

The book of Revelation gives us an outstanding picture of a people who had discovered the incomparable treasure of Jesus. It is a dramatic episode of revelation and worship and sits as the climax of the sixty-six books of the Bible written by forty authors over 1500 years. In this apocalyptic finale we see a window into heaven that foretells the conclusion of history, showing how our story intersects with God's eternal purposes.

The Revelation gives us a snapshot of the zealous worship of a burgeoning movement of Christians amidst a culture awash in idol worship — an ancient culture that in many ways bears a striking resemblance to modern times. Rome was a study in contrast; a mix of tens of millions of slaves who had been captured in Rome's military victories juxtaposed against an excessively rich ruling class. Christians were tempted to go with the flow of an idol worshiping culture.

For a first-world Christian like me, it's hard to imagine life in an emperor-worshiping culture, but it's not hard to relate to the Laodiceans who John addresses in chapter three. John writes to these believers, "You say, 'I am rich. I have everything I want. I don't need a thing!' And you don't realize that you are wretched and miserable and poor and blind and naked" (Rev 3:17 NLT).

The Laodiceans had once been on-fire Christians but had become self-satisfied consumerists. They had lost sight of Jesus, their true treasure. Their love for him had grown cold and their faith had grown lukewarm. Just as it is for us today, their challenge was to stay focused on Jesus as their Treasure, for "For where your treasure is, there your heart will be also" (Matt 6:21).

For me, the only way to make Jesus the center is to follow a discipline of being a "treasure seeker." In my daily routine of reading and prayer, I look through a window to heaven. Even if the window is only open a crack, it makes all the difference. Other-worldly beauty rattles me out of my complacency and indifference. It keeps me from settling for a materialistic view of reality. Don Williams says of Revelation that it "is out to subvert the way early Christians view reality. It is a frontal assault on the gods and goddesses of the Roman empire."[4] For us, Revelation serves a similar purpose, assaulting the gods and goddesses of the twenty-first century.

Jesus or Caesar

I can't imagine living in a country that required me to worship the president, but that's what the early Roman Christians faced. They lived in a time when emperor worship was mandated by the government. Domitian, a totalitarian ruler who brutally persecuted the Christian church, is said to have built numerous statues of himself and demanded that he be addressed as "our Lord and God" (*dominus et deus*). Not to acknowledge the Caesar as divine was considered treasonous. Yet because this group of Christians had seen how *worthy* of worship Jesus was, they openly proclaimed his divinity and the Book of Revelation is a picture of two kingdoms in conflict.

For early Roman Christians, loyalty to Jesus was very dangerous. Worship of a Jewish upstart like Jesus of Nazareth was an insult to the Roman authorities and proclaiming a kingdom other than Rome's was to pick a fight with the emperor. For that reason, John the apostle was exiled to the island of Patmos for his missionary work, and we read of Antipas (Rev 2:13), who was martyred at the hands of Domitian. According to tradition, he was slowly roasted to death in a bronze kettle.

We know nothing of this kind of risk in the twenty-first century western world. Persecution and martyrdom have reached an all-time high in the past century in Africa and Asia, but I experience no threat for worshiping Jesus in North America. This is both good and bad. It's good because I have freedom to worship, bad because I'm part of a larger culture of Christianity that is not distinct from the rest of society. Much of the church today is a bland, watered-down version of first century Christianity. It's easy to be lulled to sleep in the lap of luxury. When there are no negative consequences for worshiping Jesus, we forget how privileged we are to know him.

The biggest religious event in the emperor cult was called the Roman Triumph. Rome's army was an awesome war machine, devouring neighboring nations at will. When the armies returned home from a military campaign, they paraded the captured soldiers naked in the streets behind the decorated chariots of the Roman general or emperor. The Caesar was portrayed as "victor and savior." (Savior or *sōtēr*, meant "the one who brings good fortune.")

The distinguished dignitaries would dress in magnificent costumes of triumph, using design motifs taken from the temple of the god Jupiter, which was a popular cult in that time and place. As the procession of conquerors and slaves passed by, the Roman citizenry would sing of the greatness and power of Rome. "Great is your power and wealth and honor!" they shouted as the rulers of the land processed in their regal finery.

Against this backdrop of emperor worship, the followers of "the Way" are exalting a different King. Because the Christians had seen a much more glorious King than the Caesar, and a far superior country than their earthly one, because they had seen the Lamb who was slain who had " ... purchased men for God from every tribe and language and people and nation" (Rev 5:9), they boldly worshipped Jesus, attributing to him the same qualities for which the Roman Imperium was exalted:

In a loud voice they sang: " ... Worthy is the Lamb, who was slain, to receive power and wealth and wisdom and strength and honor and glory and praise!" ... "To him who sits on the throne and to the Lamb be praise and honor and glory and power, for ever and ever!" (Rev 5:12,13).

When the heavenly worshipers are saying "thou art worthy,"

they were thinking about the infinite worth of God and letting it saturate their hearts and minds. The songs from Revelation became part of the worship liturgy of the Roman Christians. By singing these songs, they passed through a portal into the light of the invisible kingdom. They sang as citizens of an invisible country that was far superior to the glory of Rome.

This band of first century believers, so tiny in comparison to the loyalist Roman population, knew that they were a kingdom of priests in a spiritual nation that would outlast even this world-dominating Roman empire. They had seen the unrivalled glory of the resurrected Lord, the worthy Lamb. From then on, their lives became a fountain of worship. From that point on, they were living for a heavenly reward.

Desperation or Discipline

If we skip ahead through the next few chapters of Roman history we find the Roman emperor Constantine converting to Christianity in the early fourth century and ending the persecution of Christians. It's fascinating to note that only a few years after Constantine's conversion we see the advent of monasticism. The first century Christians had banded together in secrecy to worship and encourage one another in the faith, their times of corporate worship offering an oasis and a safe hiding place.

Yet after Christianity was legalized there were no more cruel emperors who crucified Christians and threw them to the lions. No longer was desperation for survival a catalyst for corporate worship. One of the major factors in the rise of monasticism was the need to establish regular habits of consistent corporate worship. Devout Christians were looking for ways to stay focused on Jesus and to live faithful lives, so monasticism became one popular choice.

I don't believe becoming a monk is the right answer for most of us, but choosing a disciplined life of worship is the right answer for any Christian. We all need to bring structure and consistency to both our public and private worship. It's the only way to keep the bright vision of Jesus always before our eyes. Without it, we default to the gods and goddesses of our age. We lose sight of eternity.

The progression from persecution to monasticism as a catalyst for worship in early Roman times points out a few aspects of human nature — we tend to be lazy and easily distracted. When life becomes easier, our felt need to seek God decreases. This was true for the Laodiceans who had "lost their first love," and it's true for us now.

In my relatively carefree middle class existence, I must find ways to "behold the Lamb of God" everyday if I'm going to keep a fire of love for Jesus burning in my heart. To create a pathway for Jesus to shape my character and the choices of my life, I have to live as a Treasure seeker. I need regular experiences of life-giving worship, as described here by Richard Foster: "To worship is to experience reality, to touch Life. It is to know, to feel, to experience the resurrected Christ in the midst of the gathered community."[5]

> Henri Nouwen once asked Mother Teresa for spiritual direction. Spend one hour each day in adoration of your Lord, she said, and never do anything you know is wrong. Follow this, and you'll be fine. Such simple, yet profound advice. Worship is the act of the abandoned heart adoring its God. It is the union that we crave. Few of us experience anything like this on a daily basis, let alone for an hour each day. But it is what we need. Desperately. Simply showing up on Sunday is not even close to worship. Neither does singing songs with religious content pass for worship. What counts is the *posture of the soul* involved, the open heart pouring forth its love toward God and communing with him.[6]

In our busy world, we are so easily overwhelmed with other activities and seemingly important priorities. But the spiritual discipline of worship is for everyone.

God intends the Disciplines of the spiritual life to be for ordinary human beings; people who have jobs, who care for children, who must wash dishes and mow lawns. In fact, the Disciplines are best exercised in the midst of our normal daily activities. If they are to have any transforming effect, the effect must be found in the ordinary junctures of human life: in our relationships with our husband or wife, our brothers and sisters, our friends and neighbors.[7]

In the absence of life-threatening oppression from an anti-Christian government, we must make the choice of worshiping together. In the absence of feeling desperate for God, we need to make daily choices to touch the life that is truly life, found only in God. We must draw a line and not allow worship to be trumped by other pursuits. The only way I can stay passionate for Jesus the King is by worshiping him, both privately and publicly.

Revelation and Worship Lead to a Change in Behavior

Tim Keller, pastor of Redeemer Presbyterian Church in New York City, describes the alternate reality we see in John's Revelation. Jesus invites the apostle John to "open the door and come in." John sees heavenly worship, and he sees where history is going. He describes our universe as "an alternate side-alley reality," and heaven as "the main street of reality." In the main street of heaven, we see a world that makes our world look insignificant and temporary.

John brings us with him on this tour of heaven, helping us get out of the back alley of life on earth and into the mainstream of reality, to see how things are from heaven's perspective.

Tim Keller describes the progression from revelation to worship to a change in behavior: "There is an awe, which leads to a joy, which leads to a change in behavior, which leads to a major investment of yourself in that object."[8]

Several years ago my family spent three months in Hong Kong with a group of former drug addicts who had found Jesus. Many of these were members of an infamous gang called the Triads. Chung Jai was the leader of the ministry campus on which we were staying. Before he met Jesus, Chung Jai was one of the toughest, most feared of all the Triads. When he found Jesus he became one of the gentlest, most sensitive and compassionate men you'll ever meet. These are the dynamics of genuine worship. There is a fundamental change in our nature, behavior and our goals.

When we find the treasure of Jesus, and yield to him, he transforms us. Some things that were once paramount lose importance. We see eternity and build our lives around it. What's at stake is far more than singing a few songs on a Sunday.

Seeing Leads to Bowing

Our sense of privilege as worshipers is expressed in humble surrender before the holy One.

In the Book of Revelation, we see the multitudes as "They fell down on their faces before the throne and worshiped God" (Rev 7:11). One of the Hebrew words translated "worship" literally means "fall down," itself a symbolic — and actual — act of surrender.

In chapter four, the twenty-four elders who saw the glorious Lord cast their crowns before him. We all know that crowns represent leadership, power, and authority. In laying down their crowns, these leaders were handing over control. Herein lies a key point of worship for all believers: worship always leads to the surrender of control. You cannot worship without casting down your crown and losing control. Says Tim Keller:

> Anything that is the most important thing "has the crown" … If you live for power, power has got you under control, if you live for control, control has got you under control … the person who is desperate for acceptance is controlled by the people he or she seeks to please.[9]

William Sperry writes, "Worship is a deliberate and disciplined adventure in reality. It is not for the timid or comfortable. It involves an opening of ourselves to the dangerous life of the Spirit."[10] It is "dangerous" because it requires us to let God sit in the drivers seat while we become a passenger.

These first century Christians had died to this world, to the power of sin, to their needs and desires. They had seen many of their brothers around them die for the sake of the gospel. They had decided to live for God's dreams, desires, and will. And it was because of all this that they were not afraid to die again.

They would have been familiar with the earlier writing of Paul to the church in Rome, in which he gave a definition of worship: "Therefore, I urge you, brothers, in view of God's mercy, to offer your bodies as living sacrifices, holy and pleasing to God — this is your spiritual act of worship" (Rom 12:1).

As one friend of mine so aptly put it: "It's not worship until *you* are the sacrifice, until *you* are on the altar."[11]

Keeping Our Eyes on the Prize

We see fervent devotion among the early Christians, but we also see indifference.

John could have been writing to directly to the 21st century church in North America when he said, "You say, 'I am rich; I have acquired wealth and do not need a thing.' But you do not realize that you are wretched, pitiful, poor, blind and naked" (Rev 3:17). Surrounded and enticed by wealth, their love for God had fallen into decay.

The church in Laodicea (modern day western Turkey) was the wealthiest city in that region during this era. "It was widely known for its banking establishments, medical school and textile industry."[12]

John confronts these believers with three metaphors that directly apply to their local situation. Laodiceans took great pride not only in their financial wealth, but their extensive textile industry and a well-known eye salve. John steers them back to true wealth, righteousness and revelation: "I counsel you to buy from me *gold* refined in the fire, so you can become rich; and *white clothes* to wear, so you can cover your shameful nakedness; and *salve* to put on your eyes, so you can see" (Rev 3:18, emphasis added).

Jesus offers the salve of his Holy Spirit to take away sin's deception that so easily blinds us. And he offers us his pure robe of white as he calls us to offer our bodies as instruments of righteousness. The pathway to this renewal of worship is an intimate meal with Jesus, the one who says: "Here I am! I stand at the door and knock. If anyone hears my voice and opens the door, I will come in and eat with him, and he with me" (Rev 3:20).

This scripture is often used as a prelude to an altar call for non-believers. But it wasn't written to unbelievers. This is Jesus' offer to come and sup with believers whose affections for him have waned. It is a powerful picture of intimate fellowship, of friendship, of the God who seeks a relationship of mutual love with us. His honesty may begin with a "rebuke and discipline," but it leads to peace and well-being.

The life of worship is marked by continually turning away from distractions and back to our true treasure. It is marked by habitually remembering the privileged position and purpose we're called to — bearing the image of God in a broken world. And it is marked by a regular use of "eye salve" to help us see our magnificent God.

Staying Focused on the Treasure Doesn't Happen by Osmosis

To set our minds on things above, where Christ is seated is a discipline of worship that alters our view of daily life, we need to fill our mind with the story of God. The book of Revelation gives us fantastic — as well as sometimes bizarre — images to fill our imagination with the realities of heaven. Like much of the rest of

God's living word, Revelation can saturate our imagination with a picture of God in all his glory and of the wonderful destiny for the followers of the Lamb. That perspective changes the way we live today. As Paul says, " … Let God transform you into a new person by changing the way you think" (Rom 12:2).

In describing the Bill Clinton-Monica Lewinsky sexual affair in the White House, an American politician said, "Righteousness doesn't stand a chance against the imagination."[13] This statement is obviously made by a man who hasn't experienced resurrection power. Of course, the power of the human mind to fantasize is great. John Calvin said, "The human heart is a factory of idols … Everyone of us is, from his mother's womb, expert in inventing idols." But are we powerless to overcome sinful thinking?

Not according to scripture. Imagination is part of the creative nature God gave us and He doesn't want us to be afraid of it or defeated by it. God's reality as seen in the Revelation baptizes our imagination and replaces narrow-minded thinking and sinful fantasizing with a life-defining eternal picture.

In his book *Renovation of the Heart*, Dallas Willard says, "The process of spiritual formation is one of progressively replacing those destructive images and ideas with the images and ideas that filled the mind of Jesus himself."[14] If we feed our minds and spirits with the beauty of God, our imagination can run wild with good things.

To change our behavior, we must intentionally practice spiritual disciplines. James Bryan Smith, in his book *The Good and Beautiful God*, prefers the term "soul-training exercises" instead of spiritual disciplines. "The problem is not that we do not want to change, nor is the problem that we are not trying to change. The problem is that we are not training."[15]

For centuries, sincere Christians have found ways to develop healthy habits for spiritual formation. In Richard Foster's classic book *Celebration of Discipline* he lists three major categories of the disciplines: the Inward Disciplines of meditation, prayer, fasting and study; the Outward Disciplines of simplicity, solitude, submission and service and the Corporate Disciplines of confession, worship, guidance and celebration.

Foster describes the purpose of the disciplines as "liberation from the stifling slavery to self-interest and fear."[16] The word "discipline" may immediately conjure up images of sour-faced religious people who never have any fun, but Foster makes it clear that "Joy is the keynote of all the disciplines."

I have found that transformation by the Holy Spirit is supernatural but also very gradual, that "the speed of information is very fast, but the speed of godliness is very slow."[17] There are fantastic moments of revelatory breakthrough, but changing my behavior happens slowly.

I'm painfully aware of sin reigning in my body when I lapse into a spirit of greed or struggle with resentment towards someone who has mistreated me. I see ingrained patterns of sin in my life, ways of thinking that are not Christ-like. Sheer willpower won't enable me to conquer my weaknesses. I need real inner change. Without ongoing spiritual formation, our dark inward parts will at times be expressed in our behavior:

> "We have no intention of exploding with anger or of exploding with anger or of parading a sticky arrogance, but when we are with people, what we *are* comes out. Though we may try to hide these things with all our might, we are betrayed by our eyes, our tongue, our chin, our hands, our whole body language. Willpower has no defense against the careless word, the unguarded moment."[18]

To seriously confront the unsanctified areas of my life, I have to intentionally give myself to spiritual disciplines. This isn't "pulling myself up by my bootstraps" by an act of self-will. It is cooperating with the grace of God by praying, meditating, studying, serving, submitting, confessing and worshipping, etc. None of these "soul-training exercises" would be possible or fruitful without the help of the Holy Spirit. He is there to help us pray, to give us understanding and to give us the desire to do what is right.

Righteousness *does* stand a chance if we organize our lives to include spiritual disciplines. Our man Terry Herbert had an incredible breakthrough when he found the Anglo-Saxon treasure. But he found it only after years of consistently waving his metal detector across countless damp acres of farmer's fields. While it is true that Jesus takes the initiative to rescue us, it will take lots of digging to unearth all the riches of glory he has in store for us. It will take years of pursuing him and the things that are important to him. The journey of worship is part adventure and part discipline. None of it is about luck, quick fixes or instant highs.

Is Jesus our passion or is he a hobby on the side? Does he rate somewhere around watching your favorite sports team or shopping for new clothes? If he really is our passion, we'll make a point of saturating our minds with his truth. We'll spend time in a quiet place, inviting wisdom work it's way into our hearts. We'll gather with other believers to experience the incarnate Christ in our midst. We'll find ways to use our time, treasure and talents to serve others. We'll work every day to "cast down our crowns" and remember the alternate but permanent reality of heaven.

Jesus is always standing close to us, ready to give us salve to put on our eyes so we can see his kingdom. He's always standing at the door and knocking, ready to come in and eat with us. He promises to keep changing us from glory to glory if we'll keep seeking His treasure: "So all of us who have had that veil removed can see and reflect the glory of the Lord. And the Lord — who is the Spirit — makes us more and more like him as we are changed into his glorious image" (2 Cor 3:18 NLT).

Chapter 4
Prayer:
Conversations with God

I believe the most adequate description of prayer is simply talking to God about what we are doing together ....
— Dallas Willard

This quote helps me. In fact, it completely transforms the way I see prayer. It deflates the feeling of intimidation and unplugs the legalism that can generate so much heat in me. I think Jesus has a much kinder view of the subject than I do. And I also think I am not alone.

"If you want to pray better, you must pray more," said Mother Teresa.[1] She was right. The only way to get to know God is to talk to him and to listen to him. We learn to pray by praying. Prayer — like meditation and worship — is our route to approaching God, and these three disciplines are as essential to the Christian life as air or water to our bodies.

In my first years of knowing God, I had lots of very dynamic times of prayer. I didn't know what I was going to do with my life so my prayer times were a glorious mix of feeling desperate for God's guidance and finding the gift of his presence. In those formative years the foundation was laid for a strong relationship with God through prayer, worship and soaking up the word of God.

Since then, prayer has been both a blessing and a struggle. The good times have been the setting for many precious encounters with God — words, conviction of sin, specific guidance and visitations from the Holy Spirit. I have learned for myself that prayer and worship are inseparable, in many ways synonymous. To worship is to submit to God, which is precisely what happens in prayer. In prayer, we tell God how great He is. In our reverence for him, we gladly place ourselves at his service. Whether in words or in song, the heart is the same: prayer is worship and worship is prayer.

As for the struggle, well, we'll come onto that soon enough. In this chapter I will touch on just a few aspects of the huge subject of prayer, passing along some highlights of my prayer journey and quoting many writers who expertly and eloquently expound on the dynamics of prayer. My emphasis is on relational and listening prayer and overcoming frustrations in a becoming a praying person.

Legalism Isn't the Answer

While I've had a regular routine of prayer for many years, there was a time when I was bound up in legalism, never thinking I had prayed enough. Being a first-born son, highly conscientious with a strong work ethic, I became dangerously legalistic about prayer in my early years of following the Lord. On the days that I prayed much, I took pride in the amount of time I prayed. I was filled with a mixture of genuine love for God mixed with pride in my own works. A by-product of that was a critical attitude towards those I perceived to be less devoted. Like the tax collector in the Luke 18, I was foolishly confident of my own righteousness and I looked down on everyone else. My critical spirit was the rotten fruit of pride and legalism.

Another ill effect of a legalistic approach to prayer is that we can never do enough. If we feel that praying is a way of earning God's love, we begin to resent the time, and even resent God, because we can't live up to the measure that we perceive he is requiring of us. Feeling guilty about not praying enough doesn't accomplish anything.

The prayer time loses life when we're filled with guilt because we couldn't reach our goal *or* we're filled with pride because we *could* reach our goal. If we have a contractual versus a relational approach to prayer, when we've prayed, and "done our part of the bargain" then we may feel that God owes us something. It's duty, not relationship.

Devotions — that word we use to describe a quiet time of prayer and/or study — can easily degenerate into an outward form or method, both a subtle form of legalism. Heartfelt and honest devotion isn't about punching a time clock or logging a certain number of hours per week. We don't have devotions to earn favor from God and we don't owe devotional time to God. But if we're impassioned by a desire to please him in our daily occupation and relationships, we will find a way to pray.

Method Is Not the Center of What We Do

Charles Finney said of developing a life of prayer: "The key is devotion, not devotions." His point was that if our first priority in life is to honor God in all we do, we *will* pray.

Says Finney:

> Devotion is the state of heart in which everything — our whole life, being and possessions — are a continual offering to God, that is, they are continually devoted to God. True devotion must be the supreme devotion of the will, extending out to all we have and are — to all times, places, employments, thoughts and feelings … Now remember, nothing short of this standard is devotion in you! Bear it in mind that no particular acts of zeal or gushings of emotion or resolutions to change, or promises of future obedience — constitutes devotion.

My highest goal is to please God with my life. To do that, I have to learn what is on his heart. So I talk to God. If you're dependent on him, you talk to him. There's no way forward in a truly devoted life without asking God for help, wisdom, and forgiveness.

Dallas Willard describes this dynamic very well:

> I believe the most adequate description of prayer is simply talking to God about what we are doing together ... Prayer is a matter of explicitly sharing with God my concerns about what he too is concerned about in my life. And of course he is concerned about my concerns, and in particular, that my concerns should coincide with his. This is our walk together. Out of it I pray.[2]

Tackling big challenges in daily life gives me a lot to pray about. As a freelance minister, a lot of my work — worship recordings, books and itinerant work — comes directly from my own initiative. That involves a lot of planning and decision-making that requires prayer and listening to God. As a husband and father of eight children, I have a lot of responsibility. This drives me to prayer, offered in short interludes throughout my day.

Here is an excerpt from the introduction in David Winter's book, *Closer Than a Brother*, to Brother Lawrence's book, *The Practice of the Presence of God* regarding a relational verses transactional approach to prayer:

> Stop putting your trust in human rules, devotional exercises, and acts of penance. Instead, exercise a living, obedient faith in God. Live as though he were beside you and with you all the time — as indeed he is. Seek to do what he wants, as and when he commands it, and make his command your joy and chief pleasure. The person who lives like that will be fully human, completely Christian, and genuinely happy.[3]

As I've read about the prayer lives of many different Christian leaders, I'm so encouraged to find out that many of them, like me, feel like a beginner at prayer even after many years of knowing God. The widely respected Catholic writer, Thomas Merton said, "We do not want to be beginners. But let us be convinced of the fact that we will never be anything else but beginners all our life!"[4]

The English preacher Leslie Weatherhead said:

> I have always found prayer difficult. So often it seems like a fruitless game of hide and seek in which we seek and God hides. I know God is very patient with me. Without that patience I should be lost. But frankly I have to be patient with him. With no other friend would I go on seeking with such scant, conscious response.[5]

Knowing that even the greatest preachers struggled in prayer helps me take a more grace-filled attitude to the challenge of prayer. A high percentage of Christians struggle to pray effectively. Zondervan, the Christian book publisher, did a survey requesting input on peoples' prayer lives — only twenty-three out of 678 people responded that they had a satisfactory prayer life.[6]

What do we do with this? If we beat ourselves up for our immaturity in prayer it won't get us anywhere. Dallas Willard encourages us not to attempt heroics in our prayer life:

> It is much harder to learn if we succumb to the temptation to engage in "heroic" efforts in prayer." This is important. Heroism, generally, is totally out of place in the spiritual life, until we grow to the point at which it would never be thought of as heroism anyway.[7]

I figured out a long time ago that I stand no chance of ever impressing God with acts of piety. He loves me, period. That sets me free to pray, even if my prayers are very simple and brief. Richard Foster gives a wonderful illustration of God's delight in our simple prayers. It's like a mother delighting in the crude drawing of her four-year old girl. The drawing is so crude that you can't even figure out what it is. From an artistic perspective, the drawing may be ugly, but the adoring mother tells her daughter, "That's beautiful, darling!"

How encouraging that our Lord is *full* of grace towards his children who, like babies distracted by shiny baubles, we lose focus on our Father even when we're sitting in his lap. He loves us and listens to us even in our weakness:

> For we do not have a high priest who is unable to sympathize with our weaknesses … Let us then approach the throne of grace with confidence, so that we may receive mercy and find grace to help us in our time of need (Heb 4:15-16).

Persevering When God Seems Distant and Prayers Aren't Answered

There cannot be many situations more difficult than when you feel like God is neither listening to you nor anywhere near you. In times like this prayer can feel like a chore, like going through the motions. Frederick Buechner describes this feeling: "I was less like a man praying than a man *being* a man praying."[8] His prayers felt mechanical rather than organic. We must constantly remind ourselves that God doesn't see prayer as a performance, that it doesn't matter what we feel. God highly values our prayers in spite of the emotions we attach to them.

We all know that the sense of feeling distant from God is built into this earthly life. We catch glimpses of heavenly glory and then the clouds hide the sunshine from our view. God mysteriously grants and withholds his presence. Some people frequently experience God through their senses, and others rarely if ever have any sensations in prayer. Simon Guillebaud picks up on this and points us back to C.S Lewis:

> C. S. Lewis talked of how sometimes people experience extraordinary times of intimacy and closeness to God. However, God "never allows this state of affairs to last long. Sooner or later he withdraws, if not in fact, at least from their conscious experience, all those supports and incentives. He leaves the creature to stand up on its own legs — to carry out from the will alone duties which have lost all relish. It is during such trough periods, much more than during the peak periods, that it is growing into the sort of creature he wants it to be."[9]

Uncomfortable as it may be, the truth is that God may let us suffer the withdrawal of his presence as a way of leading us to maturity. It's one way he helps us become the people he wants us to be.

It is precisely because of this that the New Testament presents prayer as a long, arduous battle. Jesus tells a story of a widow nagging a judge and a man pounding on his neighbor's door for bread after he and his family have gone to bed. Any parent who prays for their children for decades for protection, wisdom and guidance understands this idea. As you watch your children grow up, you know that you can't control them. You want them to have a heart that seeks God, but only God can do that, so you fight for them in prayer. In praying for our kids when they seem to be floundering in their faith, my wife Linda says, "It's in the hard times that I learn about faith — the faith of Abraham, who believes that he is the father of many nations even when he is without any children, and just about dead."

Paul urges us to be Christian soldiers who wear the full armor of God, praying in the Spirit on all occasions. He urges Timothy to endure hardship like a soldier, to toil like a farmer, to compete like an athlete. Jesus says, "pray and don't give up." He treasures our long-term loyalty and expects us to keep going through the seasons of silence and dullness.

Surrendering Control

Ours is a world of instant everything. We're accustomed to getting what we want and getting it right now. Our culture doesn't teach us the value of deferred gratification and as a result we feel entitled to fast service and are ready to complain if we don't get it. We are fast losing our sense of perspective, like the man I heard about who was promised in-flight wireless internet access by the airline he was flying. This was the first time wireless internet would be available on any airline in the world. When the internet connection didn't work right away, the man was disgusted and complained bitterly. We act like spoiled children when our enjoyment of modern day conveniences is interrupted. I see the ugliness of my own impatience when I'm on the phone with a customer service representative who can't solve a simple problem on my visa bill.

This is where prayer comes in. We give up our control of the conversation; we learn patience. In prayer, we find the place of humility. We wait before God; we let him be God. We can't manipulate God. We are fragile, and He is strong. We are incompetent to change things, and he is sovereign. He is holy, and we are flesh. It shouldn't be surprising that we feel so small in prayer. Feeling "small" is akin to a quality Jesus' applauds in the Sermon on the Mount — meekness. "Blessed are the meek, for they will inherit the earth" (Matt 5:5). "Inheriting the earth" sounds pretty good to me.

God likes to hang out with the lowly. He says in Isaiah: "I live in a high and holy place, but also with him who is contrite and lowly in spirit, to revive the spirit of the lowly and to revive the heart of the contrite" (Isa 57:15). Prayer is all about us becoming more Christ-like as we say no to our fleshly impulse to dominate our world. Simon Tugwell says that in praying we "stop playing God": "God is inviting us to take a break, to play truant. We can stop doing all those important things we have to do in our capacity as God, and leave it to him to be God."[10]

Honesty in Prayer

An entry from my prayer journal reads: "Jesus, help me not retaliate against the circumstances of life. Forgive me for making threats when my kids mess up. Help me die to sin and live for righteousness. Forgive me for sinful words."

God knows everything about us. In prayer, we are only ever telling him what he already knows. So for prayer to be authentic, it must be honest. C. S. Lewis said: "We must lay before him what is in us, not what *ought* to be in us."[11] Here is one of those mind-boggling truths about the real Jesus — I can talk to him about *anything* that's happening in my life and he loves me just the same. It helps me to tell him how inadequate I feel for the tasks ahead of me, to unload my fear of the future, my struggle with lust. None of these things surprise him. I experience his acceptance as I speak honestly with him.

When Jesus says to the Samaritan woman that the Father is looking for "true worshippers," the word 'true' means "real and genuine" in contrast with the symbolic and typical.[12] This woman got the shock of her life when Jesus told her " ... You're right! You don't have a husband — for you have had five husbands, and you aren't even married to the man you're living with now ... " (John 4:17-18 NLT). In spite of what he knew about her, he offered her living water. Jesus was inviting her into a relationship with God unlike anything she had heard of. No longer would worship be about the exterior features like the location of worship service.

This woman couldn't fake anything in Jesus' presence and get away with it. Nor can we. We can't fool God. He is the wonder of wonders who knows the "real me" and yet who still accepts me. That inspires floods of gratitude everyday, and it gives us courage to be honest with God, knowing that no sin will disqualify us from being his beloved children.

Lewis writes: "The prayer preceding all prayers is: May it be the real 'I' who speaks. May it be the real Thou that I speak to."[13] The real "me" is a very ordinary person. (I always find if funny that people around the world think I'm some kind of "holy man" because I've written a few good worship songs. They don't know the real me).

God loves ordinary words spoken by average people. We need not put on airs or change the tone of our voice, or even speak in complete sentences when praying to God. He understands even our groans. When my wife is sick, "Lord, please heal Linda" is sometimes all I pray. Jesus was the champion of short prayers, raising Lazarus from the dead with just three words.

To worship him rightly, we must see him accurately. To offer prayers "in spirit and truth," we must lay our hearts bare before God. Abraham Joshua Heschel writes: "We cannot make him visible to us, but we can make ourselves visible to him."[14]

Worship that God accepts is worship offered on his terms: He requires honesty and authenticity. Coming to prayer pushes us towards self-examination. David prays, "Search me, O God, and know my heart; test me and know my anxious thoughts" (Ps 139:23). Worship isn't a place to hide from God; it's a place to be found by God. True worship will pull us out of hiding. Intimacy involves revealing the deepest part of your being to another, even when it's not pretty.

Confession of sin is liberating. The thing the binds you is the thing that frees you if you'll only acknowledge it. The moment you come to him broken and honest, he frees you.

Thy Will Be Done

Prayer is more about God getting his way than us getting ours. As I sit and ponder what I want to ask of God, I wonder how pure my motives are. I wonder how closely my desires line up with God's desires, and often I don't know. So, "Your kingdom come, your will be done" is one of my most frequent prayers.

Philip Yancey is honest about being re-directed by God in his prayers:

> I have discovered that God wisely answers prayer in a different way than I envision. I pray that my book will win a prize and instead find I need to improve my writing. I pray to get rich and instead find that money would be a curse distracting me from more important things. After enough of these lessons, I adjust my immature prayers in the light of what I have learned from knowing God through meditation.[15]

"Be slow to pray," says Eugene Peterson:

> Praying puts us at risk of getting involved with God's conditions … . Praying most often doesn't get us what we want but what God wants, something quite at variance with what we conceive to be our best interests. And when we realize what is going on, it is often too late to turn back.[16]

In the famous story of Daniel and the Lion's den, Daniel knew that God was able to deliver him from death, even in a pit of hungry lions. But he also said to king, "But even if he does not [deliver us], we want you to know, O king, that we will not serve your gods or worship the image of gold you have set up" (Dan 3:18). Daniel didn't presume to know God's will. His choice to worship wasn't conditional on the type of answer God would send.

I live in a nice house. The house payments aren't onerous, but sometimes I wonder if God will continue to provide enough income for us to live here. If God wants to, he can give us enough to live here. If not, we will accept that as his choice and his way of guiding us to sell the house and find something simpler. And we would still be very blessed. In any case the best I can pray is this: "Thy will be done, Lord!"

Listening Prayer

In his book on prayer, Philip Yancey says, "Sometimes I wonder if the words I use are the least important part of prayer." He describes prayer as "a time to keep company with God."[17] In most of my prayer times, I do a lot of listening. I'm listening for any insights that God might whisper to me. I'm thinking about a passage of scripture and how that changes the way I approach the day or the year ahead of me. In prayer and meditation times, I let the teachings of an inspirational leader from church history soak in.

Prayer is like a conversation between two people in which

each person's words are influenced by the others' comments; the direction and topic of conversation are influenced by both God and me. Eugene Peterson compares the partnership of praying with the Holy Spirit's help to a Greek verb tense in which the speaker contributes but doesn't control: "Prayer takes place in the middle voice. The middle voice is that use of the verb which describes the subjects as participating in the results of the action." The people talking influence but don't control the outcome. Says Peterson: "We neither manipulate God, nor are manipulated by God. We are involved in the action and participate in its results but do not control or define it."[18] We are united with Jesus through his indwelling Spirit; out of that mutuality of spirit, we listen and act, whether it is through prayer, speech or service.

Brother Lawrence makes a similar point when he suggests that we:

> … take the position in prayer before God of a dumb helpless beggar at a rich man's gate. It is the beggar's responsibility to be alert to the rich man's moves. In the same way, make your times of prayer times of submission. Fix your thoughts on him whether you speak or keep quiet. Watch for his every move.

Prayer is about listening attentively, and only then responding.

As we "watch for his every move," the name of a friend who is sick with cancer and in need of prayer may come to mind. You may suddenly remember a coworker you haven't seen in a long time — it's God's way of nudging you to pray for her. Ole Hallesby says, "Prayer has one function and that is to answer "yes" when Christ knocks."[19]

Prayer is a way of developing our friendship with God. It's not just to accomplish things. Joyce Hugget shares her epiphany of realizing the value of listening prayer:

> … it had never occurred to me that God wanted me to linger in his presence so that he could show me that he delighted

in me. Until now, my prayer had been vocal, busy, sometimes manipulative, always achievement-oriented. To kneel at the foot of a cross and allow music to wash over me so that I could "just be" with God in stillness which convinced me that "he is," that "He is God" was a new experience. But to "waste time" for God in this way changed my life, changed my view of God, changed my perception of prayer, changed my understanding of listening to God.[20]

One way I "put up my spiritual antennae" is to pray in tongues. Evidently, Paul prayed frequently in tongues, but privately rather than in church: "I thank God that I speak in tongues more than all of you. But in the church I would rather speak five intelligible words to instruct others than ten thousand words in a tongue" (1 Cor 14:18-19).

Paul describes praying in tongues as an activity of his spirit, but not his mind: "For if I pray in a tongue, my spirit prays, but my mind is unfruitful. So what shall I do? I will pray with my spirit, but I will also pray with my mind ..." (1 Cor 14:14,15).

I don't fully understand what's happening when I pray in tongues, but somehow my spirit is engaging with God's Spirit. I don't know what to pray but God does. Praying in tongues is a pathway for asking according to his will.

Finding a Routine

My regular habit is to rise at around 6:30am. I have a cup of coffee and read scripture and various books inspired by scripture. Reading God's word and gifted authors expounding on scripture spurs me on towards prayer. A mixture of reading, listening and praying works best for me. Sometimes I include musical worship, playing and singing a few favorite songs or singing spontaneously.

Now that Linda and I are finished with the babies-and-toddlers stage of our lives, it's easy to keep a regular discipline. Just a few years ago it was more challenging to carve out times to pray. In describing those early years, Linda says, "Quiet times were a bonus. I needed to know that there was help, wisdom, strength and anointing 24/7." She has also said to me, "I didn't have very many quite times. Lots of *crisis* times and *chaos* times, but few quiet times." Now that our youngest child is eight years old, Linda *does* have a regular quiet time but she says, "When I have quiet times and time to contemplate I often doze in and out of prayer. Praying and listening while I work and while I play is usually more effective."

In preparing to write this chapter, I ran across some notes I made some years ago describing the flexibility required for parents of young children:

"My daily discipline is sometimes interrupted by a two-year old who gets up earlier than usual. (While preparing this talk, my two-year old bit my five-year old's finger and I went to break up a fight)."

I have many friends who leave for work very early in the morning, so early morning prayer and study doesn't work for them. Each one of us has to find a pattern that works best. I know that without a regular prayer and study time I would lose my bearings, lose my reference point. There's nothing like being in God's presence, nothing quite like having a living, vital experience of the love and character of God is essential to be able to keep walking the path of faith. Faith for day-to-day living is like water in a leaky bucket; we have to keep going to Jesus to fill up the bucket.

Paul prayed for the Ephesian church members: "I pray that out of his glorious riches he may strengthen you with power through his Spirit in your inner being, so that Christ may dwell in your hearts through faith … " (Eph 3:16,17). Wasn't Christ already dwelling in their hearts? Yes. Did they need more? Of course they did. We always need more of God.

In the internet age, you can spend the whole day 'surfing'. There's enough funny stuff on Youtube to entertain you all day long. You can make Facebook the center of your life. It's easier than ever to let prayer be squeezed out. If we don't have focused time with God, we lose our edge. Not to pray is to say that we don't need God, that we can handle things by ourselves. "If we grasp the importance of prayer," writes Simon Guillebaud, "it will undergird our very existence and act as the engine-room for all our activities, such that we will be too busy not to pray."[21]

It seems like I spend a lot my life "coming back to the heart of worship" as Matt Redman puts it. I need to re-center my life on Jesus every day. I'm just like everyone else — I feel pulled away from the pursuit of God by the counterfeit gods of this world. So I go directly to the well of living water. I go to God's word to find what is real, what is lasting. There I find my Father. There I find his instructions for living my life.

It is only when I slow down long enough to absorb God's love and truth that I find food for my soul and nourishment for the journey. "All our ancestors agree that without silence and stillness there is no spirituality, no God-attentive, God-responsive life."[22] There's nothing like being with God, meditating on his marvelous attributes, thanking him for all he has done for me. Sometimes I find great refreshing in singing simple songs of love and devotion — just God, me and the guitar or piano. The simple joy of melody lifts my soul and enlightens my mind to the presence of Jesus. I see that Jesus is alive.

On summer mornings in Vancouver, after a long, cold, rainy winter and spring, I often pray and read in the early morning on my front porch. I turn my face towards the sun, basking in the warmth it brings in the cool morning air. I hear a chorus of birds singing their various God-given songs. I see the majestic mountains in the distance, and I thank the One who made them. I marvel at God's faithfulness through my life, his tender care despite my smallness in his great creation.

Conclusion

A prayer from my journal, 2002: "A lifelong quest to be God's friend: God, help me to be your friend; to be with you, to please you, to love you. May I give you my best, may my eye be single, focused on you."

Chapter 5
Partners with God

God-friendship is for God-worshipers; they are the ones he confides in. (Psalm 25:12)
— The Message

Linda was recently reading the book of Exodus. God spoke to her through the "pillar of cloud" imagery from that book and she shared with me:

> The Israelites had to wake up every morning check "the cloud" everyday to see if they are moving or staying. My first response to reading that was "that sucks." You never know what's going to happen. How do you get anything done? How do you settle down? Then Lord said to me, "well, would you like to stay somewhere I'm NOT?" When He put it to me like that, my response was "I want to be where you are. If you want us to go, I'm ready to go.[1]

Linda and I have lived in seven different cities in our twenty-nine year marriage. We've listened for our "marching orders" and tried our best to follow the Lord. Linda is naturally more of a "settler" and I'm more of an adventure seeker. We've tried to submit to God and one another and move when the cloud is moving.

Worship at its core is about relationship with God. As we have seen in the last chapter, prayer is a vital element of that relationship, and across the next few pages we will look at what it means to know and worship God and *do life* with him and for him. This is the pattern for all the great worshipers of the Bible and all the outstanding figures in church history — they listen and obey. I'll share a few stories in this chapter about very specific direction we've received from God, about the way that we — and others — have been worshipping and watching for the cloud.

An Ordinary Man

In Luke's account of the birth of Christ we meet Simeon, simply described as " ... a man in Jerusalem named Simeon. He was righteous and devout ..." (Luke 2:25 NLT). He is not a priest or prophet, he holds no official office. Yet Luke says Simeon " ... was eagerly waiting for the Messiah to come and rescue Israel ... " (Luke 2:25 NLT) and that " ... the Holy Spirit was upon him" (Luke 2:25 NLT). His heart was tuned in to the priorities and plans of God. He was the kind of man who made a habit of listening to God.

The Lord had promised Simeon that " ... he would not die before he had seen the Lord's Messiah" (Luke 2:26 NLT). On the day Mary and Joseph brought the baby Jesus to the temple to dedicate him, " ... the Spirit *led him* [Simeon] to the Temple ..." (Luke 2:27 NLT, emphasis added). How exactly did the Spirit lead him? We'll never know. Perhaps Simeon just *knew* he had to go the temple that day. We do know that when Mary and Joseph showed up, Simeon was there.

Simeon took the baby in his arms and praised God, saying:

> Sovereign Lord, now let your servant die in peace, as you have promised. I have seen your salvation, which you have prepared for all people. He is a light to reveal God to the nations, and he is the glory of your people Israel! (Luke 2:29-32 NLT).

Simeon was a common man who loved God with all his heart. His deep devotion made him ready to receive the Lord's messages and he had cultivated a lifestyle of responding to the urgings of the Spirit. For Simeon, following an impulse from God to go to the temple on this day was natural.

God is looking for today's equivalents of Simeon: "a woman who lives in Chicago who is righteous and very devout"… "a teenager who lives in Atlanta who is righteous and very devout" … "a man who lives in Hong Kong who is righteous and very devout." As we respond to the ideas God plants in our thoughts, He will set up divine appointments like the one Simeon had with the newborn Jesus. Then, we become messengers for the Lord.

Here's a fact for you: God speaks to ordinary people. Moses wasn't an eloquent speaker, but he "spoke with God as a man speaks to his friend" and then led God's people to freedom from slavery. Along the way, God led Moses with specific instructions.

David, a renowned worship musician and psalmist, was conscripted to lead Yahweh's armies. He received specific instructions from God at crucial moments as a leader. He had no plans, no strategy, no greater wisdom than dependence on God's direction.

Paul, the apostle, had a conversational relationship with God. Jesus commissioned him to go the Gentiles, and spoke to him many times on his missionary journeys, telling him where to go and not to go, and what he could expect in certain places. God spoke to Paul about both the big picture of his life and about specific day-by-day plans.

Intimacy and Obedience

Partners talk about the work they do together. Like any good Senior Partner, God lets his partners in on the process of planning, making decisions and moving forward. Any wise manager cheers on his workers and points them in the right direction with encouraging words. Yet these days we talk less about God being some kind of Senior Partner figure and instead the expression "intimacy with God" is commonly used to describe close friendship with God. Many of our worship songs paint pictures of intimacy with God — hearing his voice, feeling his presence and knowing him more deeply. But how can we really hope to be "intimate" with God?

Respect, reverence and obedience are at the heart of this intimate relationship. When applied to our relationship with God, 'intimacy' has a different shade of meaning than for human relationships. Intimacy with my wife, my kids and my mother, while similar in some ways, are all unique. All these relationships resemble my relationship with God but are also very different.

One of the most powerful books in Scripture on friendship and intimacy with God is John's gospel. In chapter 14, Jesus promises to be intimate with his disciples: "And I will ask the Father and he will give you another Counselor to be with you forever" (John 14:16). And a few verses later, " … He who loves me will be loved by my Father, and I too will love him and show myself to him" (John 14:21). These are great promises — God says he will be close to us!

But that's only part of the story; Jesus only promises to be intimate with those disciples *who obey him*. In chapter 14, Jesus says the same thing *three times* in a row. He's really trying to make a point here.

> If you love me, you will *obey* what I command. And I will ask the Father, and he will give you another Counselor … (John 14:15-16, emphasis added).

> Whoever has my commands and *obeys* them, he is the one who loves me. He who loves me will be *loved by my Father*, and *I too will love him* and show myself to him (John 14:21, emphasis added).

> Jesus replied, "If anyone loves me, he will *obey* my teaching. My Father will *love him*, and we will *come to him and make our home* with him" (John 14:23, emphasis added).

For Jesus, true love for God is expressed in obedience. Usually we put the emphasis on God's unconditional love, on the fact that he loves us in spite of our failings. As true as this is, it's not the whole story.

In the verses above Jesus is saying to his disciples, and to us, "do you want to be intimate with me, close to me? Then do what I say. Do you want to experience my love, receive revelation from me? Then do as I say."

We have many songs these days about being in the Father's warm embrace and being filled with His comforting Spirit. I love those songs. But in our culture of narcissism, we could be led to believe that intimacy with God is all about *feeling* loved. It's as if we believe that if *we can get a warm, fuzzy experience in worship then we have been intimate with God.* I really enjoy every *feeling* that comes from worshiping Jesus, but friendship with God is bigger than that. Feelings make for a lousy compass.

> "You are my friends if you do what I command. I no longer call you slaves, because a master doesn't confide in his slaves. Now you are my friends, since I have told you everything the Father told me. You didn't choose me. I chose you. I appointed you to go and produce lasting fruit, so that the Father will give you whatever you ask for, using my name" (John 15:14-16 NLT).

In this particular passage, there is a strong connection between being a *friend* of God and bearing fruit. If the energy of our life is devoted to obeying God (v. 14), and sharing God's love (v. 17), *then* Jesus calls us his friend.

Jesus describes his ongoing conversation with his Father: "For the Father loves the Son and shows him everything he is doing … " (John 5:20). This is in the context of Jesus' healing ministry. Jesus couldn't do anything without the Father.

Jesus said he came not to do his own will, but the will of his Father who sent him. To get his marching orders, Jesus listened to his Father. And his Father spoke. This was a very natural exchange between Father and Son. Family members talk to one another —

that is how they express their love, and share their lives together. That is how covenant relationships are lived out.

If we were doing our best to love God with all our heart and love our neighbor as ourselves, why *wouldn't* he speak to us to help us on our way? God doesn't expect us to undertake the mission of serving him in an isolated state of *ex-communicado*.

Specific Instructions Given to Paul

In Acts 16, we see Paul traveling through the region of Phrygia and Galatia. They had been " … the Holy Spirit had prevented them from preaching the word in the province of Asia …" *(*Acts 16:6 NLT). When they were opposite Mysia, they attempted to go into Bithynia, " … *but again the Spirit of Jesus did not allow them to go there*" (Acts 16:7 NLT); so, passing by Mysia, they went down to Troas. During the night *Paul had a vision*: there stood a man of Macedonia pleading with him, and saying, " … *Come over to Macedonia and help us!*" (Acts 16:9 NLT). When he had seen the vision, he immediately tried to cross over to Macedonia, being convinced God had called them to proclaim the good news to them.

God clearly communicated to Paul and his traveling companions. In his partnering with Jesus, Paul needed to get his marching orders from the General of the army. While on his way to Jerusalem, the Lord warns Paul of hardships: " … in every city the Holy Spirit warns me that prison and hardships are facing me" (Acts 20:23).

As a creative person, I have lots of ideas and many of them are bad ones! Last year I had an idea to do a series of Christmas worship concerts. It seemed like a good idea. I contacted a few friends about forming a band for these events, and I made a list of churches to contact to present the idea.

When it was time to start sending emails and making phone calls to book these events, I didn't feel right about it. Several times

I sat down to begin the process of contacting people, but I kept getting a feeling God was holding me back. In hindsight, I'm so glad that I followed this hunch. When December came around and I had finished a very heavy season of travel, I desperately needed a break. After an exhausting three months of ministry on the road, I wouldn't have had energy for a series of Christmas concerts. God stopped me from going overboard with my idea factory. I wish I could say I've always stopped long enough to hear him say "no." God has given "hunches" to his people throughout history to help them make the right decisions.

To hear the whispers of God, we simply have to listen. We have to be smart enough to know that we don't know all the answers. To rush into doing our own plans without listening for God's input is presumptuous. I frequently pray "Lord, keep me from going down the wrong road. Keep me from striving to accomplish my plans when you have a better idea."

Others Who Listened

Philip was a disciple who was actively engaged in preaching the gospel, another man who knew what it meant to respond to the words of Jesus. As a man of action in God's kingdom, he was poised to receive instructions from the Lord. Here we see a remarkable story of specific guidance: "Now an angel of the Lord said to Philip, "Go south to the road — the desert road — that goes down from Jerusalem to Gaza. *So he started out …*" (Acts 8:26,27, emphasis added).

Understanding that it's always a good idea to obey when God instructs, Philip went down the road and met a court official of the queen of Ethiopia. Then, God spoke again: "The Spirit told Philip, 'Go to that chariot and stay near it'" (Acts 8:29). God gave Philip *very specific instructions*. And *as he obeyed*, God gave him more information.

I've found that it works this way in my life. I respond to a word from God, or at least what I perceive to be a word from God, and after step one, he gives me step two. I usually make a lot of mistakes along the way, but he faithfully re-directs me.

King David was another one who received specific instructions from God. David was trying to figure out where to live, so he asked the Lord, " … David inquired of the LORD. 'Shall I go up to one of the towns of Judah?'" he asked. The LORD said, "Go up." David asked, "Where shall I go?" "To Hebron," the LORD answered" (2 Sam. 2:1). David needed to know where to live, so he simply asked God.

In 1983 I was driving out to Twentynine Palms, California to visit my wife who was visiting her mother. Along the way the Lord told me "go help at the new Vineyard in Santa Barbara." It seemed like a clear word. So we drove up to Santa Barbara to meet with the pastor. Before long, we moved there and I became a volunteer intern pastor while my wife worked as a nurse.

Several years later, we were living in Canada. While visiting Anaheim, the Lord spoke to me about moving again. While driving onto a freeway onramp, God said, "someday, you're going to live here." That was the last thing I expected. I was just about to begin a new job as a senior pastor of a church in Surrey, British Columbia. Four years later, we moved to Anaheim where I worked in a large Vineyard church.

I've joined up with Jesus and his cause. I'm doing the best I can to follow him. He gives me fuel for the journey by speaking to me in a myriad of ways. Dallas Willard says "our union with God consists chiefly in a conversational relationship with God while we are each consistently and deeply engaged as his friend and co-laborer in the affairs of the kingdom of heaven."[2]

His speaking is not as loud and frequent as I would hope, but as I look through my journal and see what he has said, I see how strong and consistent his words are. Of course, his still small voice is only one way that he speaks. His written word is alive and powerful, always available, and always relevant in directing my life. And the counsel of friends and elders is indispensable.

Moses Receives Ongoing Encouragement

I can think of few people in the Bible that heard from God more than Moses. Moses had a difficult life-assignment from God; he was to lead a huge group of grumbling people through the wilderness. It didn't matter how many times God spoke to Moses along the way, he needed ongoing encouragement.

After numerous miraculous revelations and miracles — the command to set the Hebrew people free, his staff that morphed into a serpent, manna from heaven, and water coming from a rock, just to name a few — Moses asked to see God's glory. He wanted reassurance that God's presence was still with him.

We all need that reassurance, over and over again. We don't stand head and shoulders above the crowd like Moses did, but we are no less God's *friends*.

As a father, I am delighted when I see my kids taking initiative to care for their younger siblings. When my kids were younger, I would heave a sigh of relief when an older brother rescued a toddler from an impending fall and injury. "They're getting it!" I'd say to myself. In these moments I thanked my maturing teenagers, cheering them on, giving them more reason to keep showing compassion. I guess this is just a pale reflection of the way that God sees us.

One word that God has spoken many times to us is "I have called you here." I find it very encouraging when God reminds me that I'm in the right city and the right church. Recently, I was attending a Bible study and God's presence came to me in a beautiful, unexpected way. Again he spoke those words: "you are in the right place."

Moments of revelation stay with me for a long time. When

God personalizes his word to us — when he speaks directly to us in our spirit — we are powerfully strengthened, encouraged and comforted.

Chapter 6
God Talks to His Friends

Prayer is simply talking to God. He speaks to us: we listen.
We speak to him: he listens. A two-way process:
speaking and listening.[1]
— *Mother Teresa*

Friends of God

They call us arrogant. They call us fools. They call us deluded. Some people think it's presumptuous to believe that almighty God would speak to us. Dallas Willard quotes actress Lily Tomlin, summing up the problem: "Why is it that when we speak to God we are said to be praying but when God speaks to us we are said to be schizophrenic?"[2]

And yet speaking to his people is precisely what God does. The Bible tell us that God speaks, church history tells us that God speaks and I'll bet that to some degree you know it to be true in your own life. If God is all-powerful and all knowing, then he certainly knows how each of our "tomorrows" is going to unfold. Is it really so presumptuous to think that God would talk to his friends and family?

"You are my friends if you do what I command," said Jesus "I no longer call you servants, because a servant does not know his master's business. Instead, I have called you friends, for everything that I learned from my Father I have made known to you" (John 15:14,15). Jesus has chosen to give us inside information — to let us in on what he is doing and planning.

God talks to his friends, and it is this idea of friendship that is vital to grasp. When friends talk, it is a lot more than one friend telling another what to do. Communication between friends is about connection, being together, being of the same heart and mind.

When God gives me a tip on something unusual that's coming the next day, or when he gives me a revelatory word that shows me how to pray for one of my friends, it gives me *confidence*. Not confidence in my abilities, but an assurance that he is with me, helping me every step of the way.

The Love of a Family

The imagery in the Bible that describes our relationship with God is very diverse; he calls us co-laborers, servants, heirs, children and friends. Many of these metaphors are familial relationships: parent-child, sheep-shepherd and husband-wife. In all of those relationships, there is ongoing dialogue, the kind that nurtures and strengthens the relationship.

Put another way, what kind of marriage would *exclude* intimate conversation? — only a really bad one. If the cords of conversation are cut between Linda and me, it doesn't take long before we're in conflict. If our responsibilities eclipse our friendship, we wander down parallel but separate roads and find ourselves in different worlds. But if we take time to talk, we stoke the fire of our mutual love and commitment to one another. Family members talk to each other. Fact.

And while we are on the subject, what kind of parent-child relationship would *exclude* communication? — only a heart-breaking one. There is a direct correlation between broken homes and broken communication. When a father and son never talk, how can love be given, how can trust be engendered? Without two-way conversations, a loving attachment can't be built and nurtured.

The gospel of the New Testament models intimate conversation with a loving Father. We see Jesus listening to his Father all the time for what to say and do. Though God is called "gracious and compassionate" throughout the Old Testament, Jesus is the first to address him with the personal language of Abba, a term of endearment that was used in Jesus' time to address one's earthly father.

Eugene Peterson's description of the resurrection life in Romans 8 of *The Message* is especially touching: "It's adventurously expectant, greeting God with a childlike "What's next, Papa?" God's Spirit touches our spirits and confirms who we really are. We know who he is, and we know who we are: Father and children" (Rom 8:15, *The Message*).

Studies on child development show that children need consistent one-on-one contact with their parents for healthy emotional and mental development. Children thrive on attention. They need to regularly hear their parents say "I love you." They need to feel affirmed by a listening, responsive parent. Without this kind of loving care, children feel insecure. Without a nurturing parental presence, they aren't happy and don't play well with their siblings or other kids.

Just as kids blossom under the constant affirmation of parents, so we as God's children thrive on personal contact with our loving heavenly Father. Without our Father's assuring words we don't know who we are or how we fit in our Father's world. Paul echoes this with a clarion call to experiencing God's love. He prays that his churches would experience this same union with Christ, this same personal knowledge of God's powerful love:

I pray that out of his glorious riches he may strengthen you with power through his Spirit in your inner being, so that Christ may dwell in your hearts through faith. And I pray that you, being rooted and established in love, may have power, together with all the saints, to grasp how wide and long and high and deep is the love of Christ ..." (Eph 3:16-18).

Jackie Pullinger, lifelong missionary to Hong Kong, has been a great inspiration to me. I recently heard her share a story[3] of how her personal prayer times often go. She uses the Lord's Prayer, beginning with "My Father" and saying to him "Lord, you are so wonderful, so beautiful," as she meditates on the Lord's goodness. Then the Father says to her "You are so wonderful ... you are so beautiful." This goes on for a long time, back and forth, each one speaking to the other about how special and beloved and precious they are.

After a while, Jackie asks, "Can we talk about work now?" The Father says "no." He wants her just to listen to him say how special she is — just to sit and wait. So she continues praising the Father and resting in his love, and then after another several minutes, she asks again, "Can we talk about work now?" And he replies "Not now." After some time she asks again, "Will we ever talk about work?" And he replies "Maybe not." Very often he will say "maybe not." It's not that he doesn't care about what's happening with the work of helping people, it's just that he wants her to be continually be filled up with a fresh dose of his revealed, personal love.

Jackie's life is all about helping people in need. For forty-plus years she has lived in Hong Kong, helping the poorest of the poor. The Father has a priority of helping her take a breather from serving others to shower his love on her.

Jesus said that he and the father would *make their home* with those who love and obey him (John 14:23) and that his Father would reveal himself to each one of us (John 14:21). What a picture of warmth and intimacy. Home is where we know unconditional love and acceptance, it's where we can completely relax and be ourselves, a place to talk about anything and everything. In my home, I talk to my kids all the time. Surely our Father wants to talk to his children!

With my teenagers I talk about the things they're doing — their music, what's up in school, the sports they love. I'm interested in what my kids are doing because I love them. My conversation with them isn't limited to commands or instructions. What a sour relationship it would be if all I ever said was "take out the garbage." Just being with my kids and having a good time laughing and playing games is sometimes the best medicine for the soul. My presence with them communicates love and mutual enjoyment and this helps build a foundation for all the challenges and conflicts of family life.

Hanging out with toddlers is something I really miss. When my son Ian was three years old, he wanted to be with me no matter where I was or what I was doing. He would come running into my office, jump on my lap and say, "show me some pictures!" — His own birthday pictures got the biggest response. When I was gardening, he insisted on having his own shovel to dig alongside me. If I was going on an errand, he was thrilled to come along. He was enthusiastic about doing what I was doing, just because he got to be *with me*. Along the way, we talked.

When I put my kids to bed, I kiss them, pray for them, and tell them I love them. If I know how to do this for my kids, surely our Heavenly Father desires to speak his words of comfort to us.

It's mind-boggling to think that God could speak millions of different messages to millions of different people, all at the same time. But scripture reveals him as the all-seeing, all-knowing, self-revealing God. We see many God-encounters with people all through the Bible, and as "a kingdom of priests" we are all eligible for these divine breakthroughs. We don't earn the right; God gives it to us freely.

Dallas Willard describes our interaction with God as a "freely cooperative relationship between mature people who love each other with the richness of *agape* love."[4] While the fruit of our union and conversation with God is good works, it isn't the only topic of conversation. Our Father is interested in our well-being, and he has purposed from eternity past to lavish his love on us. So he finds lots of ways to communicate his love, not just his commandments.

Examples From the Bible and Church History

Encounters between God and his people are common throughout the Bible and in church history. Abraham, Moses, Paul and Peter all had mystical experiences with God and Paul considered revelatory experiences to be a part of normal Christian life.

Beyond the Bible it is possible to see a pattern that emerges as you read the stories of the most influential leaders and writers in church history. Most of them had profound experiences of God that launched their journey of faith. Tangible communication with God is commonplace, as the lives of George Fox and John Wesley make clear.

George Fox lived from 1624 to 1691 in England. He was raised in the Church of England but his spiritual thirst was never satisfied within that tradition. He founded "the Religious Society of Friends," better known as the Friends or the Quakers. Fox is known for emphasizing every Christian's direct experience with God. He describes the indwelling Holy Spirit as the "light of Christ within" and "Christ as inward Teacher."

The obvious scriptural basis for Fox's teaching is Jesus' parting words to his disciples: "But the Counselor, the Holy Spirit, whom the Father will send in my name, will teach you all things and will remind you of everything I have said to you" (John 14:26).

Because Fox taught people to be directly dependent on the Lord himself — and less tied to church authorities — his message was vehemently resisted by the Church of England. For most of his life his teaching was banned by the state church. He was beaten, stoned and tortured for his views of Christian spirituality.

Fox's model for hearing from God is finely balanced with respect for the authority of Scripture. While he is known for promoting the believer's direct experience of God's living presence, he did not elevate experience above scripture. The first four of his "Seven Elements in Our Life with God" are summarized as follows:

1. Every true Christian has direct, immediate experiences of Jesus.

2. These experiences are best understood by relating them to evidences from Scripture.

3. These experiences not only confirm current leadings but also provide new insights as we move through life.

4. Scripture teaches us how to relate our experiences of the historical Jesus with the leadings of the inward Christ.[5]

Soon after George Fox's period of prominence, another towering figure in church history came onto the scene: John Wesley (1703-1791). Wesley was the founder of the Methodist Church movement and a pioneer in starting churches throughout the United Kingdom emphasizing discipleship and personal accountability.

Like Fox, Wesley was a faithful Anglican, but became deeply agitated when he realized that thinking rightly about God wasn't enough. Hungry for assurance of his salvation he began a long period of diligent praying and searching for God. After a long period of prayer, he was forever transformed by an encounter with God at a meeting of Moravians in the south of London.

Up until that time he adhered to "three-point Anglicanism,"

which recognized the primary authority of Scripture with the secondary authorities of reason and tradition. After his life-changing encounter with God he included "experiencing God" as a fourth primary point in following Jesus. It was a message that remains just as relevant today:

"Wesley states that heart religion is confirmed by direct, immediate, inward experiences of God. Just as we know physical reality because of our natural senses, we know spiritual reality by our supernatural senses."[6]

Wesley was not unaware of emotionalism in certain sectors of Christianity. His healthy respect for scripture kept him from over-emphasizing the personal, direct experience of God as he had witnessed both in England and on the East coast of the United States. "Wesley realized that "experience" did not contradict Scripture but served to organize, illuminate and apply the truth of it to our life."[7]

The stories of George Fox and John Wesley highlight the importance of the many biblical examples of people encountering God. They remind us that knowing God is more than adherence to a body of truth. Engaging with God touches the deepest part of our souls. It is helpful to trace God's consistent self-revelation throughout history, lest we think that God-encounters are reserved only for Bible times, or limited to modern day Charismatic church movements. God's visitation is commonplace throughout every era.

The evidence of scripture and history is clear: we all have access to God and every one of his children can hear his voice. On the other hand, as I look at history I see some well-known preachers and saints who had amazing and extraordinary God-encounters. Most of us won't receive appearances of the crucified Christ experienced by such people as St. Francis of Assisi or Julian of Norwich. Saints and preachers such as St. Francis are a gift to the church in all generations. Their extraordinary encounters with God point the way for us towards intimacy with Jesus during this life and make us long for the bliss of heaven.

Seeing the God Who Sees Us

One of my favorite Bible stories that demonstrates God's desire to communicate his loving concern and awareness of our circumstances is the story of the Egyptian woman, Hagar (Gen 16:4-14). Hagar is the servant to Abram's wife, Sarai. When Sarai cannot conceive a child, she suggests that Abram sleep with Hagar to produce the child that God had promised to give. But when she becomes pregnant, Hagar despises Sarai. Sarai reacts angrily, treating Hagar harshly. Then, Hagar runs away into the desert to escape Sarai's abuse. Then the angel of the Lord appears to Hagar and begins by correcting her: " ... Return to your mistress and submit to her authority" (Gen 16:9 NLT).

The angel hasn't come only to rebuke, but to encourage. He promises that Hagar will have " ... more descendants than you can count," saying " ... the LORD has heard your cry of distress." (Gen 16:10-11). In God's compassion, he saw the pain and predicament of this Egyptian slave woman, and came to speak to her, guide her and rescue her. Though she had acted disrespectfully towards her mistress, God forgave and blessed her.

Before that God-encounter, Hagar likely saw God as distant and unconcerned. She was a foreigner, and not part of the chosen line of Abram. But after that experience with God, Hagar referred to the Lord, who had *spoken to her*, as " ... the God who *sees me*," for she said, " ... *I have seen the One who sees me!*" (Gen 16:13 NLT, emphasis added).

For me, this is a profound story that illustrates what it's like to *see the Lord*. I *know* He sees me. It's like a child who has lost her way wandering in the desert, and her father comes looking for her.

The child is frantic with fear, but when she sees her Daddy coming to her rescue, and looks into his eyes, she *sees the one who sees her* and everything changes.

When God sees us in our time of need, and takes initiative to speak and make a promise to us, we never see him the same again. From that time on, we see him as present, aware and ready to communicate with us. Like Hagar in her time of need, we think of God as *"the One* who *sees us."*

Hagar's dramatic encounter with the angel of the Lord isn't comparable to my daily experience. On occasion I've had very powerful encounters with God, accompanied by various physical phenomena, but mostly I hear him speaking in a " … gentle whisper" (1 Kgs 19:12). Like a butterfly that flutters into view and is gone in a few seconds, his whisperings are usually brief and gentle.

The Various Ways God Speaks to Us

Of course the scriptures are a primary source and the most reliable means of God speaking to us. We can see a scripture and it hits us like a ton of bricks, but at times God speaks through pictures in the mind's eye. With me these are usually faint images; seldom are they vivid and in "technicolor." To another person he speaks through intense feelings followed by a flood of ideas that tumble out of the heart and into a journal. Other people "hear" a word or phrase or idea go through their mind, but it's not an audible hearing — it's more of a knowing.

The thing to remember is that God is infinite; He speaks to people in diverse ways. I won't attempt to give an exhaustive list. Some people have very little emotion attached to hearing from God, while others gush with tears. Some people dream dreams, others see visions (Acts 2:17) and others have a simple but profound sense of knowing truth from God.

God can speak to us through a movie or a novel or a formation of clouds in the sky. A few years ago at the national Canadian Vineyard conference in Manitoba, someone in the meeting gave a word about "God's hand being on us." At the same moment, Rik Berry, a pastor and gifted artist, was on the platform and had just finished painting a prophetic picture of God's hand upon us. Then, someone said "look up in the sky!" Rik came out from under the band shell overhang to see a cloud formation in the shape of a hand with distinct fingers. The cloud was right over our outdoor meeting place, confirming the prophetic words through a natural phenomenon.

The Difference It Makes

Previous to my awakening to God as a teenager, I had a vague knowledge of God as "up there somewhere." Then he turned the lights on. Before, his written words were only an abstract idea. Then they became living words, daily bread for my soul. He kept on speaking to me, sometimes with surprising clarity. Sometimes I'm frustrated because I can't hear him more clearly. But he is God and I am not; he chooses when to speak.

In the seasons of silence, there are many memories of revelation from my past that instill confidence. Like monuments dotting the path I've walked, God's words and fulfilled promises bolster my confidence for today's journey. My response to God's whisperings is deep thankfulness. Constant contact with my Father makes me secure and steady. I'm able to fight off demons of discouragement because my Father is present and speaking. Though I make mistakes, he comes to me as he did to Hagar, with correction, guidance and blessing. He keeps reminding me — *I will be with you.*

This is the never-ending cycle of worship, revelation, more worship and more revelation. The more we see, the more we worship, and the more we worship, the more we see.

He Speaks Before We Ask

I'm amazed that God will sometimes take the first step, speaking to me before I call on him. This communicates that he "sees me" and is ready and able to rescue me from myriad problems, bolstering my faith for the present day.

Occasionally, just as I'm about to fall asleep, God gives me an impression such as: "It's going to be a really good day" ... or "get ready for a surprise." It's like a quick idea flashing in my head, like an exclamation point appearing in the air for a brief moment, and then it's gone. In those bedtime moments when God whispers, I'm often not praying. God takes the initiative. As I'm dozing off and my brain is going into "suspend mode," I'm startled by a clear thought. The words sound like my own thoughts, yet I know that they're coming from outside me.

When I get these nudges from God, inevitably something extraordinary happens the next day — I get a phone call from a close friend I haven't heard from for ages, I have a conversation with a coworker that is a key turning point, I receive an unexpected check in the mail, or I'm really happy because it's a beautiful sunny day — that might sound trite but it can be huge if you live in Vancouver and you've had twenty or thirty straight days of cloud and rain!

These words often come at the end of a tough day. God's gift of communication at that time lets me know two things — he sees the struggles of the present day and he has something good planned for tomorrow. In the heat of the battle, God says *I will be with you*. His words bring comfort, strength, and encouragement.

Let's get back to that first question: why would he speak to us like this? Why would he go to the trouble of saying something so specific, yet so simple? The answer is clear; because he loves us and wants us to know *he is with us*. He wants us to know that he knows everything that *is happening* and *is going to happen* in our lives. He doesn't miss a thing. His promise that we'll never be separated from his love isn't just theory, it's a reality (Rom 8:39). Our Father finds creative ways to communicate his abiding presence.

I Will Be With You

Over and over again in the Bible God tells his people "I will be with you." To Isaac, God said " ... I am the God of your father Abraham. Do not be afraid, for *I am with you ...*" (Gen 26:24, emphasis added). To Moses, who was desperate for a guarantee of God's presence and favor after the golden calf incident, God said " ... I will personally go with you, Moses, and I will give you rest — everything will be fine for you" (Ex 33:14 NLT, emphasis added).

To Joshua, who had some awfully big shoes to fill after Moses passed away, God said, "So be strong and courageous! Do not be afraid and do not panic before them. For the LORD your God will personally go ahead of you. *He will neither fail you nor abandon you*" (Deut 31:6 NLT, emphasis added). The list goes on, because more than anything else we need to know that God is with us. When he speaks to us, revealing that he sees our personal needs at specific moments in time, we're comforted and strengthened.

Sometimes all we need is to know that God is with us. Sometimes all we need is to be reminded of the fact that we are a child — and a friend — of God.

Can you picture Jesus walking into the room right now, smiling as he sees you, and reaching out to embrace you? Can you imagine what it would be like for him to look right into your eyes, giving you his full attention? Can you feel his genuine concern and love for you?

Jesus would listen intently to your every word, picking up every nuance, gesture, and emotion. He would completely understand what you're going through. And then he would respond to you, telling you just what you need to hear. You would feel safe and secure in his love and you would know that *he is with you.*

Can you image anything more precious?

Chapter 7
Be Like Little Children

Anyone who becomes as humble as this little child
is the greatest in the Kingdom of Heaven (Matt 18:4 NLT).
— Jesus

Ruben and Rachel were only seven years old. The twins had been following Jesus, wide-eyed with wonder, from the moment he arrived in their little town in Galilee. After seeing one miraculous healing, they stuck to Jesus like glue. They had to sneak away from their parents to follow this amazing man all through their little town.

It was the Sabbath Day and a large crowd of people surrounded Jesus. In the group were his disciples and a few Pharisees. The twins elbowed their way through the throngs of people and made it to the front just in time to hear Jesus say, "Stretch out your hand!" to a man with the withered hand. When he stretched it out his hand, it was healed! Gasps and exclamations erupted from the crowd of onlookers.

"Wow!" cried Ruben. "Look what Jesus did!"

The kids had never seen anything like it. Right before his eyes, people were being healed.

On another day, they saw Jesus feed thousands of people from a little boy's lunch.

"Did you see all those leftover baskets of bread?" shouted

Rachel, full of wonder. "That's totally amazing! What's he going to do next?"

Awestruck, Ruben and Rachel wanted nothing more than to be close to Jesus, to give him their full attention and soak up every moment.

Of course, the story of Ruben and Rachel is fictional, but Jesus said the kingdom of heaven belonged to children like Ruben and Rachel:

> … Let the little children come to me, and do not hinder them, for the kingdom of heaven belongs to such as these (Matt 19:14).

> … Unless you change and become like little children, you will never enter the kingdom of heaven. Therefore, whoever humbles himself like this child is the greatest in the kingdom of heaven (Matt 18:3-4).

The "kingdom of heaven" is not reserved for the "afterlife;" it is here right now. It intersects this earthly realm and we can receive the blessings of heaven and be conduits of those blessings today. Yet there is a catch; to do so, we must be like humble children.

Children are full of expectation

Unlike the twins I've never seen Jesus in person. But I've seen him heal people many times, not just from inner pain, but from physical ailments that disappeared. But I've also experienced a lot of disappointment — unanswered prayers, shattered dreams, and the daily grind of living in a world that is tainted with evil. After years of attending church, it's easy to come to worship with a low expectation of *really* seeing Jesus. I've heard the Bible stories and I've seen the power of God many times, but expecting Jesus to do miraculous things today is still difficult. Keeping that childlike optimism is hard.

It takes dogged determination to keep returning to the prayer Jesus taught us to pray: " … Our Father in heaven, hallowed be your name, your kingdom come, your will be done on earth as it is in heaven" (Matt 6:9,10). In this, the only prayer Jesus specifically instructed his disciples to pray, Jesus tells us to pray that his rule and reign would come right now. How can we, as worldly wise adults, embrace such unbridled expectation?

The Kingdom Is Near!

Ruben and Rachel would have heard Jesus say: "The kingdom is near you!" They saw the *demonstration* of this kingdom power by multiplying the fish and loaves to feed the hungry. The message was clear: the in-breaking power of the kingdom to heal, save and deliver is within our reach.

How can we regain this childlike expectation that Jesus' kingdom is here? One way to stir up our faith is to meditate on the historical reality of God's wonder working power in the Bible and in church history. To really see Jesus, just check out the undiluted kingdom of God in the gospels and the book of Acts. At Pentecost, the people were filled with faith and a pervasive spirit of worship: "Everyone was *filled with awe*, and many wonders and miraculous signs were done by the apostles" (Acts 2:43, emphasis added).

Here is a principle we see repeated numerous times in church history — a renewal of worship is accompanied by an outpouring of God's Spirit for healing and salvation. A few examples are the sixteenth century with Martin Luther, the Wesleyan revival of the 1800s, and the early 1900s in the Azusa Street revival in Los Angeles. In all these cases, dynamic worship in song was accompanied by outpourings of the Holy Spirit to empower and renew God's people.

We can increase our childlike expectancy of God's visitation by revisiting these chapters in church history in which worship was thriving and the Holy Spirit was moving powerfully. One such outpouring of God's Spirit in recent times came to the Anaheim Vineyard in the 1970s and '80s.

Todd Hunter, now a bishop in the Rwandan Diocese of the Anglican Church, is a former Vineyard church planter. Hunter speaks first on the distinctive quality of the early worship of the Anaheim Vineyard:[1]

> For 25 years I've traveled all over the world; I've participated in worship services, conferences, seminars, retreats and just about every other setting in which Christian worship takes place. In my judgment, the worship in the early era of Calvary Chapel/Vineyard Yorba Linda stands out way above the rest — it is of a completely different nature.

Hunter says that the three distinguishing characteristics of early Vineyard worship were: intimacy with God, the manifest presence of the Holy Spirit, and a culture of expecting God to visit his church powerfully in every time of worship.

He describes the congregation's desire for intimacy and eager anticipation as it looked forward to worshiping together.

> We literally could not wait to get to church; to be in the congregation, to worship, to see what God would do today, etc. We felt anticipation and we had legitimate hope that God would visit us in worship because he was consistent in doing so.[2]

> Many people walked into worship services for the first time and were caught up into the cycle and the atmosphere it created without ever giving it a conscious thought, except in hindsight: "what just happened to me; why do I feel so loved and so full of love, so close to God, so willing to pour out my heart to God in worship, to serve others, etc?"

Todd explains that it wasn't about the music, it was all about knowing God: "I don't ever remember anyone walking out of the gym and remarking about the band, the great guitar licks, the cool piano chops or the amazing vocal performances. It was all about feeling and knowing the presence of God and responding to him in worship."

We can't recreate past moments in history. In His sovereignty, God moves one way in one season, and then another way. Yet the truth of Jesus' words are still real today: "the kingdom is near you" (Matt 3:2, 4:17, 10:7). With God's help, we can see what Jesus saw: "To Jesus' eyes this is a God-bathed and God-permeated world. It is a world filled with a glorious reality, where every component is within the range of God's direct knowledge and control."[3]

Jesus-style worship means to invite the blessings of heaven to bring change today. We can start with the push-to-the-front-row kind of eagerness we see in Ruben and Rachel.

The Spirit of Adventure

I have a ten-year old son named Ian. Ian loves adventure, whether he gets it through books, movies or action characters. But he doesn't just want to read about something that happened once a long time ago. He wants to enter into the story and become one of the characters. So he goes into the backyard with his friend and they act out the roles of their heroes, even quoting lines from the movies as they fight. It's not a story anymore, it's real life. They don't care how they look. They just go for it.

This is what childlike faith can do. We enter into the acts of Jesus, so it's not just a story from long ago. We throw caution to the wind and reach out our hand to pray for someone or speak to someone. In kingdom activity, we learn by doing. If childlike faith wins out over adult constraint, we might just do something Jesus-like. It's not about whether we're going to win or lose. It's about doing what our hero does. We jump in the pool with both feet and learn to swim.

In the sixth chapter of John, we see a boy who took a leap of faith. When five thousand hungry people were gathered to listen to Jesus teach, and it was time for lunch, there was only one young boy who had brought his lunch. Peter's brother, Andrew said, "There's a young boy here with five barley loaves and two fish. But what good is that with this huge crowd?" (John 6:9 NLT).

I'm not the most generous person in the world; I'm still learning. I find the idea of sharing my lunch a little troubling. If I pack my lunch for a picnic, I want to *eat my own lunch*. When it's lunchtime, I'm *hungry!* Why should I share my food with anyone else? They could have planned ahead and brought some food, but they didn't. Why should I rescue them? But this little boy just gave it away, despite whatever doubts were in his mind or whatever criticism and taunts we coming from his friends.

I'm guessing this was the first time this boy was asked to share his lunch with five thousand people. It was a brand new challenge, a brand new step. This little boy didn't have to understand everything going on in this mob scene of hungry people before he was willing to participate. Someone asked for help, and he gave it. Childlike faith won the day. He didn't reason his way out of an act of generosity.

If we need to figure everything out before we'll take a step of faith, we won't get very far. If our priority is self-protection and self-preservation, we won't give much at all. But look what happened when this little boy took a step of faith. He took a risk and five thousand hungry people were fed. That's pretty good fruit for one little boy.

Do the Obvious

One advantage that Ruben and Rachel had over us is that following Jesus was by far the most exciting thing in town. Today we live in an age of computer games, television and i-pods. We're pulled away from hungering for God by a thousand different things.

I recently participated in a weekend worship conference in Australia called "Building a Tabernacle." The imagery is taken from the Old Testament tabernacle, which was a place for God to dwell, a place to meet with God. During the weekend, we spent a lot of time worshipping; that was the main priority. We taught from the Bible, but the first priority was to exalt God through singing and meditating on him, and to open our hearts to his Spirit and voice.

This is a simple, childlike act — setting aside many hours over a few days to sing songs of love and adoration to God. Many people were greatly refreshed by this time. In one worship time, God profoundly touched me with a sense of his royal majesty. Once again, He gave me an other-worldly experience of sensing his holiness and transcendence as King of Kings.

To walk in childlike humility, we must set aside time to be with him and worship him. The spiritual discipline of worship requires a submissive surrendering of our agenda to adore God, to let the reality of God sink deeply into our souls. We need to give him our full attention, to drop everything to do what Rachel and Ruben did; behold the Master's ways and works. This is the humble pathway to experiencing the wonders of his kingdom in the here and now.

My daughter Jessica isn't a child anymore — she's eighteen years old and quickly becoming an adult. I recently bought a book for her called "The Reason for God: Belief in an Age of Skepticism" by Tim Keller. She couldn't put it down. Not only did she immerse herself in the book but she found Keller's website and downloaded dozens of his sermons on podcasts. One day she devoured three of his messages in half a day.

Later in the summer she took a week-long Christian worldview course. Everyday she came home bursting with excitement about what she had learned. Her hunger for truth, and her less busy summertime schedule allowed her to be filled with truth, to sit at the feet of Jesus and soak in his word. There was space in her life, and she chose to fill it with Jesus instead of constant entertainment. Childlike behavior doesn't have to stop when the toys get packed away in the attic.

Children Know They Have a Lot to Learn

When the disciples asked, "Who is the greatest in the kingdom of heaven?" (Matt 18:1). Jesus said they needed to *change* and become like children to enter the kingdom of heaven. The world pushes us towards being the "greatest" but Jesus says, "humble yourself" like a child.

One of the definitions of "humble" is *unpretentious*. Kids know they have a low rank in the hierarchy of power, even within their own families. They know they have a lot to learn (though sometimes they won't admit it). Most of the time little children know that they need their parents. They might love sword fighting or dressing up, but they also gravitate to the safety of their mom or dad's lap. When pain hits, they gravitate to the source of their comfort and love. As adults we learn to respond in more sophisticated ways, losing out in the process.

Kids will ask for clarification when they are unsure what something means, and while we believe that we are done with being educated, the time that kids spend at school often leads them to be better suited to learning more about the nature and character of Jesus. Our minds can be closed while theirs remain wide open.

In the book of Romans, right after Paul tells us how to live a life of worship, he says, " … Do not think of yourself more highly than you ought … " (Rom 12:3). When you're seven years old and only four feet tall, you know you're not the king of the mountain. When you're six feet tall, it's harder to admit you have a lot to learn.

Imagine Ruben and Rachel and their parents listening intently to Jesus teach a lesson that would become perhaps his most famous sermon. A huge crowd had gathered, so Jesus hiked up the hillside with his closest followers. Further down the hill, the twins strained to hear every word, pick up every nuance.

God blesses those who are poor and *realize their need for him,* for the Kingdom of Heaven is theirs. God blesses those who mourn, for they will be comforted. God blesses those who are humble, for they will inherit the whole earth (Matt 5:3-5 NLT, emphasis added).

After this lesson, the seven-year-olds would have asked their parents many questions. I hope that their parents would have filled in any gaps in their understanding, making clear that childlike dependence on God is the kingdom way, no matter how old you are. I hope that they grew up to know that feeling a need for God means we are "blessed" and that being "blessed" means so much more than just being "happy." A blessed person is one who is to be envied and emulated. It's a term of congratulation and recommendation. If you do these things, you are to be congratulated. In the short term, you may not see great visible rewards, but you will win in the long run. You will have a rich relationship with God.

This short teaching alone contains a wealth of insight into being a follower of Jesus. After over three decades of following Jesus, this simple truth still astounds me and calls me to a healthy self-examination. God never wants me to be self-sufficient. I can only find his blessing if I realize my need for him. Self-sufficiency leads to being full of myself instead of being full of him.

Little Children Don't Hide Their Feelings

I love the uninhibited freedom of a toddler. They make the funniest noises, say the funniest things, and they have no idea that it looks silly. When my daughter Elizabeth was younger, she would start dancing as soon as I put a CD on the stereo. Her two-year old version of break dancing was hilarious to watch, but in her mind she had all the right moves. She also "danced" in her chair while eating without a shred of embarrassment.

Dallas Willard explains how we learn in adulthood to hide our true feelings: "Interestingly, "growing up" is largely a matter of learning to hide our spirit behind our face, eyes, and language so that we can evade and manage others to achieve what we want and avoid what we fear. By contrast, the child's face is a constant epiphany because it doesn't yet know how to hide feelings."[4]

As adults, we often don't want people to know what we're thinking, and we never want to look silly. We want to fit in and be respected; after all, we have a reputation to protect. Admittedly there is a time for everything — including a time to keep our thoughts to ourselves — but there is also a time to be honest with our friends and with God. Childlike humility will free us from a prison of self-protection so we can open up — to laugh, to cry, to tell someone our biggest dreams, or to confess our sin and be healed.

Some attitudes *repel* God's presence, like pride and unbelief. Other attitudes *invite* God's presence and activity in our hearts, like humility and faith. May God give us faith like a child to believe that He exists, that His kingdom is all around us, and that he rewards those who sincerely seek him. May we throw unbelief to the wind and choose to believe that He actually is almighty God; that he can do the same things today that he did in the first century and in the revivals of the centuries past. May we expect him to act like God in us, bringing his kingdom to earth through us.

Chapter 8
Living a Grateful Life

Thankfulness is a secret passageway into
a room you can't find any other way.[1]
— Mark Buchanan

These following words are from Brother Yun, a courageous evangelist from a poor village in the Henan Province of China.

> The five of us were placed in a prison cell inside the police station. The temperature was well below freezing. There was no heating at all, and they had taken my coat and thrown it in the snow. We shivered and our limbs turned blue. We almost fell unconscious. Our frozen handcuffs cut like knives into our swollen wrists.
>
> I used the handcuffs to knock on the door and the iron windows. As I looked around I saw a broken wooden box in the corner of the cell. Inside it was an old drum. I beat the drum with my handcuffs and made a loud noise. At the top of my voice I sang Psalm 150 ... the more I sang the more I was filled with joy. I stood up and praised the Lord. Gradually my frozen hands and feet regained feeling and I wasn't cold anymore. The four brothers knelt down on the floor and earnestly prayed for China. The piercing wind whistled loudly outside, but inside our cell, weeping and the groans of intercessory prayers were heard.[2]

In his youth, Yun became one of China's house church leaders and experienced horrific opposition as he preached the gospel. His story of devotion to Jesus is amazing and inspiring. Worshiping the

Lord was his lifeline as he suffered persecution and imprisonment — just like the apostle Paul. He learned to be thankful regardless of his circumstances.

Brother Yun's prison ordeal is a miraculous story of what happens when a person chooses to give thanks in a horrible situation. How can you become warm in below freezing temperatures when you've been tortured and have no coat? That's a miracle.

Any trials I have are puny by comparison. Compared to the monumental obstacles that Brother Yun and the apostle Paul faced, like beatings, hunger, shipwreck, and sleepless nights, my problems don't really seem like problems at all. Nevertheless, my troubles can defeat and depress me unless I persevere with an attitude of thankfulness.

Most of my trials are just minor aches, pains and frustrations. Yet I can so easily fall into a pessimistic attitude. It doesn't take a major calamity to get me down; a minor predicament will do the job. While working on writing this chapter, the hard drive on my six-month old computer died. Six month-old computers aren't supposed to die, but mine did, taking my backup copies with it. Losing computer data isn't a life-threatening problem, like the amazing story of brother Yun. Nevertheless, it's hard to "rejoice in the Lord always" when your computer freaks out on you. What did I *feel* like doing in that situation? Throwing my #@%*! computer out the window and smashing it into a million pieces!

The challenge of being grateful in a time like this requires me to surrender control and look at things from God's perspective. I have to humble myself to a sovereign God who would allow the inconvenience of lost computer data. To come through with a winning attitude, I have to take a few steps back from my situation and think about how God sees it. Having done that, it really is possible to live a joyful, thankful life.

If I can trust God for the things I can't understand instead of ranting and raving, I can actually have peace. And I'm a lot easier to live with. Gratefulness, and the humility it requires, is a pleasing offering to God.

No End to Problems

Life is full of problems. If we wait for them to go away before we choose to be thankful, we might be waiting our whole life. In his book "The Road Less Traveled," Scott Peck begins with this statement:

> Life is difficult. This is a great truth, one of the greatest truths. It is a great truth because once we truly see this truth, we transcend it. Once we truly know that life is difficult — once we truly understand and accept it — then life is no longer difficult ... . Life is a series of problems. Do we want to moan about them or solve them?[3]

Sometimes we can solve our problems and sometimes we can't, but moaning isn't a good option. Some people suffer great difficulty yet possess great joy, while others who have easy lives are always complaining. What a tragedy when we live joylessly no matter how good we have it.

This brings to mind the story of Fanny Crosby. Fanny (1820-1915) was a famous hymn writer who penned great songs like "Blessed Assurance." When Fanny was an infant with an eye infection, a quack doctor treated her with a hot poultice. From that moment on, she was blind. For most people, such a tragedy would be the end of a happy life. But Fanny saw it as a blessing; something that God used for his glory. She said that unless she had gone blind, she probably never would have written hymns. Her blindness limited her participation in many activities of life. This forced her into developing the spiritual side of her life.

As a result, she wrote thousands of hymns, some of which endure as favorites in churches today. Ms. Crosby was also a vigorous preacher and tirelessly cared for the poor. Because of

Fanny's stubborn persistence to rejoice in the midst of difficulty, she enjoyed a fruitful, fulfilling life. A horrible medical tragedy wasn't the end of her happiness. Fanny's life shows us that you don't have to be miserable while you suffer.

Getting God's Perspective

Let's take a look at what scripture says about living a life of thankfulness; the hindrances to gratefulness, the keys to being grateful and the fruit of continual praise.

Over and over again, God tells us to always be thankful. To the Thessalonians, who were undergoing all kinds of persecution and trial, Paul writes: "*Always be joyful.* Never stop praying. *Be thankful in all circumstances,* for this is God's will for you who belong to Christ Jesus" (1 Thess 5:16-18 NLT, emphasis added).

The psalmist says, "I will always have hope" (Ps 71:14) and "My mouth will tell of your righteousness, of your salvation all day long." (Ps 71:15). But hold on a minute, isn't it a little unreasonable that we should *always* give thanks, *always* have hope, *always* rejoice, no matter what is happening? Yet the stories of Paul and brother Yun and many other show us that it is possible. God knows what we can handle; he wouldn't burden us with commandments that are impossible to keep.

While in prison in Rome, Paul writes to his beloved Philippians, encouraging them to "Rejoice in the Lord always. I will say it again: rejoice!" (Phil 4:4). Faced with all kinds of obstacles, Paul was determined to keep rejoicing no matter what happened.

For Paul, it was all about perspective. He saw himself as a servant of Christ, one who belonged to God and lived to glorify him. In many of his letters, Paul introduces himself as a "servant of Jesus Christ." A servant's job is to please his master. Praise, and the simple trust that underlies it, is pleasing to God. Paul's view of life transformed his prison into a sanctuary of praise. Paul was single-minded in his determination to trust that God is sovereign in every situation.

On his trip to Asia, Paul and his team " … faced conflict from every direction, with battles on the outside and *fear on the inside*" (2 Cor 7:5 NLT, emphasis added). Paul was afraid. He struggled just as we do. But he kept the right perspective. Take a look at Paul's grasp of God's purposes in allowing suffering:

" … We were under great pressure, far beyond our ability to endure, so that we despaired even of life. Indeed, in our hearts we felt the sentence of death. [WHY, GOD?] But *this happened that we might not rely on ourselves but on God*, who raises the dead" (2 Cor 1:8-9, emphasis added).

Paul saw the ultimate purpose for his suffering; God wanted his faith to grow. To depend on God is to worship Him. To rely on him when we can't understand why He is allowing tough circumstances is to worship him.

In those incredibly trying moments a lesser man than Paul would have had a sour attitude, questioning just what kind of God would expect so much suffering to be heaped upon one person. Indeed, God could have prevented Paul's shipwreck, the nights without sleep and days without food, but he didn't. He could have taken out the Judaizers who undermined Paul's teaching and led astray his converts with legalistic teaching, but he didn't.

Though Paul suffered days of despair, he could see everything through the lens of God's sovereignty. As Mark Buchanan says: "You cannot practice thankfulness on a biblical scale without its altering the way you see. And the more you do of it, the more you find cause for doing it."[4] For Paul, it didn't matter that he was in jail. God used that for good by spreading the Good News to the prison guards and others who came to hear Paul preach.

But God chose to allow Paul's house arrest to continue, and

Paul saw it as an *opportunity* to preach to his visitors rather than a hindrance or defeat. Ultimately Paul was sent to the gallows, but even that was okay with this servant-apostle! Paul saw God as being in control. That's huge. You can't rejoice or be content if you question God's choices for your life and his ability to make the right things happen.

Rejoicing While House-Cleaning

When we resist God's plan for our life by complaining instead of rejoicing, we push away his blessings. My wife Linda shares a personal story that illustrates this:

> After several hours of cleaning my big house I was feeling resentful that I had didn't have any help. And the Lord told me that it was the exact kind of resentment that I used to feel living in the house of my step-mother. Because her love wasn't enough, I wanted my real mom's love. So, not only did I miss out on my real mom's love, I couldn't get my step-mom's love either because I was so resentful. So then, while cleaning my house, I was delivered from a complaining attitude and not being able to receive God's blessing in my big house. God showed me that I'm not able to receive blessing when I'm resentful. He delivered me of resentment.

She explains the connection between the past incident and the present:

> The root of the resentment over house-cleaning was my childish response to the step-mother situation. If you have childhood pain, you tend to make decisions based on that pain. When God reveals that issue, you can be freed from your bondage to the past pain issues.

Just a few weeks ago there was another house-cleaning incident that gave evidence of Linda's changed attitude. I was playing a round of golf with two of my sons. I called Linda to say "I love you." She was in the middle of cleaning the bathroom as I was enjoying the beautiful out of doors. She said, "It's okay, it's a *nice* bathroom. And forty percent of the people in the world don't even have a toilet." How's that for clear perspective? (Not to mention her unselfishness in blessing me to play golf while she's cleaning).

Linda says, "Two things that have brought death to me are self-pity and complaining." So she avoids them like the plague. Jackie Pullinger said it like this: "Self-pity is a very unattractive missionary quality."

Brother Lawrence

In the seventeenth century a lay brother named Brother Lawrence joined the Carmelite Monastic order. Previously a soldier for several years, in the monastery he became famous for practicing the presence of God. His work included washing dishes and preparing food for his brothers. In an expression of absolute trust in his Father for his future job assignments, he said: "I do not know what God wishes to do with me; I am always very happy."[5]

Wow, that's amazing! For most of us, not knowing God's plans is a source of anxiety. For Brother Lawrence, it didn't matter. He was happy no matter how the Lord might lead. Brother Lawrence was happily surrendered to work at whatever task might be given to him.

I struggle to stay in that place of absolute trust. I get uptight about not knowing what's going to happen next month and next year. I like to make plans and work towards goals. I become frustrated if my plans are waylaid. But when I realize that my main job is to love God and love people, I can relax and be happy. Gratitude flows naturally.

Grumbling or Praise

Think about the tragic result of a generation of grumblers who followed Moses into the desert. They forgot what God had done for them, and became ungrateful. Though God delivered them from hunger with supernatural provision of manna and quail, though he opened the Red Sea and cut off their attackers, though he brought water from a rock to quench their thirst, still they hardened their hearts.

In Psalm 95, God describes this generation: " ... your fathers tested and tried me, though they had seen what I did" (Ps 95:9). This is the latter part of the psalm, and the first part shows us how to counteract that hard heartedness. We sing for joy to the Lord, shouting out loud to him, coming with thanksgiving, music and song. Grumbling flees as we approach God's throne with gratitude.

God made himself easily visible to Moses and the Hebrews; in a pillar of cloud by day and a pillar of fire by night. It didn't require a special time of meditation and the Hebrews could see with their own eyes a physical representation of God's presence. Time after time, God came through with supernatural provision. When they needed water, God turned bitter water into sweet.

Yet despite all these miracles, the people quickly forgot about these demonstrations God's amazing love. When faced with a new problem the people had the gall to ask Moses questions such as, " ... Why did you bring us up out of Egypt to make us and our children and livestock die of thirst?" (Ex 17:3). When they came to a place where the water wasn't drinkable, they asked, " ... Is the Lord among us or not?" (Ex 17:7). Instead of gazing on God they focused on the problem.

There's no substitute for simple trust in God. When that's out of whack — when we fail to remember our place in the scheme of things — our foundation for peace crumbles. To worship God is to acknowledge every day that he gives us life and breath and the ability to work. He gives us our daily bread. To worship God is to attempt to please him at all times. "Without faith it is impossible to please God ... " (Heb 11:6). Our simple trust that he will provide is pleasing to Him.

Isn't it interesting that God provided manna (bread) for the Hebrews in the desert only one day at a time? They couldn't store it overnight or it would rot. I guess God wanted them to learn to trust him literally for their *daily* bread. In the grip of unbelief, we want our "yearly bread" all prepared and stored up in advance. But that would remove the need for faith.

While it would feel more comfortable to have a year's salary in the bank, that's not the kind of comfort God promises to all of us. He promises a divine peace *despite* our circumstances. The apostle Paul chose to be content with food and clothing (1 Tim 6:8). What are we adding to the "must have" list before we'll be content?

So many times I've let myself become rattled by the storms of life. It's because I still fail to remember that God knows my every need. He is tenderly leading me like a shepherd. I forget that "he is our God and we are the people of his pasture, the flock under his care" (Ps 95:7). My gaze still slips away from the One who has the power to create or destroy. Though he has helped me countless times in unpredictable ways, I haven't mastered the art of always fixing my thoughts on Him.

Peace on the Foreign Mission Field and in Child-Raising

Jesus said, "In this world you will have trouble..." Then he said, " ... But take heart! I have overcome the world" (John 16:33). Remembering and choosing to think about God's unstoppable love will soften our hearts and remind us that he is indeed with us. This is the pathway to the place of rest.

Finding the place of rest requires humbling ourselves: " ... let us kneel before the Lord our Maker" (Psalm 95:6). It takes effort and discipline to keep our minds on him. In trying times I pray, "I repent from unbelief and I choose to remember your faithfulness." Sometimes I do this ten times a day when things get tough. I can't wait for a time of solitude to refocus on him.

J. Hudson Taylor was a pioneer of missions in China. He faced tremendous opposition, including death threats from his persecutors. He had so much responsibility and so little help from co-workers. You would expect him to struggle to be at peace. Yet a coworker said of him: "He was an object lesson in quietness. He knew nothing of hurrying. He knew there was a peace that surpasses understanding. He answered every letter (piles of them) with faith that was simple and continuous."[6]

This kind of peace isn't reserved for famous missionaries. It is the fruit of developing a habit of taking time to draw near to God and think about his goodness. In the car, surrounded by toddlers, or at the kitchen sink, we can receive from him.

My wife has found Jesus in the crucible of child-raising:

> Twenty years of interrupted sleep and breast feeding babies through the night is the crucible to create silver and gold in my character. It's a refining fire. I find that God speaks in times of crisis. He speaks to me when I'm in pain or even when I'm panicking. I believe it's true that I can burst into the throne room of God at any moment, even with all my baggage, my garbage, my un-prettiness in tow. I find that God speaks in the midst of the grind. I grow in character as I do hard things. It's here that I learn about faith — the faith of Abraham, who believed that he was the father of many nations even when he was without any children, and just about dead.[7]

> Trusting God is about contentment versus fantasy. You fantasize about being somewhere else but God wants you here. This is a discipline of the mind. We say, 'If only I could have more worship time, or have this or that, then everything would fall into place.' As with the Israelites, so it is for us; whining is a sin. You're missing out because God is already with you.

She realized:

> there's no mother-in-law to help, and Andy is gone on a ministry trip. There is no "plan B." There wasn't going to be days off or vacations from taking care of the kids. I had to live at a pace at which my life restored itself. It was all about

being flexible, not having long lists of agendas, looking for God in the middle of exhaustion, pain and discouragement and *finding him* in those places instead of avoiding those places by entertaining myself.

Linda says:

> Just by turning to God, and meditating, there is transformation. A lot of religions use meditation and repetitive sayings but there's no power to transform. But we are invoking the power of the Holy Spirit, which is the spirit of transformation when we yield our heart and mind. The whole idea is that pain, suffering, injustice are not only stopped, they are transformed into something that gives God glory.

Linda shares another episode of parenting in which she let go of her right to a distraction-free worship time at church:

> There's a child in my backpack, one at the breast, one on my lap, and we were resting and singing, moving and clapping in the presence of God all together. I would have people come up to me and comment about how patient I was. I thought 'worship has become a very me-centered event.' It's not right that people feel they can only worship God when they're undistracted. When does that ever happen for a mother of eight? It must be true that you can worship in spite of distractions."

Linda wasn't waiting for the perfect opportunity to worship. She grabbed for God every chance she got.

Don't Be Anxious

It is never God's will for me to worry. *Never!* "Do not be anxious about *anything*, but in everything, by prayer and petition, with thanksgiving, present your requests to God. And the peace of God which transcends all understanding, will guard your hearts and minds in Christ Jesus" (Phil 4:6-7, emphasis added).

I'm a naturally worrisome person, but that's the "old me" talking. To worry is to resist God's will. To worry is to take matters into my own hands. To worry is to refuse to trust God. So I must intentionally resist and repent from anxiety. " … Do not let your hearts be troubled and do not be afraid" (John 14:27). That means we can actually have power over feeling troubled, with God's help. With dogged determination, we can hang onto God's truth with a spirit of thanks. We may have to "struggle with all his energy" as Paul did, but we can do it.

Paul says to Timothy that he should "Endure hardship with us like a good soldier of Christ Jesus" (2 Tim 2:3). Soldiers endure lots of discomfort in the battlefield. They don't give into their feelings of pain, but choose to do what's right. To worship God continually requires acting the opposite of how we feel much of the time.

Eugene Peterson describes it like this:

> Feelings are great liars. If Christians only worshiped when they felt like it, there would be precious little worship that went on. Feelings are important in many areas, but completely unreliable in matters of faith."[8] Peterson quotes Paul Scherer, who writes: "The Bible wastes very little time on the way we feel."[9] Peterson continues: "We think that if we don't feel something there can be no authenticity in doing it. But the wisdom of God says something different, namely, that we can act ourselves into a new way of feeling much quicker than we can feel ourselves into a new way of acting. Worship is an act which develops feelings for God, not a feeling for God which is expressed in an act of worship.[10]

When Brother Yun and his friends were in a freezing prison cell, they probably didn't *feel* like praising God. But they knew it was the right thing to do, and God met them powerfully as they chose to give thanks.

In his wonderful book "Champagne for the Soul," Mike Mason talks about the discipline of choosing to rejoice. "One must choose joy, and keep on choosing it under all conditions until gradually it becomes a habit, a self-sustaining reality." Mike writes:

> We must resolve deep within, "nothing will stop me. I'm fixing my eyes on Jesus and not letting anything interrupt my joy in him" .... Happiness is not happenstance, but rather it

involves a profound spiritual discipline. If I want to be strong, I don't sit around waiting until I'm strong enough to lift weights; rather, I lift weights in order to become strong.[11]

Mason goes on to say that a message about always rejoicing is necessarily about spiritual warfare. Maintaining a positive attitude requires a feisty, fighting spirit. To live in constant gratefulness, you must "Put on the whole armor of God so that you can take your stand against the devil's schemes" (Eph 6:11).

Forget the Past and Move On

To live a thankful life, we must forget the failures of the past. "… Forgetting what is behind and straining toward what is ahead, I press on toward the goal to win the prize for which God is called me heavenward in Christ Jesus" (Phil 3:13-14).

Think of all the famous Bible characters who made *big mistakes* and were then blessed big-time by God. Moses — a murderer, Abraham — a liar, David — an adulterer and murderer. All of these men were forgiven by God and then had to forgive themselves, forget the past and press on with praise.

Paul made some big mistakes prior to knowing Jesus. His mission was to track down Christians keep them from worshiping Jesus. He stood by as Christians were killed. This looming memory could have haunted and condemned him, crippling his effectiveness. Instead of being bogged down by regret, he turned it into a praise opportunity.

I've made so many big mistakes in life, and I make little mistakes every day. Ministry mistakes, financial mistakes, relational mistakes; I've messed up in all kinds of ways. But stressing out over my bad decisions is not going to fix anything. To rejoice in the present, I have to forget what's behind. "… Each day has enough trouble of its own" (Matt 6:34) — agonizing over yesterday's blunders will only drag me down.

Conclusion

God has blessed me in so many ways. I have a wonderful family and a good income to support them. He has enabled me to enjoy my work and when I take time to remember God's blessings to my wife, kids and me over the past twenty-nine years of married life, I am amazed, overwhelmed and humbled.

Yet I can find so many things to complain about. Things like broken computers, and my gradually decaying body. The only way I can overcome a complaining spirit is to continually make the choice to rejoice in the Lord. It's up to me to think about the things that are excellent and worthy of praise (Phil 4:8). That's the path to joy and peace.

Is there something that's stifling your heart of thanks? Maybe you've had heartbreaking setbacks in life, so I don't want to minimize your problems. Maybe you've lost a child, lost a job, or lost a spouse. I'm not offering pat answers that lead to instant joy, but we can all learn from the saints of the past who chose the path of humility and gratitude, even in the face of overwhelming odds. We can find inspiration from Brother Yun, Fanny Crosby and the apostle Paul. They all suffered but found a way to be thankful instead of miserable.

We all have to decide: "What are we going to think about?" You can fret about your physical pain, the strained relationships in your extended family, the unpaid bills, or the question marks about your future career. Or you can think about God's ability to take care of you in the midst of those tensions. You can think about God's gift of life and his sustaining power that enables you to breathe another breath.

May God grant you the gift of gratefulness so you can peacefully live in the tension of unanswered questions and an uncertain future. May you experience the peace that passes understanding as you bring your requests to God with thankfulness.

Take five or ten minutes and think about what God has done for you through your lifetime; let the litany of God's wondrous works in your life lift your spirit and launch you into praise. The habit of rejoicing, learned through prolonged hour-by-hour practice, is the antidote to many ills. It's the cure for anxiety and for dwelling on past mistakes. It empowers us to see the future with eyes of faith.

Chapter 9
Worship and Suffering

*I wonder ... it scares me, but ... do we ever
get to know God but through suffering?*
— Glenn Hansen

Jesus said, "... In this world you will have trouble ..." (John 16:33). He was right, of course. If you haven't yet experienced tragedy and trauma, someday you will. Life is no picnic. Instead it feels at times more like a series of problems, both large and small. As soon as one problem is solved, another one pops up. One bumper sticker reads: "Life is hard and then you die."

So that's it, is it? This chapter's going to be nothing more than a series of miserable reinforcements of the endurance race that we call *life*? No. You see, life in Christ is not futile. While traveling this worship journey we will suffer collisions, accidents and sickness. We may be robbed or raped. We may end the race prematurely and leave behind a church full of bewildered mourners. But, among all these unknowns about the way ahead, one thing is sure: there is a way to worship throughout the journey, no matter how hard it gets.

God has provided us with a manual for getting through tough times. The laments that we find among the Psalms reflect the true feelings of a range of people who struggle and honestly pour out their pain to God. We see people being unfairly treated and attacked, and others tormented by physical sickness.

It's amazing that only a minority of the Psalms focus on joyful praise and thanksgiving. Based on the songs we hear in church, you would think that ninety percent of the Psalms would have a joyful tone. But at least sixty of the 150 Psalms are laments, and some scholars even classify seventy percent of the Psalms as laments. The moods of the Psalms swing wildly from vengeful anger to joyful praise, from self-righteousness to depression and back to joy again. One thing they are not is a continual multi-mix of hi-tempo happiness.

God includes so many laments in the Psalms because he knows we need him in our discouraging and devastating times. He made us and the world we live in; he knows we're going to suffer. God affirms us in our frailty by giving us the language of the laments. They show us how to cry out to him for help, to pour out our complaints, and even to be angry with him.

Tough situations in life cause despair, frustration, depression, anger at God and at people, and feelings of abandonment and rejection. The psalmists' shocking freedom of expression gives permission to let our hair down before God, not to pretend or put on a façade. No matter what we're going through, there is a Psalm to help us be honest with him.

A Series of Personal Letters to God

Philip Yancey gives some very helpful guidelines for reading the Psalms in his book "The Bible Jesus Read." Yancey explains that the psalms are "not meant to be studied as much as to be absorbed … it is more about forming us and less about teaching us." In reading the Psalms, it is "as if we are looking over the shoulder of the writer, seeing their spiritual journals."[1]

The laments give us an up-close look at people in pain and in danger who are trying to reconcile their beliefs about God with the seeming contradiction of being abandoned by him. When we see the psalms as personal journals, the vacillating emotions of the psalmists make sense. Life is like a roller-coaster — always up and down.

Seeing God's acceptance of people in pain in the Psalms takes the pressure off me to always feel happy. God calls us to be joyful but doesn't expect me to always feel a bubbly sort of happiness. The laments help us stay on the path of worship even in "the valley of the shadow of death." We grow closer to God in the process.

Glenn's Story

The best way I can illustrate worshipping through suffering is to tell you the story of my friend, Glenn Hansen. His journey is a beautiful example of someone who goes into the depths of despair and comes out on the other side loving God. In a fourteen-year period, Glenn's life was punctuated by all kinds of family sickness and death. He suffered violent ups and downs through these years. But he kept his heart soft and pliable before God. Looking back, he thanks God for the gift of a soft heart.

In Glenn's response to tragedy, we see a living example of worship and lament. We see the importance of real gut-level honesty. We see that it's not wrong to be mad at God. We see a 'life-of-Job' type of teachable heart. We see that being in a "school of suffering" is part of God's choice for us. We see the question God puts before us: is our love for him conditional on things always going well for us?

We see that we're ultimately not in control. We have to make the choice — will we worship even when it feels like God has pulled the carpet out from under us? Even while grappling with devastating loss, Glenn found a way to worship. In Glenn's life, we also see numerous examples of God's presence "showing up" in response to his making a tough choice to worship. Finally, we see the heart of a warrior who refuses to be stomped on by the evil one.

I met Glenn Hansen in 1985 shortly after moving from California to British Columbia. He and his wife, Ann, were good friends to Linda and I. Glenn is a gregarious, fun-to-be-with sort of a guy, and Ann was a lovely quiet personality. Soon after we met, Glenn finished his college degree and was honored with the title of class valedictorian. Their lives as a young married couple were full of joy and promise for a great future. At that time, they knew nothing of the depths of heartache and suffering they would undergo in the years to come.

The Hansen family moved to New Zealand in 1987 where Glenn became a pastor in a small, rural Assemblies of God church. They had three beautiful daughters, Leah, Erika and Abby, and a baby boy named Dominic. Then Grace, their fifth child, was born with Down's syndrome.

Glenn describes the time of Grace's birth: "Surprise and shock. This was huge. It's grief. Your world has been altered significantly. I came face to face with the reality that we are not ultimately in control of our lives … that bad things happen to good people."[2]

As a pastor who was comfortable in the role of teacher and counselor, all of a sudden Glenn knew he didn't have all the answers: "I can remember feeling like I was exposed as a hypocrite. 'Here's pastor Glenn, he knows how life works.' Then, wait a minute … this wasn't part of the plan." Glenn says:

> At that time I drove twenty-five minutes everyday to the hospital where Ann and Grace were staying after the emergency C-section that brought Grace into the world. During that daily ride I poured out my heart to God over and over again through the song, "Will You Worship."[3]

Deep in my soul is a tug of war, I'm struggling to know what this life is for

I try so hard to stay in control, to hold back the tears, to not let go

I don't know why I hang on so long

When I know the question you are asking me

Will You worship, will you bow down before your Lord and King?

Will You love me, will you give me Your heart, your everything?

Right here and now, I make my choice, with all my love I will answer You

I will worship, I will bow down, before my Lord and King

I will love You, I will give You My heart, my everything

Glenn knew that God was asking him, even in your suffering, "Will you worship, will you bow down?"

This song gave Glenn a way to say "yes, I will worship" in his time of great pain. He relates, "To have words and melody that can connect your heart to God is *life* in that moment. It does us good to speak, even better to raise our voice in song." Glenn chose to humble himself despite the seeming unfairness of it all. In effect, he was saying, "God, I can't understand why you are allowing this but I believe you are good."

The birth of Grace was just the first of many dark valleys that Glenn and Ann would walk through. Shortly after Grace was born, Glenn's two-year old Dominic suffered bouts of illness for six months. He started to have seizures and shortly after that he was diagnosed with an aggressive and rare cancer of the brain lining. He died less than 48 hours after the diagnosis and there was never any chance of treatment. This was a couple of months before his third birthday. I remember that Glenn called me from

New Zealand when Dominic's body was still lying on the bed. He was cherishing every moment and memory of Dominic's short life. He was slowly saying goodbye. You can imagine their sorrow in losing their only boy.

Glenn explains the progression of tragedies:

> It was really, really difficult. Dominic died on March 1, and we buried him March 5. At the same time, one month-old Grace had battled near fatal pneumonia, was on life support for eight days and in intensive care for three weeks. My parents flew out (from Canada to New Zealand) on March 17. That same night, Grace was again rushed to the hospital. There were firemen administering oxygen in my house as I stood shaking on my front porch. Shortly after this, Grace was diagnosed with Leukemia. Six months of intensive chemotherapy was required.

Honesty with God

Rather than clamming up and letting his feelings stay buried inside him, Glenn followed the pattern of the laments; he said to God exactly what he felt. Glenn's honesty was like the writer of Psalm 88:

> ... my eyes are dim with grief. I call to you, O Lord, every day; I spread out my hands to you. Do you show your wonders to the dead? Do those who are dead rise up and praise you?" (Ps 88:9-10). In effect, the psalmist was saying to God almost with a mocking tone, "How can I praise you when I'm dead!?

Glenn remembers:

> Through this I had to get real with God. I walked up Mt. Victoria in Wellington and started to talk to God: "God, are

you there? Are you real? Do you see us? Our son is dead and our daughter is in the hospital."

I was walking up the switchback trails towards the music conservatory at the top and I cried out to God, "Could you *just give me a sign?*" The words hadn't even left my mouth when I heard someone from a distance say, "How is your little girl?"

I saw that a woman had parked her car nearby. I said to her, "how do you know I have a little girl?"

She said, "I work in the hospital; I'm a security orderly." Then she just jumped in the car and left. It hit me that God had answered my prayer for a sign. *I put my face in my hands and wept uncontrollably because God showed up.*

Glenn's cries of agony remind us of the psalmist:

My God, my God, why have you abandoned me? Why are you so far away when I groan for help? Every day I call to you, my God, but you do not answer. Every night you hear my voice, but I find no relief .... Do not stay so far from me, for trouble is near, and no one else can help me (Ps 22:1-2; 11).

Pouring out our complaints to God is part of our genuine worship, along with asking for deliverance, and telling him we trust him.

Moving to Canada

The Hansen family returned to Canada in May of 1999 after being in New Zealand for twelve years. Several months after the turmoil of an international move with four children, they were beginning to get settled. But one year after the move, Ann was diagnosed with cancer. For six months she received chemotherapy treatments, then radiation therapy.

Glenn shares a remarkable story during of God's intervention during this heartbreaking time:

In the aftermath of Dominic's death, a stressful international move, and Ann's twin-sister Jane's death after a long battle with cancer, I was working at Trinity Western University. Ann was through with her chemotherapy treatments. Finally, I could let down a little bit, and I became the weak link in the chain. I was gutted. I had to face my own stuff.

One day I came home and was absolutely racked with anxiety. I walked into a neighbor's garage and I was doubled over in pain. I could barely straighten up. I said to my friend, "I think I'm going to need you to take me to the hospital to get a tranquilizer." At that moment I was a complete wreck; I thought I was going to end up in a mental institution. I thought, *there's no way I'm going to be able to provide for my kids*. But then I went into my house and I was all alone.

Then God broke through. Glenn says:

> Something inside me *just spoke*. I started to prophesy. I stood in the room and yelled, "No way, Satan! I am Glenn Hansen! I am a blood-bought son of the most high God! I have a unique destiny! I am making unique footprints on this world!" I just stood up and walked out of the house and said to my neighbor, "Look at me, I am clothed and in my right mind."

Glenn was experiencing demonic oppression mixed with depression and post-traumatic stress. In that moment, the Holy Spirit gave him a word of life, bubbling up from inside him. By speaking this word, he took a stand against the devil's schemes. Instead of acting like a victim, he rose up like a warrior, proclaiming a word of defense and a proclamation of victory.

Again Glenn recalls the gift of God's presence, "When you get *real* with God, he is there. *I was delivered.*"

The Last Chapter

Glen's story skips ahead to 2008. After several years of being free and clear of cancer, Ann was diagnosed with a rare and aggressive type of cancer, the sort which Vancouver General Hospital only treats about four times a year. Glenn says:

> We knew this was really bad. The day after I took Ann to VGH, I was at home sitting on the red couch. Someone

sent me an e-card about Ann's situation. I expected a lot of "cheese." But I opened the audio e-card and heard the sound of rushing waves. The caption read, "as the waves of the sea, he comes to us with grace upon grace for our every need." In that moment I lifted my hands and the presence of God came to me. I didn't want to admit what I was doing, but I knew I was letting Ann go. God was gracing me to let Ann go.

Even in receiving a digital greeting card, Glenn was quick to respond to the tender initiative of God's comfort.

In this period after the discouraging diagnosis, Glenn is honest with God about his inability to handle this trauma:

One day Ann was sleeping upstairs because she was uncomfortable. I was downstairs on the couch. I was thinking, *Ann is going to die.* I was trying to imagine "what will it be like?" I said, "God, I don't know how to do this because I'm just a man. I don't know how to watch my wife die." Somehow I found comfort in speaking those honest words.

God Is Good

Through these ordeals, Glenn learned to relinquish control of his life to God:

We spend so much of our time trying to control everything and trying to manipulate God to bless us. How often do we worship to somehow place God in our debt? Then we have to come to grips with the question "who is the real God" and "is he good?" And I say "he is good."

In spite of all of Glenn's grief, his conclusion was, "he is good."

Many Christians believe that "God is an angry judge. If you do well, you will be blessed; if you sin, you will be punished."[4] There's a line in the movie *Sound of Music* that is spoken from this perspective. Julie Andrews' character, Maria, has just realized that the "captain" and father of the seven children she was caring for is in love with her and that she will be spending the rest of her life married to him. She sings, "Somewhere in my youth our childhood, I must have done something good" to deserve this blessing.

Is that the heart of God? Are we rewarded for good deeds and punished for bad deeds? The Bible teaches us that the righteous are rewarded, but there is no promise that God's people will be spared from suffering and that we can earn such things as a good spouse.

Jesus addressed this question in the gospels. He explains whether suffering is caused by human cruelty or a natural disaster, the root cause is *not* the sin of those who suffer:

> About this time Jesus was informed that Pilate had murdered some people from Galilee as they were offering sacrifices at the Temple. "Do you think those Galileans were worse sinners than all the other people from Galilee?" Jesus asked. "Is that why they suffered? Not at all! And you will perish, too, unless you repent of your sins and turn to God. And what about the eighteen people who died when the tower in Siloam fell on them? Were they the worst sinners in Jerusalem? No, and I tell you again that unless you repent, you will perish, too" (Luke 13:1-5 NLT).

Again in the gospel of John, when a boy is born blind, Jesus was asked by his disciples:

> Rabbi … why was this man born blind? Was it because of his own sins or his parents' sins?

> "It was not because of his sins or his parents' sins," Jesus answered. "This happened so the power of God could be seen in him (John 9:2-3 NLT).

Jesus saw it as an opportunity for God to be glorified in the healing of the blind man.

Who Are We Going to Worship: God or our Agenda?

To believe that our good behavior will guarantee God's blessings is tantamount to believing we can control God and our world. God didn't give me eight healthy children who are still strong today because I was an especially good Christian. Nor did Glenn lose a child and his wife because of his bad behavior. That's not the way it works. In fact, Jesus says that our Father " … causes his sun to rise on the evil and the good, and sends rain on the righteous and the unrighteous"(Matt 5:45).

Why would God set up his universe in this way? What kind of a response is he looking for? We can answer that by looking at the lives of people who witnessed many miracles yet never learned to please God by trusting him. The Hebrews who followed Moses into the desert saw wonders upon wonders of God — a pillar of cloud by day and fire by night, manna from heaven, water from a rock, the Red Sea parting. What kind of fruit did this string of miracles produce in their lives? Not much, evidently, because they never stopped grumbling about the discomfort of living in the desert. They never stopped doubting that God would provide, even though he had proven himself over and over again. They never grew to trust God, and they never entered the promised land because of their unbelief.

" ... Without faith it is impossible to please God ... " (Heb 11:6). God is looking for a people who will believe him. He is looking for mature love that is freely given even when our lives take a turn for the worse. He is looking for people that will accept the mysterious twists and turns of life and not require an answer to every question right now. He is looking for a people who will trust that He will eventually bring justice, even if it's not in this present life. "We must know God or perish. But unless we know God as ultimate mystery we do not know God at all."[5]

Glenn figured out that it's easy to create an illusion, a god of our own making, who we expect to serve our agenda. But that's not who God is. Glenn shares this valuable lesson:

> You have to answer the question, "Is God just there to make your life good and to bless you or is God *really God*? Can he do or allow what he chooses to do and allow? Are you OK with that? I think we're going to ask that question time and time again in our lives. Who are we going to worship — God or our agenda? Are we going to worship the real God, or the god who we *thought* was God?"

After Job lost his entire family, the Bible says of him, " ... Job did not sin by charging God with wrongdoing" (Job 1:22). Job's worship wasn't dependent on his circumstances.

Vulnerability

It would be a lot harder to swallow the bitter pill of life's tests if Jesus himself hadn't undergone the most cruel punishment of all. "Jesus not only *explains* suffering, he *experienced* suffering."[6] Even Jesus " ... learned obedience through what he suffered" (Heb 5:8). Jesus came down from heaven, humbly took the form of a man, and then suffered the shame and agony of crucifixion. We'll never be able to fully understand how vulnerable Jesus felt.

We get a taste of how vulnerable Glenn felt during his long ordeal. Glenn shared with me, "I think there's something about having *your heart laid bare.*" He quoted the psalmist: "A broken and contrite heart, O God, you will not despise" (Ps 51:17). In his brokenness, Glenn found God.

Jesus doesn't ask us to undergo anything he hasn't already undergone himself. And he promises to be *with us* through it all. Over and over, Glenn says, "In the moment when you *choose to worship God,* he shows up in a profound way." For many, the closest experiences with God are in the toughest times.

Though many receive a touch from the "God of all comfort" in their grief, herein lies another mystery: some of us won't always experience such a tangible touch of God's love when we say "yes" to God in our pain. Though the Father will never forsake us, sometimes we may *feel* forsaken. God tests us in different ways.

At one point in our chat, Glenn used the imagery of attending a school to describe his journey: "This isn't a game; we're playing for keeps. You have to decide; do you want to play in the big leagues? Do you still want to go to this school and pay the tuition?"

The "school" of hard knocks that Glenn is talking about is one that every famous Bible character attended. It's one that every leader in church history has studied in. It's a school that's attended by every devout Christian person who has lost a job, lost a loved one, or lost their health.

Attending this school develops godliness in us: "Consider it pure joy, my brothers, whenever you face trials of many kinds, because you know that the testing of your faith develops perseverance. Perseverance must finish its work so that you may be mature and complete, not lacking anything" (Jas 1:2-4).

In this school of faith, God gives us tests. Life is full of tests. The book of Job teaches us about tests from God. After losing all of his children and falling ill, Job felt like he was *constantly* being tested and said to God:

> What is man that you make so much of him, that you give him so much attention, that you examine him every morning and test him every moment? Will you never look away from me, or let me alone even for an instant?" (Job 7:17-19).

Yet while Job felt hounded by God, he never cursed him.

The pathway to godly character is a long and arduous one. Philip Yancey quotes Soren Kirkegaard, who says Christians reminded him of, "schoolboys who want to look up the answers to their math problems in the back of the book rather than work them through." Yancey says, "We yearn for shortcuts but shortcuts usually lead away from growth, not toward it."[7]

Our Father Carries Us

Glenn shares another experience of hearing from God in worship:

> I remember another time about seven or eight years ago. Grace had just about died from pneumonia, Dominic got sick and died, Jane [Ann's twin sister] got sick and died, and Grace got Leukemia. Ann had been through an earlier bout with cancer. I was in worship chapel on a Friday, and *in a moment,* God showed me through the words of a song that

even though I had been through all this hard stuff, I still had a heart towards God. *But it wasn't because of me.* It was because of God's kindness leading me towards repentance. I was not bitter and twisted, and strung out, angry and bent out of shape, hating God. Why? Because *he had kept my heart.* And what did I do at that moment? I put my face in my hands and I wept and I worshiped.

When we're too weak to do all the right things, God's strength takes over: "He believes even when we cannot. He prays even when we cannot. We participate in *his* faith."[8] Paul wrote to the Galatians, "I have been crucified with Christ and I no longer live, but Christ lives in me … I live by faith in the Son of God, who loved me and gave himself for me" (Gal 2:20). The phrase "by faith in the Son of God" can also mean "by the faith *of* the Son of God." It's Jesus' faith working through and for us. Sometimes we feel like Glenn did, unable even to believe. But the Father carries us, and we ride on the wings of Jesus' faith.

Knowing the God of All Comfort Through the Power of Music

I've written tons of worship songs, and a handful of them have impacted the church in many countries. Occasionally I'll receive an email from someone who has been touched by God through one of my songs. The overwhelming majority of emails I've received are from people who have been comforted and encouraged by God in a time of suffering.

One night while in England on a ministry trip I began to write a song called "Yet I Will Praise." The impetus for the song was a picture I saw in mind's eye of a mother who was terribly distraught over a tragic accident involving her child. I wrote this song from the perspective of that mother:

"Yet I Will Praise"[9]

I will praise you Lord my God
Even in my brokenness I will praise you, Lord
I will praise the Lord my God

Even in my desperation, I will praise you Lord
And I can't understand all that you allow
I just can't see the reason, but my life is in your hands
And though I can't see you, I choose to trust you

Even when my heart is torn, I will praise you Lord
Even when I feel deserted, I will praise you Lord
Even in the darkest valley, I will praise you Lord
And even when my world is shattered
And it seems all hope is gone, yet I will praise you Lord

I will trust you Lord my God, even in my loneliness,
I will trust you Lord; I will trust the Lord my God
Even when I cannot hear you, I will trust you Lord
And I will not forget that you hung on a cross
Lord you bled and died for me, and if I have to suffer,
I know that you've been there,
And I know that you're here now
And I know that you're here right now

In the aftermath of the 9/11 attacks on the New York twin towers, two different people sent me videos of the burning twin towers accompanied by this song. This video was played in local churches to help American Christians grieve the loss of so many lives.

I also received an email from a young lady in South Africa whose husband had been shot to death in front of her when he tried to stop a car-jacking. She and her husband were newly married when he was murdered. She wrote to say that God was helping her through her grief through this song.

Jenn from Arizona wrote me a card saying:

> Three weeks ago my husband and I gave birth to our first child (Atlee Ryan). She was only nineteen weeks old … sadly she didn't live. It has been the worst period of our lives, but I have found comfort in your song "Yet I Will Praise." I have

listened to it over and over. I am trying to make it my prayer during this time of intense grief.

Another type of email I receive regularly is people asking permission to record one of my songs. Most of these requests are routine, but reading Sara Richardson's email made me cry.

Here is her story. When she was ten years old, Sara was diagnosed with a rare bone cancer, called *osteosarcoma*, in her leg. On her website, she says:

> My life went from music lessons, gymnastics, and schoolwork to months of chemotherapy treatments, major surgeries, and hospital stays. Nationwide Children's Hospital in Columbus, Ohio became my second home. I lost my long, beautiful hair from the chemotherapy and I had to use crutches to get around for about a year as my leg slowly healed.[10]

Tragically, after years of cancer treatment, her doctor said there was no other choice but to amputate her leg. She was crushed to hear that report.

> Even though losing my leg is the most trying thing I have ever had to face, my life is anything BUT miserable and disabled. I have a prosthesis that I can walk with and I enjoy many adaptive sports such as skiing, rock wall climbing, and rifle-shooting … . I love meeting other people with similar challenges as mine. It is a huge blessing to talk to new cancer patients facing amputation, answer some of their questions, and show them how they can still live life to the fullest despite a missing limb.

What a tremendous example of worship in the midst of hardship. Sara says with gratitude, "It is a miracle I am alive, and I don't want to waste any second of my life." Sara's attitude also brings to mind the words of Abraham Lincoln, who said, "people are just about as happy as they make up their mind to be." While some people seem to be "career complainers," griping at the smallest inconvenience, others are like Sara, who can see the best even in the worst of situations. As a pre-teen and teenager, Sara battled cancer, and fought her way through it with worship.

Jenn and Sara and the others mentioned here had to *choose* to be grateful. When they stepped towards God, he stepped towards them to bring his comfort. Thanks be to God for his amazing gift of the Holy Spirit working in partnership with the beauty of music. Through this channel, God's words and healing bypass the defense mechanisms of our minds and touch the deep hurts in our hearts.

We Know God Through Suffering

In my interview with Glenn, he said at one point: "I wonder … it scares me, but … do we ever get to know God *but* through suffering?" This thought is echoed by many people, including Joni Eareckson Tada who wrote: "When life is rosy, we may slide by with knowing about Jesus, with imitating him and quoting him and speaking of him. But only in suffering will we *know* Jesus."[11]

Paul said, "I want to know Christ and the power of his resurrection and the fellowship of sharing in his sufferings … " (Phil 3:10). Our intimacy with God deepens as our troubles are multiplied. Paul had such a deep connection with Christ that it often seems unattainable to the average Christian. But Jesus is just as near to us has he was to Paul. If we *really* want to say along with Paul, "For to me, to live is Christ and to die is gain," (Phil 1:21), then we will press into knowing him in good times and in bad.

I'll close this chapter with one more Pauline-sounding quote from Glenn Hansen:

> In worship I've found out more and more that our lives are really about him. Our lives are lived in response to his love. I realize how significant worship has been in my life — how it has been a track to run on. Because really, when push comes to shove, we are here to worship.

Chapter 10
Contentment vs. Greed

There are two ways to get enough; one is to continue to accumulate more and more. The other is to desire less.
— G. K. Chesterton

It is arguable that materialism is the single biggest competitor with authentic Christianity for the hearts and souls of millions in our world today, including many in the visible church.[1]
—Craig L. Blomberg

Compared to the average person on the globe, I live in luxury. I live in a beautiful house in a very nice neighborhood. All of my family's basic needs are met, plus more. I have every reason to be content with the lot God has given me. But sometimes I get sucked into looking at what my neighbors have that I don't and feeling envious.

Envy is defined as "painful or resentful awareness of an advantage enjoyed by another, joined with a desire to possess the same advantage."[2] The author of Ecclesiastes observes this phenomena: "Then I observed that most people are motivated to success by their envy of their neighbors. But this, too, is meaningless — like chasing the wind" (Ecc 4 NLT).

We all know what envy looks like in our own lives. We see fancier cars, bigger houses and more recreational toys. We see people that seem to live carefree lives and something pulls at our hearts, even though in reality they're not *really* carefree. That's part of the deception. When I focus on material things, I sometimes forget the essential truth of who I am — an eternal person with an eternal destiny.

Our culture feeds our imagination with a desire for more, more, more. When our imaginations run wild, fed by the media and fuelled by our own lusts, we succumb to the spirit of envy and greed. These desires are cleverly repackaged by the media, leading us to a place where our values become subverted: "Covetousness we call ambition. Hoarding we call prudence. Greed we call industry."[3]

An Age-Old Problem

Envy and greed are ancient urges, bred into humankind in the fall. Around 1,000 years before Christ, during King David's reign, Asaph was one of the key worship leaders. In Psalm 73, we get a glimpse into Asaph's struggle to stay free from envy and bitterness. While the "wicked" around him were enjoying the easy life, he was struggling to get by. Asaph had to fight to stay pure, to keep a right perspective, just like us.

He honestly tells us about his envy of the rich. He is disgusted with their selfish, godless behavior. Embroiled in anger, Asaph almost slid down the slippery slope:

"But as for me, I almost lost my footing. My feet were slipping, and I was almost gone. For I envied the proud when I saw them prosper despite their wickedness" (Ps 73:2-3 NLT).

These passages from Asaph's story could just as easily be descriptions of the rich and corrupt people of our day:

> They seem to live such painless lives ... They don't have troubles like other people; they're not plagued with problems like everyone else. They wear pride like a jeweled necklace ... These fat cats have everything their hearts could ever wish for! .... Look at these arrogant people — enjoying a life of ease while their riches multiply (Ps 73:4-7; 12 NLT).

This passage brings to mind certain professional athletes that have been in the news in the past few years. The top players get out of college at twenty one years old and because of their extraordinary talent, and they quickly sign contracts for multimillions. They are the cream of the crop and some of them become infamous for their shameful behavior — sexual assault, drug abuse and disgusting conceit. They haven't had to "pay their dues" and work their way up the ladder in pro sports because they're so talented. Fabulous fame and huge wealth is handed to them on a silver platter. Their fans worship them as kings of sport.

Whether its self-absorbed athletes and actors, businessmen who build their empires on the backs of the poor or tyrannical dictators who slaughter thousands at will, there is no lack of people who have been tainted by money, power and fame.

We might wonder as we look at these people what it would be like to be them. We might think that if only we had the salary/looks/profile of some celebrity or other that we would have it made. We can spend hours on these daydreams, all the time giving in to the spirit of greed that is so prevalent in these times. The sticky web of "the deceitfulness of riches" can easily entangle us.

Why does it bother us?

There are rich people all around us. Some of them are obnoxious and arrogant and many are not. Why did this bother Asaph so much? Why should this bother us? One reason it bothers me is that I'm vulnerable to the same lusts in which others so openly indulge. When I judge others for their greed and pride, it's only a reflection of that same tendency in me.

In his letter to the church in Colosse, Paul says " … Don't be greedy, for a greedy person is an idolater, worshiping the things of this world" (Col 3:5 NLT). A definition of greed is: "a selfish and excessive desire for more of something (as money) than is needed." Wanting more than we need is so common in our culture that we do it without thinking about it. And then we wake up to God's reality.

Paul the Apostle describes what happens when people refuse to acknowledge God's existence. "Their lives became full of every kind wickedness, sin, greed, hate, envy …" (Rom 1:29 NLT).

When we read this terrible list of sins, we think " … such derelicts these people are!" But Paul cautions us: "You may think you can condemn such people, but you are just as bad, and you have no excuse! When you say they are wicked and should be punished, you are condemning yourself, for you who judge others do these very same things" (Rom 2:1 NLT).

Conflict and Resolution

As Asaph's story unfolds we see him in incredible conflict. He's trying to figure it all out, to make sense of seeming injustice and unfairness. Reading between the lines Asaph is asking: "Why do good things happen to bad people? These people mock God, and deny his existence!"

Caught in a moment of rage he questions whether he has made a big mistake by following the narrow path of worship and purity: "Did I keep my heart pure for nothing? Did I keep myself innocent for no reason?" (Ps 73:13 NLT).

He sees all the self-indulgent fun that the ungodly are enjoying and thinks about what he is missing. "Maybe I should just eat, drink and be merry like the rest of them. If it feels good, maybe I should just *do it*." In deep despair, he's vulnerable to temptation. He's forgetting that the wages of sin is death.

Asaph can't believe God would really let such horrible injustice happen. He is full of questions and confusion; there are no immediate answers. His frustration reaches a boiling point, and for a while he blames and questions God: " … Does the Most High even know what's happening?" (Ps 73:11 NLT) Asaph sees no justice: "So I tried to understand why the wicked prosper. But what a difficult task it is!" (Ps 73:16 NLT).

Does it bother you that there are a small percentage of highly privileged in the world and billions of "have-nots?" Is it fair that your rent that is so high you can barely make the payments, while your landlord is rolling in the dough? Does God see what's happening, and if he does, why isn't he doing anything about it? Does he see the terrorism, the rape and murder, the oppression of the poor that runs rampant in our world? Why does evil seem to win the day so much of the time?

A few years ago I delivered a check from our church to a refugee family who had no money for rent or food. They came to Canada from a war-torn third world country. The head of the family was earnestly looking for work, but to no avail. It didn't seem fair and I still have questions about the way things worked out for them. Didn't God make all people equal in his sight? Why do so many people try so hard to make ends meet, only to end up on welfare, while the rich keep getting richer? So many of our questions will remain unanswered this side of heaven. We can only trust God will make it all right in the end.

The Turning Point: Worship

Asaph's saga takes an abrupt turn for the good when he goes to church one day:

> Then I went into your sanctuary, O God, and I finally understood the destiny of the wicked. Truly, you put them on a slippery path and send them sliding over the cliff to destruction. In an instant they are destroyed, completely swept away by terrors. When you arise, O Lord, you will laugh at their silly ideas as a person laughs at dreams in the morning (Ps 73:17-20 NLT).

When Asaph went into God's sanctuary and reflected on a life of righteousness and its rewards, everything shifted. As he opened his heart to God in worship, he got a whole new perspective. This is worship as Paul describes it in Romans 12. Real worship will " ... transform you into a new person by changing the way you think. Then you will learn to know God's will for you, which is good and pleasing and perfect" (Romans 12:2 NLT).

Worship is a *safe place;* living there keeps us away from the slippery slope of greed. Dallas Willard describes it this way:

> Worship is the single most powerful force in completing and sustaining restoration of the whole person .... Worship is at once the overall character of the renovated thought life and *the only safe place for a human being to stand*[4] (emphasis added).

Just by turning to God, and meditating on the truth, Asaph's feelings and outlook on life shifted dramatically. All of a sudden, he was at peace. Though he couldn't explain the present injustice, he knew that God would eventually right every wrong. Asaph saw that ultimately there is no reward for the unrighteous. The pleasures of the unrighteous are short-lived and fleeting.

When he saw life through God's eyes, Asaph realized how hardened his heart had become:

"Then I realized that my heart was bitter, and I was all torn up inside. I was so foolish and ignorant — I must have seemed like a senseless animal to you" (Ps 73:21, 22 NLT).

A *senseless animal!* Sound familiar? It does to me. When I lose perspective and harden my heart, I get angry and frustrated and complain about things I want but don't have. It's impossible to think clearly when we're full of anger at others and God. When we insist on knowing all the answers, we put ourselves in God's place. Only he knows how everything fits together, how all the wrongs will be made right.

The Path Of Purity

The very first verse of the psalm is a huge key here: "Truly God is good to Israel, to those whose hearts are pure" (Ps 73:1 NLT). When we return to purity, to complete devotion to God, we can *see* again. "Blessed are the pure in heart, for they will see God" (Matt 5:8). When there is no conflict of loyalties, no mixture of motives, and no hypocrisy, we can be content.

Are we citizens of heaven or earth? For a while, we live in both worlds, but Peter urges his brothers and sisters to live as *aliens* in this world: "Dear friends, I warn you as 'temporary residents and foreigners' to keep away from worldly desires that wage war against your very souls" (1 Pet 2:11 NLT).

When he succumbed to the spirit of Greed, Asaph's soul was ravaged by the evil one. His own evil desires opened a door for spiritual warfare that wreaked havoc in his soul. Though there was truth in his assessment of the ungodly, it was mixed with his own envy and greed. He stood in judgment against others, and so placed himself at odds with God.

Asaph's story shows us that only one kind of love can *win;* the love of our Father *or* love for the things of this world. The two simply cannot co-exist. In his lapse into greed, Asaph had no compassion for his self-absorbed neighbors. If we are living in love, we'll have compassion for everyone, even the unjust. "Do not love this world nor the things it offers you, for when you love the world, you do not have the love of the Father in you" (1 John 2:15 NLT).

Nearness to God Is The Answer

This psalm resolves so beautifully as Asaph once again finds contentment in being a simple child of God, delighting in the Lord.

> Yet I still belong to you; you hold my right hand. You guide me with your counsel, leading me to a glorious destiny. Whom have I in heaven but you? I desire you more than anything on earth. My health may fail, and my spirit may grow weak, but God remains the strength of my heart; he is mine forever (Ps 73:23-26).

The NIV Bible says " ... God is ... *my portion* forever" (Ps 73:26, emphasis added).

What a turnaround! In the classic pattern of a psalm of lament, the worshipper moves out of despair into an entirely different frame of mind; his eyes are opened to another reality. His pain hasn't disappeared, but his bitterness is no longer blurring his vision of God. He regains his grasp on life.

When Asaph remembers who he belongs to, life makes sense and he claims, *"I still belong to you."* So much is contained in those few words. To jolt myself out of crazy thinking I sometimes speak these words to myself: "I belong to you, Lord. I am yours. I repent from thinking I am my own boss. I repent from self-centered living. The only place I want to be is with you."

In Asaph's reunion with the Lord we see a picture of intimate friendship, God holding his right hand. Asaph has broken out of his spiritual stupor. He comes close to God, finding comfort and strength. And don't forget that this all started when he went into God's sanctuary. He made the choice to seek God, and God met him. A humble heart opens the way for intimacy with God.

Asaph's sense of responsibility as a leader of God's people also kicked into gear. He had too much integrity to let his temper tantrum control his life, and because he had built his life on righteousness, he couldn't possible betray himself and those around him. The storm clouds of bitterness disappeared when he repented.

The Man in the Cardboard Box

When we compare ourselves to those who have more than us we are tempted to complain. When I've traveled internationally and seen how much I have in comparison with most others I have been jolted into repentance for complaining about a lack of cash flow. And when I see how happy and content the poor can be, I'm convicted of my sin of materialism.

My friend Mac Jardine and his wife lived with the poor in Hong Kong for several years. Mac's favorite story is that of a very special old Chinese man. Mac liked taking rice boxes to street sleepers and on one such day, he and some Chinese friends visited a very old man in his "home," a box about the size of a refrigerator carton, located on the top of an old high rise building in the central part of the city. Mac relates what happened:

> We climbed up many flights of stairs to his home and gave him a rice box. I saw that he was blind, but had a huge smile on his face! I asked the guys why he was so happy. The old man responded, with an even bigger smile, that he had had such a wonderful day with Jesus! It amazed me that he had almost nothing except two cats, was completely blind and yet was so happy.

Mac learned a lot from this old man about being content in simply knowing Jesus; being satisfied because God is *"holding my right hand."* This poor man shows us where true riches are found — in experiencing God's love and being thankful no matter how humble our home may be.

He may have owned almost nothing, yet — or perhaps we should say 'therefore' — he had an amazing intimate friendship with Jesus. There was very little to distract him from basking in the presence of his loving Father, so he was free of the entanglements that most of us battle. Though he had no earthly comforts, he was free of envy and bitterness.

Is knowing God enough for us? Or do we require some other condition to be met before we'll be content? For the man in the cardboard box, it was good enough to be *near to God.* These words of Asaph the psalmist could have been written by this man from Hong Kong:

> Whom have I in heaven but you?
> I desire you more than anything on earth (Ps 73:25 NLT).

Asaph sees heaven. He sees the futility of wanting a perfect life on earth. He sees the shortness of this life compared to an eternity with God. He allows the joys of the future age to break into his present existence. He chooses to treasure God over *anything* on earth.

In addition to his emotional turmoil, Asaph has another problem; he is physically sick. He says, "I get nothing but trouble all day long; every morning brings me pain ... My health may fail, and my spirit grow weak, but God remains the strength of my heart; he is mine forever" (Ps 73:14, 26 NLT). He was facing his own mortality, staring at a sickness that may have proved fatal and it brought his life into sharper focus. Realizing that only unseen things are eternal he came alongside God where he could find a permanent refuge. The lust for earthly luxuries no longer held him captive because the end of his earthly life was right around the corner. Why worry about the things that we can't bring with us?

At the conclusion of the Psalm, Asaph writes: "But as for me, how good it is to be near God! I have made the Sovereign LORD my shelter, and I will tell everyone about the wonderful things you do" (Ps 73:28 NLT). Asaph shows us the way to contentment. He went into God's sanctuary of worship and humbled himself, purifying his heart from envy. With clean hands and a pure heart, he could once again see God clearly. He found his real treasure once again.

> Others may climb to the top of the corporate ladder ...
> but as for me it is good to be near God.
>
> Others may indulge in endless extravagant luxuries ...
> but as for me it is good to be near God.
>
> Others may never have to worry about earning a paycheck ...
> but as for me it is good to be near God.

While traveling this road of worship, like Asaph I sometimes forget who my traveling partner is. I'm distracted by enticing attractions along the road, lured in by the adventure and treasure I might find on a side street. Then I realize I just want to stay on the main road with Jesus. I don't want to be burdened with any extra baggage that I might pick up on a different route.

May God give you contentment as you draw close to him and let him take your hand. May you overflow with joy like the man in the cardboard box because you have the privilege of walking with Jesus all day long.

Chapter 11
Worship, Contentment, and Addiction

After all, don't we have the ability to take the initiative
to frame our own future? Aren't we in charge of our own destiny?
Can't we become anyone we want, do anything we want, go
anywhere we want? Independence
and autonomy are the watchwords of our day,
not dependence and submission.
— Gary Beebe, Longing for God[1]

In my teens and twenties, I wrote hundreds of songs and produced self-financed recording projects. I led worship in my own church, mostly as a volunteer, and occasionally did concerts in other churches. I didn't earn income from my music, but I was happy to be using my gifts wherever I could.

In the late 1980s and 1990s, I took on more responsibility as a senior pastor of a local church and then as a worship pastor in a mega-church. I wrote several worship songs that became popular across a broad spectrum of church denominations. After ten years of learning the craft of songwriting and using those songs mostly in my own local church, all of a sudden my songs were being published.

At the same time I began to travel widely to lead worship in large conferences, both in the U.S. and internationally. I was frequently ministering in front of large crowds of people. After many years of using my worship gifts in relative obscurity, all of a sudden I had opportunities to lead worship for large numbers of people and make worship recordings that were widely distributed.

Why the résumé? Because in the midst of the excitement that surrounded these big things that God was doing, I battled to keep my motives pure. Ironically, the fruit of intimacy with God — my songs and musical gifts — made me vulnerable to self-promotion. The same gifts that I practiced in obscurity in my first ten years of ministry had now led me to a place of tension, with righteous ambition and selfish ambition on either side.

Though I was doing my best to serve God with a pure heart, I enjoyed the admiration and recognition that came from writing popular songs. Having tasted success, I found it to be an intoxicating wine, and eventually I learned to fight fiercely against serving my own agenda. As the Proverbs says, "the crucible for silver and the furnace for gold, but man is tested by the praise he receives" (Prov 27:21).

The Search for Significance

I suppose that it won't come as a surprise to read that all this was about my own insecurities. The root of my vulnerability to the lust for prominence was a search for significance. I wanted to be someone important, to have real value. Because of this, my music ministry threatened to enslave me, to become an addiction.

Our culture teaches us to find our self-worth through our accomplishments. We live in an age in which pursuing personal goals at all costs is celebrated. In his book "A Long Obedience in the Same Direction," Eugene Peterson says that *ambition* in America:

> … has been made into a monument, gilded with bronze and bathed in decorative lights. It has become an object of veneration …. Our culture encourages and rewards ambition without qualification. We are surrounded by a way of life in which betterment is understood as expansion, as acquisition, as fame. Everyone wants to get more. To be on top, no matter what it is the top of, is admired.[2]

In ancient times, selfish ambition was seen as a vice; today it is seen as a virtue.

Moreover, North America is the land of opportunity in every sector of the marketplace. It's where people come from hundreds of other countries to find their fortune, to climb their way up the ladder of success. It's the home of big business and huge Christian ministries, with pastors and singer-songwriters who are household names. These kinds of opportunities are a setup for addiction. Gifted individuals who are looking for significance through a career, a cause or a ministry may find their connection to God supplanted by another attachment. The waters become muddied and the motives even more mixed.

Addictions

In his book "12 Steps With Jesus," Don Williams explains that every single one of us struggles with addiction. "We medicate the emptiness, loneliness and pain in our lives through [addictions]. *We use them to find our self-worth, justify our lives and validate what we do and even who we are.* They [addictions] become functional idols — the real objects of our worship."[3]

Gerald May describes the pervasive reach of addiction:

> The same processes that are responsible for addiction to alcohol and narcotics are also responsible for addiction to ideas, work, relationships, power, moods, fantasies and an endless variety of other things."[4] ... "Addiction exists wherever persons are internally compelled to give energy to things that are not their true desires. To define it directly, addiction is a state of compulsion, obsession, or preoccupation that enslaves a person's will and desire. Addiction sidetracks and eclipses the energy of our deepest, truest desire for love and goodness. We succumb because the energy of our desire becomes attached, nailed, to specific behaviors, objects or people.

Don Williams shares his story of addiction in his early years of ministry:

> I became addicted to people, their opinions, their views of me and their acceptance … Along with my addiction to people and ministry, I became addicted to crisis. It elevated my mood. It gave me a purpose larger than myself. It threw me into action … I could problem solve, reach out to people and, again, receive the validation I so desperately needed … I was addicted to my adrenaline. I was also addicted to caffeine and sugar. My drugs of choice were legal stimulants that kept me going.[5]

Ministry is a good thing, but addiction to ministry is a bad thing. At this point in Don's life, it was an escape. It had power over him, and it displaced God's authority. Being successful, even by the world's definition of success, isn't necessarily a bad thing. Making a lot of money in your job isn't necessarily a bad thing. Thank God for devoted Christians in every sector of business and industry who generously support Kingdom endeavors. God gifts some people with great intelligence, vision and ability in these areas. But God has a better plan than for us to be devoured by our attachment to an occupation, a recreational activity or a relationship.

Idolatry — A Good Thing Taken Too Far

Addiction and idolatry are closely related. They both involve attaching ourselves to an object, person or activity in an unhealthy way and it is true that idolatry — defined as "excessive or blind adoration, reverence, devotion" — takes many forms.

To keep from becoming overly attached to other "gods," I've found N. T. Wright's five points of idolatry[6] to be very helpful. Wright uses Romans 1:18-25 as a basis for this teaching. The people described in Romans 1 don't acknowledge God or thank him, therefore their minds were blinded to the truth and they became enslaved to the worship of created things. Though the people Paul is describing in this chapter are not Christians, the dynamics of idolatry work the same way for Christians.

Point One: Perversion of the Good

Wright's first point is this: idolatry is a perversion of the good. Don Williams picks up on this:

> As Tom Wright says, an idol is, first of all, a perversion of God's good creation. Sex is good. Sexual abuse, pornography, incest, adultery and deviancy pervert it. Chemicals are good. Drug abuse perverts them. Love of country is good. Fanatical patriotism — "My country right or wrong" — perverts it.[7]

In Isaiah 44, we see the making of a meal morph into idol worship. The man in this story uses wood and fire for it's God-intended purpose, but takes it way too far when he fashions an idol and looks to that carving for salvation.

> It [the wood from a fallen tree] is man's fuel for burning; some of it he takes and warms himself, he kindles a fire and bakes bread. But he also fashions a god and worships it; he makes an idol and bows down to it. Half of the wood he burns in the fire; over it he prepares his meal, he roasts his meat and eats his fill. He also warms himself and says, "Ah! I am warm; I see the fire." From the rest he makes a god, his idol; he bows down to it and worships. He prays to it and says, *"Save me; you are my god"* (Isa 44:15-17, emphasis added).

Recreation is a healthy pursuit. Whether you choose golf, skiing, basketball, going to the rodeo or the dog show, they can all be a good way of resting and relaxing … just as long as your life is not consumed with any of these things, and as long as you are not addicted to these things.

But recreation can be a religion. Something as tame as sports can become a consuming passion that eclipses the higher priorities of eternity. Just look at soccer, whose fans will riot, trample and even — in the case of Colombian footballer Andres Escobar who scored on his own goal in the 1994 World Cup — *murder* in their misplaced devotion to the game. In the U.S. basketball, football and baseball reign supreme, with the most rabid of fans clearly worshipping their stars.

If you are an over-the-top sports fan, you know every statistic of your team's players. You spend *all* of your free time thinking about the upcoming game. If your team loses, you suffer real agony that bleeds into your mood and close relationships. If your team has a losing season, you are depressed. If your team wins, you are ecstatic. Your identity is intertwined with your team and your heroes. Wearing a jersey of your favorite team is OK, but does that loyalty define and prioritize the way you use most of your discretionary time, energy and money?

Love of sport is one of a myriad of lower loves that can consume us. Any of a thousand different hobbies could be the focus of our attention. For example, the preservation and restoration of the environment is a worthy cause, but like anything else, it can become an object of worship.

In Romans 1, Paul describes how they " ... exchanged the glory of the immortal God for images made to look like mortal man and birds and animals and reptiles" (Rom 1:23). In the absence of worshipping God, we must worship something else. We exchange the glory of God for the glory of a Harley motorcycle or the glory of an awesome wardrobe or the glory of a successful career as a musician or worship leader.

When God is not our focal point, our bodies and feelings become paramount. Our ultimate reference point becomes our feelings, appetites, and emotions. Here is the progression described in Romans 1:

> So God abandoned them to do whatever shameful things their hearts desired. As a result, they did vile and degrading things with each other's bodies. They traded the truth about God for a lie. So they worshiped and served the things God created instead of the Creator himself, who is worthy of eternal praise! Amen (Rom 1:24, 25 NLT).

The human body in today's culture has become central. This is expressed in slavish devotion to physical fitness and physical beauty.

This preoccupation with appearance is sometimes accompanied and supported by eating disorders such as anorexia or bulimia.

Dallas Willard has a great way of helping avoid this trap of finding our identity in our body-image. He explains: "We are, all of us, never-ceasing spiritual beings with a unique eternal calling to count for good in God's great universe."[8] You are not *your body*, you are a spirit-person who temporarily occupies a human body. So don't invest too much energy beautifying a body that's not going to last very long.

Sexual addictions are another fruit of being driven by our appetites and feelings. All you have to do is turn on the TV to see that "sex sells." Hundreds of millions of advertising dollars are spent in prime time television hours to advertise sex-enhancing drugs.

Being driven by our feelings also leads to statements like: "I don't feel like staying married to this person," "I don't feel like going to work today," "I don't feel like being honest about my taxes," or "I don't feel God's presence, therefore I don't feel like worshiping."

There's nothing wrong with feelings. We were created to sense, to intuit, to relate and respond. But, as Wright says, that great ability to feel can easily be perverted, placing idols at the centre of our lives.

Point Two: Idols and Identity

The second fact about idolatry is that your identity is determined by the idol, as Don Williams makes clear:

> Idols make us feel 10 feet tall. They enhance our lives. A sexual predator seduces women and feels invincible and alive. A wallflower does a few lines of coke and is the life of the party. A student joins a pro-gay or peace movement and feels powerful and important for the first time.[9]

In May of 2004 an article appeared in *Time Magazine* called

"My Wheels, My Self." It was all about defining who you are by the car you drive. A caricature of this choice of idols can be seen at a beach that I sometimes visit with my family. A parking lot next to this beach town is the hangout for a group of muscle men who like to sit on the bumpers of their "muscle cars" — vintage cars restored to perfection. You can tell these guys devote a lot of time developing their big muscles and their hot cars. It's who they are.

Perhaps cars aren't your thing. Perhaps it's your home. You are a faithful disciple of Martha Stewart, and you wake up every morning thinking about your next home decorating project. You say "I won't be happy until my house looks like *this.*"

In my early teens I went through a phase in which I really wanted to have a motorcycle. I yearned after them, coveting the motorcycles I saw, envying those who drove them and dreaming about riding one. I was depressed because I didn't have one. At this point, the desire to own a motorcycle *owned* a part of me. The same thing happened later on with girls; I thought I would be fulfilled if I had a girlfriend who was devoted to me. My desire to have a romantic partner *owned* a part of me.

I'm amazed at the worship-like quality of popular love songs I hear on the radio. The would-be lover has the ultimate power. In pursuit of romance, the pop star sings, "You are my everything" … "I can't live without you." That's worship. Ultimate worth is attributed to the prized girlfriend. The heartsick singer (and listener who buys the message) is under the illusion that this elusive relationship is the key that will deliver complete satisfaction. Obsession with a would-be lover is idol worship.

Point Three: Sacrifice

Third, idols demand sacrifice. "We offer them our time and money. Little by little, we give up our freedom, individuality, family, friends, honesty, present and future."[10] If drugs are your master, the cost is big money, and if taken to extremes you will lose your family, friends and health. If a romantic relationship is your main goal, you may sacrifice all your waking thoughts, your sexual purity and all your discretionary income to obtain your prize. Over and over, this allegiance is turned to a human idea, ideology or person.

In a message on worship, Don Williams describes how the affections of Germany were stolen from worshipping the living God and turned toward the dark power of the Nazi regime. The rise of Hitler's regime is called by some, "the black miracle of Germany." In a dramatic night time ceremony:

> Hitler amassed 100,000 storm troopers for this ceremony. A huge backdrop with swastikas was designed, lit up with torches in the dark of night. It was designed for maximum psychological impact. Hitler made his grand entrance, walking alone, with his lieutenants alone in this vast stadium.

> The people would effectively say to Hitler "strength, honor, power to you!" It cost us 60 million dead. If you give yourself to anything aside from Jesus Christ, you'll pay the consequences.[11]

Another way of saying this is "you become like the thing you worship." The devoted followers of Hitler shared his zeal to purge the world of "inferior races." In worshiping Jesus, the goal is to become more like him. But if I worship the lifestyles of the fabulously wealthy, I will sacrifice godliness for selfish gain. My heart will be set on material gain.

Point Four: Justification

And then there's this truth:

> Fourth, we justify our idols philosophically. Hugh Hefner blatantly set out to create an empire built on liberating male lust. To do so he buried himself in the Playboy mansion in Chicago and wrote his "Playboy philosophy," a dull, rambling, shallow justification for his assault on traditional morality. The drug culture creates its own ideological defense

of addiction and tries to take down a generation with it. The legalization of street drugs is continually justified by political, economic, legal and medical arguments.[12]

We look at the people around us and excuse ourselves by saying "everybody else is doing it." "I have freedom to do what I want," twisting the biblical definition of freedom to mean license to pursue whatever you want instead being freed to act for the good.

Point Five: It Never Ends Well

Don Williams explains the fifth and final aspect of idolatry:

> Fifth, our idols finally kill us. We think we have captured them; they capture us ... . Sexual liberation breeds sexual addiction, abortions and venereal diseases with AIDS as the extreme outcome. Street drugs breed addiction, gangs, violence, and huge criminal cartels that corrupt whole cities and even countries."[13] "There is a way that seems right to man, but in the end leads to death" (Pro 14:12).

Success has been my struggle, my idol, yet no matter what idol may tempt you, these principles are signposts to help steer you away from false substitutes for fulfillment and back towards God.

The Greatness of a Child

One way I fought against an addiction to success in worship leading was by immersing myself in God's definition of success. I strove to see "greatness" through God's eyes. When Jesus' disciples argued about which of them would be the greatest, Jesus cut right to the heart of the matter, confronting their selfish ambition. Jesus said, "You wanna be great? Become like a little child; if you don't, you won't even get into heaven." What is Jesus' definition of "being the greatest?" He says, "humble yourself just like this little child."

One of the lessons we can learn from children is found in Psalm

131, a wonderful prayer that presents a happy child as a model of contentment for us to emulate:

> Lord, my heart is not proud; my eyes are not haughty. I don't concern myself with matters too great or too awesome for me to grasp. Instead, I have calmed and quieted myself, like a weaned child who no longer cries for its mother's milk. Yes, like a weaned child is my soul within me (Ps 131:1,2 NLT).

This psalm is attributed to David — a king and warrior who conquered armies and ruled a nation. From the heart of this world leader comes the prayer of genuine humility and weakness. Here is a man who was endowed with a wide array of gifts — from music, to governing a nation, to military prowess.

David knew his limits; he knew where his strength came from. He didn't boast in his gifts nor did he trust his own strength, wisdom, or abilities. Yet David struggled to glory in God's strength rather than his own. Near the end of his life he ordered that a census be taken of the fighting men of Israel. This action seems to have been motivated either by pride in the size of the empire he had built or by reliance for his security on the size of his army. At the time of the census there was no immediate threat of war. It seems that David was reveling in his own power rather than God's. The penalty for this was severe, as 70,000 died in a punishing plague.

For a songwriter like me the equivalent of "numbering the army" would be "numbering my songs." I might idly wonder how many good songs I've written in the last year, and as I do so I'll be feeding some part of me that finds the parallels between my own life and the career of some well-known secular musician. But returning to the picture of a contented child with his mother helps me reject the temptation to strive for fame and fortune and cuts the comparisons short.

Eugene Petersen helpfully points out the difference between "ambition" and "aspiration:"

Ambition is aspiration gone crazy. Aspiration is the channeled, creative energy that moves us to growth in Christ, shaping goals in the Spirit. Ambition takes these same energies for growth and development and uses them to make something tawdry and cheap ....[14]

Perhaps Psalm 131 came near the end of David's life, when he could look back and see his life with clear perspective. He saw his mistakes, his selfish ambition, and in the end knew that God is not pleased with a proud, haughty heart.

The literal translation of the Hebrew in the 2nd verse of Psalm 131 is found in the King James Version: "Surely I have behaved and quieted myself, as a child that is weaned of his mother: my soul is even as a weaned child" (Ps 131:2, KJV).

What a self-effacing prayer this is, coming from a powerful king. The psalmist realizes that many projects and issues in life are outside his reach, and that it would be self-serving to venture into such endeavors. He has chosen not to strive for unreachable goals, but to be like a small child who is content to be at his mother's side.

As I look back over three decades of ministry, I see lots of high and low points — seasons of great productivity and visible outpourings of God's favor. I also remember times of depression and disappointment. There have been times of exciting opportunities in music ministry fuelled by new inspiration from heaven, and seasons of silence from God. There have been times of plenty and periods of economic strain.

Viewed within the frame of God's sovereignty, these ups and downs produce Godly results: I hope in the Lord, not in myself. I don't glory in my own strength, because I know how limited it is. Being battered by the trials of life produces a humility that results in a sustaining hope in God. As Paul wrote, " ... suffering produces perseverance; perseverance, character, and character, hope. And hope does not disappoint us because God has poured out his love into our hearts by the Holy Spirit, whom he has given us" (Rom 5:3-5).

Like a Weaned Child

My last child is named Elizabeth. Lizzie is a joy to our whole family and her older siblings love to dote on her. When she was little, Lizzie was the most content little child I've ever seen. She would hang around her mom all day, so happy to just go with the flow. She helped mom in the kitchen, and did all kinds of arts and crafts — coloring, painting, and working on puzzles. She fit the description of Psalm 131 — a small child content to be near her mother.

She didn't have to be *doing* anything to be happy; she was satisfied to just *be*. Little children don't have to be doing anything productive to be happy. It's that blissful time of life when everything is totally flexible because they don't have responsibilities.

Little children don't have their own agenda except to enjoy life as they follow the lead of their parents. I would invite Liz into the garden to "help me" or into my office to color while I worked and she'd quickly say "yes." Her carefree attitude reminded me to take time to smell the flowers and enjoy life. If we can't enjoy life, what good are great accomplishments?

I find it takes a lot of discipline to still and quiet myself "just as a small child is quiet with its mother." As a first-born high achiever, my jets are turning at a thousand revolutions per minute. Eugene Peterson writes: "It's no easy thing to quiet yourself: sooner may a person calm the sea or rule the wind or tame a tiger, than quiet oneself. It is a pitched battle."[15]

One of our goals should be to enjoy the simple pleasures of each day. Don't let your joy be choked off by your own hard-driving work ethic.

I've watched my wife wean all of my eight kids off breastfeeding. In those first few years, our kids were in food heaven. Anytime they were hungry, they buried their face in mommy's soft, warm breast and got a tummy full of sweet milk — better than hot chocolate, or richest ice cream! I can remember my babies being in a drunken-like state after breast-feeding. Those silly, giggling babies were intoxicated with their mothers' sweet milk. But after a few years of heavenly milk comes the time for weaning. You want to see anger? Just watch a baby who is being told "no, you can't have mommy's milk whenever you want it. You have to wait until bedtime." Red-faced, sweating and trembling, they shriek and wail as if to say "I want my milk and I want it *right now!*"

During weaning, the child is graduating from infantile dependency to a beginning level of independence. A weaned child is a picture of someone who has learned through painful surrender that comfort can be found another way.

Letting go of our codependent attachment to our work or our hobby can be just as hard as a baby's weaning process. If our sense of self is totally bound up in the "fix" that our work provides, it's a painful separation. If we're addicted to that "sweet milk" of our own advancement and can't be happy without it, we need to find contentment in simply being a child of God. The content, weaned child is a picture of the Christian who is secure in the Father's love and affirmation. The love of God really has been poured into your heart through the Holy Spirit; *he* will satisfy you and sustain you.

Whether your struggle with idols and addictions is work related or having to do with sexual issues, materialism or whatever, there is healing and freedom to be found in Jesus. The pathway to freedom from idols and addictions is found within accountable relationships in a strong Christian community, and in the spiritual disciplines that have been helpful to saints throughout the ages.

Just Like a Child

Several years ago when I saw how close I was to the slippery slope of self-serving ambition and pride, I wrote a song expressing my desire to return to innocence, to be untainted and pure.

"Just Like A Child"[16]

Oh let me return to the innocence, the first blush of my love for You

When I was smitten by your loveliness, and all that I wanted was You

I want to be just like a child again

I want to be just like a child again

Don't let me be tainted by my own success, or think that I've finally arrived

For what do I have that I did not receive? It's all a gift for this child

I don't want to work for the praises of men, for then I would have my reward

I'd rather seek after the treasure of heaven, and for that I must be like a child

Dancing and spinning in a field of flowers, singing and praising for hours and hours; I want to be, I want to be just like a child again

If this is your heart's cry — to be as innocent as a child — you'll be safeguarded from having a proud heart and haughty eyes. You'll be saved from the agony of getting yourself into big messes because you concerned yourself with "matters too great or awesome." You won't look at your neighbor's station in life and say "why didn't he take me along that nice road?" You'll have the joy of being content, like a small child is content at his mother's side.

Your Father has good plans for you. You can take his hand and trust him, and he will lead you in a way that is designed just for you, to bear fruit and live peacefully. "O Israel, put your hope in the Lord — now and always" (Ps 131:3 NLT).

Chapter 12
Worship and Unity:
Humility vs. Pride

A Christian man is the most free lord of all, and subject to none; a Christian man is the most dutiful servant of all, and subject to everyone.[1]
— Martin Luther

Judy and Cindy hadn't been getting along. They were both very involved in the evangelism programs of their local church. They both had a passionate heart to see people introduced to Jesus for the first time, but they couldn't agree on how to run the ministry; they had different strategies. Each woman wanted to involve a different group of workers and while both of them respected the pastor, these two ladies couldn't see eye to eye on how to carry out the vision. The tension between these women was obvious to their coworkers. Their angry exchanges of words put a damper on their team meetings. The resulting disunity was beginning to sap the team's energy to reach the lost.

This scenario sounds like a modern day church, but it's actually from the first century — the church in Philippi. I've changed the names and embellished the story a tiny bit, but most of it is taken right out of Paul's letter to the Philippians.

Settling this disagreement was one of Paul's main reasons for writing the letter. "Now I appeal to Euodia and Syntyche [Cindy and Judy]. Please, because you belong to the Lord, settle your disagreement"(Phil 4:2 NLT). I can picture our fictional characters Judy and Cindy each being passionate about their own ministry vision. Each of them felt they had the right idea. Evidently they needed to learn more deeply that love " ... does not demand it's own way ... " (1 Cor 13:5 NLT).

Unfortunately, I can think of a lot of examples of disagreement between church members and leaders. I've been a party to many a disagreement, both in church life and in all kinds of other relationships. Where there are humans interacting with one another, there will often be disagreement. What's the remedy for disharmony and how does it relate to a heart of worship?

Submission Amidst a Narcissistic Culture

Narcissism is defined both as "a doctrine that individual self-interest is the actual motive of all conscious action" and "inordinate fascination with oneself; excessive self-love." That's a pretty good description of the spirit of our age, the one that could so easily be titled "It's All About Me." Such a mindset is the exact opposite of what Jesus taught, but sadly it's highly prevalent in the church.

> Garrison Keillor once said that there are only two ways to cure raging narcissism: Have children or ... move to a foreign country where people don't care who you are or what you do.[2]

I understand the first option. Having eight kids is teaching me not to be so self-centered. Sadly, many believers in Jesus take the second option. They distance themselves from close relationships to others, thereby avoiding the issue of cooperation altogether. In so doing, they avoid God's design for becoming Christ-like. The worship journey was never meant to be a solo ride.

A pastor I know used to do a lot of marriage counseling. A woman at the church he was serving approached him one Sunday and said she wanted a divorce so she could marry her husband's brother. Needless to say, he was shocked. When he awkwardly told the woman that he would not feel comfortable doing their wedding, she angrily blurted out, "But doesn't the Bible say that God wants us to be happy?"

Gary Kinnaman, author and pastor, accurately describes the distortion of the pursuit of happiness among American Christians:

> We are obsessed with happiness and have little or no capacity for suffering and loss. After all, it's one of our "unalienable rights" — "life, liberty and *the pursuit of happiness.*"
>
> Whatever "happiness" meant to our Founding Fathers, of course, was much different from what it means today: that my country must, at all costs, protect my right to pursue, unfettered, my own happiness .... Good American Christians will sacrifice their most cherished and important relationships, will leave the church where they've known people for years, will even disobey God himself and end a marriage of twenty-five years, all in the relentless pursuit of the elusive god of personal happiness.[3]

Divorcing your spouse of two decades is commonplace in our society, but Paul explains in the book of Romans that if you *really* want to worship God, "Don't copy the behavior and customs of this world ..." (Rom 12:2 NLT). To worship is to submit to God, who *is* love. To worship him is to yield to and practice his ways of love. The most prevalent ideas of worship in the original biblical languages are translated as *service and grateful submission to God.* Submission to God leads to mutual submission among believers, in marriages, and in working relationships. We read in Ephesians: "Submit to one another *out of reverence for Christ*" (Eph 5:21, emphasis added).

Richard Foster includes "The Discipline of Submission" in his book *Celebration of Discipline.* Foster says that, "every Discipline has its corresponding freedom. What freedom corresponds to submission? It is the ability to lay down the terrible burden of always needing to get our own way."[4] Jesus is our model for "not getting our own way."

In his letter to the Philippians, Paul directs their attention to their experience with the life-giving Holy Spirit. They had tasted of God's love but there was a disconnect between receiving and giving that love. So Paul appeals to them to get in touch with the comfort and encouragement they've received from knowing Christ: "Is there *any encouragement* from belonging to Christ? *Any comfort* from his love? *Any fellowship* together in the Spirit? Are your hearts tender and compassionate?" (Phil 2:1 NLT).

Paul is in essence urging the Philippians to remember that, "the Holy Spirit has made his home in your hearts! The God of all comfort is dwelling inside you! The Father has spoken to you over and over again! He has let you know in the deepest part of your heart that you are His beloved child! As you've worshipped together as devoted brothers and sisters, he has come near to you!"

Having tasted of God's love, they had the wherewithal to *live a life of love*. When we receive the Holy Spirit, there should be a corresponding outward change of behavior. After all:

> ... if worship does not change us, it has not been worship. To stand before the Holy One of eternity is to change. Resentments cannot be held with the same tenacity when we enter His gracious light. As Jesus said, we will need to leave our gift at the altar and go set the matter straight (Mt. 5:23-24). In worship an increased power steals its way into the heart sanctuary, an increased compassion grows in the soul. To worship is to change.[5]

Being loved by God and our friends in the faith enables us to defer to one another. So Paul says:

> ... then [since you've truly received God's love] make me truly happy by agreeing wholeheartedly with each other, loving one another, and working together with one mind and purpose. Don't be selfish; don't try to impress others. Be humble, thinking of others as better than yourselves (Phil 2:2-3 NLT).

That's a radical statement. If I think of you as better than myself, then I'm going to value your opinion above my own. That's not easy to do. It goes against our natural urge to have our own way.

Several months ago I spent a few days with a team of worship arts leaders who were struggling with the sudden and shocking resignation of their senior pastor from his position of over twenty-five years. Though this man had faithfully served his church, the board of elders was forcing him out of his role. His close friends and coworkers were hurt, angry and confused about how this could be allowed to happen.

One of the ways I encouraged them was with this scripture from Philippians 2, particularly the words consider others "better than yourselves." That was the last thing they felt like doing. They were more inclined to strangle the perpetrators of this injustice, so it was a chance for them to be imitators of God. It required them to lay down their visceral reaction to injustice, a chance to love their enemies. (At least it *felt* like they were enemies). Their great challenge was to live a life of love and offer themselves as a sweet-smelling offering and sacrifice to God.

Francois Fenelon said, "Happy the soul which by a sincere self-renunciation, holds itself ceaselessly in the hands of its Creator, ready to do everything which he wishes; which never stops saying to itself a hundred times a day, "Lord, what wouldst thou that I should do."[6]

Richard Foster comments on this passage from Fenelon:

> Does that [constant yielding to God] sound impossible? The only reason we believe it to be far beyond us is that we don't understand Jesus as our present Teacher. When we have been under His tutelage for a time we see how it is possible for every motion of our lives to have its root in God.[7]

Being "under the tutelage" of "Jesus as our present Teacher" is the moment-by-moment yielding to the Holy Spirit that constitutes a life of worship. It is the submitted life, the humble life that puts

God and other first. We can't do it in our own strength, but we can do it by the real and effective enabling of God's Spirit. I love the phrase "Jesus our present Teacher." It's a beautiful description of our Friend and Mentor being always with us, ready to nudge us in the right direction. Training our souls to be always attentive to him is a lifelong process.

Let love be your highest goal

We see the same issues popping up in the church in Corinth. The new Christians in Corinth were very excited about using their spiritual gifts, and Paul strongly encouraged this pursuit. But the Corinthians' lack of concern for one another while using these gifts made it necessary for Paul to clarify, "let *love* be your highest goal! ..." (1 Cor 14:1 NLT, emphasis added).

Personal advancement and pride was getting in the way of real love, so Paul had to say "For who makes you different from anyone else? What do you have that you did not receive? And if you did receive it, why do you boast as though you did not?" (1 Cor 4:7). People were seeking an elevated spiritual status in the church through using their gifts. They were trying to impress one another.

Paul confronts this attitude in Philippi. He says, "don't try to impress others." I think that part of the problem with Judy and Cindy is that they were trying to impress others, vying for a place of greater prominence under Paul's ministry and struggling to control the ministry situation. They each had a vested interest in carrying out their own agenda because their status in the church would be enhanced if their ideas won the day. Sound familiar? The truth is that this is part of human nature.

Judy and Cindy's important goal of bringing people to Christ was eclipsing the highest goal of all; to love at all times. Their vision was clouded, the unity was gone and they couldn't see straight.

Small issues of contention became the main issues and instead of unity, there was competition. Whenever people are competing for visibility and prominence, some people will end up feeling left out. In Corinth, some people felt *left out* because they didn't have certain spiritual gifts: "And if the ear should say because I am not an eye, *I do not belong* to the body ..." (1 Cor 12:16). The less gifted ones felt like they *didn't belong*.

Paul gives the answer to this problem in the next chapter, which is the famous "love chapter" (1 Cor 13). Love is not self-seeking (church isn't all about me), love does not envy (when someone else is more gifted than me), love keeps no record of wrongs (when I feel hurt or excluded by someone's words), love always protects, always trusts, always endures (even when I've been mistreated or misunderstood by imperfect people, I'm going to make the choice to love).

You Are Not Your Own

The foundational verse for the discipline of submission is this: "... If anyone would come after me, he must deny himself and take up his cross and follow me" (Mark 8:34).

The old "you" is dead. There's a new you who is alive in Christ and who *belongs* to God. So Paul appeals to Judy and Cindy "... because you *belong to the Lord*, settle your disagreement" (Phil 4:2 NLT, emphasis added). In Christ we give up our own rights, including our right to "get our own way." To be Christ-centered is to be other-centered.

Paul put Jesus first, others second, and his own needs last. He said: "For to me, living means living for Christ, and dying is even better" (Phil 1:21 NLT). A few verses later he is " ... torn between two desires: I long to go and be with Christ, which would be far better for me. But *for your sakes*, it is better that I continue to live. Knowing this, I am convinced that I will remain alive *so I can continue to help all of you* grow and experience the joy of your faith" (Phil 1:23-25 NLT). For Paul, life was all about helping others, not his own comfort.

Love doesn't hang onto personal privileges. Our model for this is Jesus, who gave up his divine privileges. In my home, I frequently need to let go of my ideas because my wife has a different — and often better — idea than mine. In church leadership I've often had to give up my right to enact my own plans.

We have more than 33,000 Christian denominations in the world. Why? Because through the centuries church leaders haven't been able to submit to one another and lay down their own ideas. Our culture teaches us to hang on to, stand up for and fight for our rights, yet the way of love says, "let it go, love is more important." Love is not self-seeking. If love is our highest goal, then almost everything else is negotiable.

Individuals or Members of a Family?

Because we're part of a church planting movement and have helped pioneer new churches, I've been a member of eight different churches in the last thirty-five years. We've been in all churches of all sizes, from mega-churches to tiny congregations. The experiences gained along the way have taught us many things, like the fact that our culture teaches us to be extremely independent, individualistic people. My generation, the baby boomers, is especially steeped in the value of being autonomous and self-directing. The modern age celebrates the self-made man who pulls himself up by his own bootstraps and creates his own destiny.

All of this works against our call to come together as the church. We are prone to say, "I'll do it myself," "I can figure it out," and "I can be responsible for myself." I have to work at resisting this kind of thinking. I have to fight the tendency to work in isolated independence.

We don't understand and experience the kind of corporate identity that we see in the Bible. Here is a list of the many ways our identity as a *people of God* is described in the New Testament:

1. the brothers and sisters, the flock protected by the Shepherd

2. the body of Christ, a living expression of the Spirit of Jesus

3. the branches nourished by the vine, the temple of the Holy Spirit

4. a city — the new covenant community, fellow citizens with God's people

5. the household of faith, the family of God, the bride of Christ

6. building blocks in the temple in which God's royal presence lives

7. church (*ekklesia*) — "assembly," "called out ones"

8. a chosen people, a royal priesthood, a holy nation, a people belonging to God

9. God's fellow workers; God's field, God's building

If we value being part of a body, a household, a family, then we'll defer to the greater good for everyone even if it means we don't get our own way. As the parents of eight kids, Linda and I are constantly thinking about how to make things work for everyone. Whether it's placing kids in the right pairings in bedrooms, planning a vacation, sharing food or going on a hike, we constantly have to be thinking about what's best for the group, even if that means making a personal sacrifice.

A few months ago our entire family went for an afternoon to walk on the boardwalk at the beach. Our oldest child is Zachary, who is twenty-three years old and our youngest child, Elizabeth, is seven years old. As Lizzie walked with us that day, I realized that for the first time in twenty-three years of family life, we could all walk at the same pace together! No more babies or toddlers who have to be carried or pushed in a stroller! No more waiting for the stragglers!

In church and work relationships, people "walk at a different pace." Maybe one of Judy and Cindy's main problems was simply a timing issue; one wanted to eagerly push ahead with an outreach project while the other one felt led by God to wait until the team of workers was more prepared.

The body of Christ is a mosaic of individuals from vastly different backgrounds, education levels, with diverse personalities, gifts and interests. Some of us are pioneers and some are settlers. Some are hard chargers and some are nurturers. Some are evangelistic and some are pastoral. We see things differently. So we have to wait for one another, respecting the limitations and heartfelt convictions of our brothers and sisters. We have to "change the way we think" and become less independent and more community driven.

As God's beloved children, we belong not only to him but to one another. It is true that "so in Christ we who are many form one body, and *each member belongs to all the others*" (Rom12:5, emphasis added). Read it again, will you? Isn't that a radically different idea from the way our first-world postmodern culture thinks?

An astonishing example of "belonging to one another" is found in the second chapter of Acts. At Pentecost the Holy Spirit came in power and the results were far reaching. Everyone spent a lot of time together in meals, fellowship, work and worship. There was a common purse allowing everyone to share all their material possessions. Can first-world, middle-class Christians live out this value of "belonging to one another?" I'm sure it's possible but I haven't experienced it on an Acts 2 level. Not yet, at least.

Abiding in God's Love

But it is worth pursuing. We can't fully experience the benefits of God's love unless we give ourselves away. "To properly pursue love, we must strive to give it away rather than simply find it. If we don't, we endanger ourselves by becoming the ultimate consumers."[8]

If the water in a stream stops running, a stagnant pool forms. Some of the fish will die because they're not getting the oxygen and nutrients they need. Likewise, stopping the outward flow of God's love from our lives makes our spirits stagnant. When we stop being patient, gentle and kind, we receive less nurture and nourishment from God. After all, *He is love*; to act otherwise is to resist his very nature. The only way you can fully experience God's love is to always be giving it away. As Paul says: "and do *everything* with love" (1 Cor 16:14 NLT emphasis added).

We see this interdependence between harmonious relationships and the experience of God's presence in Paul's letter to the Corinthians where he tells his readers to " ... be joyful. Grow to maturity. Encourage each other. Live in harmony and peace. *Then* the God of love and peace will be with you" (2 Cor 13:11 NLT emphasis added). Put negatively, this verse implies "If you have disunity, you won't have as much of God's presence."

We can't see things properly if we're holding a grudge or embroiled in envy. I've seen the negative proof of this many times in church life when people's hearts are hardened to one another and they become closed off to counsel. Someone who was my good friend one day became my enemy the next day because they were convinced I was wrong and they *knew* they were right.

When unity is squelched, so is clear thinking and receiving wisdom from God. Paul says, "My purpose is that they may be encouraged in heart and *united* in love, *so that* they may have the full riches of *complete understanding, in order* that they may *know the mystery of God ...* " (Col 2:2, emphasis added). Without unity, we don't have full access to God's wisdom.

Spiritual Warfare and Submission

Peter describes the devil as "a roaring lion looking for someone to devour." Believe it or not, this line appears in the context of a discussion about relationships! To avoid being "devoured," Peter instructs *everyone* to humble themselves to one another:

> *Young men*, in the same way be *submissive* to those who are older. All of you, clothe yourselves with humility toward one another, because, "God opposes the *proud* but gives grace to the humble." *Humble yourselves*, therefore, under God's mighty hand, that he *may lift you up* in due time ... Be self-controlled and alert. Your *enemy the devil prowls* around like a roaring lion looking for someone to devour. Resist him, standing firm in your faith ... (1 Pet 5:5-9).

The most venomous and hurtful spiritual warfare I've experienced in the church is when relationships fall apart. People stop submitting to God and one another, and they start attacking and criticizing one another.

Pride, the opposite of humility, is a double-edged sword — cutting us off from God and one another. When pride rules us, no longer do we consider one another better than ourselves. Then the devil has a heyday. This is nothing new; the early church struggled with the same problem.

It's the same story in James' epistle. "What causes fights and quarrels among you? Don't they come from your desires that battle within you? ... . God opposes the proud but gives grace to the humble. Submit yourselves, then, to God. Resist the devil, and he will flee from you" (Jas 4:1,7).

The dangers addressed in this passage are the harmfulness of cruel words and anger, the desire to be lifted up above other people, and the struggle in submitting to one another. When we stumble in those areas, a door is opened for the enemy to wreak havoc in our relationships.

A third example of warfare in relationships is from Ephesians:

"'In your anger do not sin': Do not let the sun go down while you are still angry, and do not give the devil a foothold" (Eph 4:26-27).

Anger is often the flash point that divides Christians — in business, ministry or marriage. It is true that "Christians have never known exactly what to do with anger. Anger arises from a sense of violation: a violation of self, of agreements, of principles. It also arises when we feel a threat to our social status or a desire to control other people's lives."[9]

Evagrius of Ponticus lived in and around Constantinople in the fourth century. He was heavily influenced by Origen and wrote extensively on the psychology of spiritual devotion. Evagrius identified eight deadly thoughts that can agitate our mind and ruin our life. One of these deadly thoughts is anger:

> The most fierce passion is anger. In fact, it is defined as a boiling and stirring up of wrath against one who has given injury. It tends to lead to a preoccupation with the one with whom we are angry. It ruins our health — both physical and mental.[10]

Our characters Judy and Cindy in Philippi were likely angry with one another. I am all too familiar with this emotion of anger and I admit that I get angry in traffic jams, angry at my children and angry when I can't get quick results. The only way out of anger is confession of sin and submission to God and others. Humility and confession loosens the grip of anger.

Forgiveness and Gratitude

There will invariably be times we have to forgive one another when we're wronged. Harsh words are spoken, offence is taken and without forgiveness our relationships with God and others are stifled. Erwin McManus explains the connection between forgiveness and gratitude:

> Forgiveness and gratitude are inseparable. When we receive forgiveness, we grow in gratefulness. When we grow in

gratefulness, we are more willing to give forgiveness. Our ability to receive forgiveness is directly related to our willingness to give it. A direct benefit of gratitude is the freedom from bitterness. When we are grateful, we are not bound to grudges or vengeance.

Even as gratitude and forgiveness are inseparable, so are ungratefulness and bitterness. When we are grateful, we see and experience life with a healthy optimism. When we lack gratitude, we move toward pessimism and even cynicism. An ungrateful heart always sees what's wrong with life. The longer we live without gratitude, the more embittered we become. If we are to enjoy lives of gratitude, we must break free from the gravitational pull of bitterness.[11]

Real Worship Leads to Real Unity

A remarkable story of worship and unity comes from the life of Count Zinzendorf. Zinzendorf was born into a noble Pietistic family in Dresden, Germany in 1700. In 1722, he was approached by a small band of wandering Moravians to request permission to live on his lands. The Moravians were a refugee colony from Bohemia who were persecuted for their spirituality And Ziznnendorf allowed them to settle in the village of Herrnhut on a corner of his estate.

In 1727 Zinzendorf devoted himself to working with the Moravians, who were seriously divided. What followed was

> ... an intense and powerful experience of renewal, often described as the "Moravian Pentecost." During a communion service at Berthelsdorf, the entire congregation felt a powerful presence of the Holy Spirit, and felt their previous differences swept away. This experience began the Moravian renewal, and led to the beginning of the Protestant World Mission movement.[12]

A Moravian historian described the repentance from selfishness that filled them: "Every one desired above everything else that the Holy Spirit might have full control. Self-love and self-will, as well as all disobedience disappeared and an overwhelming flood of grace swept us all out into the great ocean of Divine Love."[13]

"On May 12, 1727, Zinzendorf addressed the community for three hours on the blessedness of Christian unity. The people sorrowfully confessed their past quarreling and promised to live in love and simplicity."

This story powerfully illustrates God's passionate desire for unity in the body of Christ. The presence of the Holy Spirit warms of our hearts and moves us to discard our own self-will in favor of unity.

Loving God and our neighbor are two intertwined and interdependent commandments. You can't be a true worshiper without being a good neighbor and sincere worship results in serving your neighbor and true devotion to your brother strengthens your relationship with God.

In chapters 12 through 15 of the book of Romans Paul explains how to demonstrate your devotion to God in relationships:

> Love must be sincere ... Be devoted to one another in brotherly love. Honor one another above yourselves ... Share with God's people who are in need. Practice hospitality ... . Live in harmony with one another ... .Do not be conceited ... . Accept him whose faith is weak ... . We who are strong ought to bear with the failings of the weak and not to please ourselves. Each of us should please his neighbor for his good, to build him up" (Rom 12:9-10; 13, 16; 14:1, 15:1-2).

All of these chapters flow directly out of the keynote passage on genuine worship in Romans 12:1 where we are told to give our bodies to God. The fruit of worship is the formation of a group of people that love and serve one another. Paul knows that it's going to take a lot of perseverance to do this, so after all these instructions on love, he says:

"May the God who gives endurance and encouragement give you a spirit of unity among yourselves as you follow Christ Jesus, so that with one heart and mouth you may glorify the God and Father of our Lord Jesus Christ" (Rom 15:5, 6).

Recently I went to hear my daughter's choir perform in a beautiful cathedral in downtown Vancouver. There were two choirs, four gifted soloists and a volunteer orchestra that was talented, but occasionally played some sour notes. I winced as I heard the clash of dissonant notes in the orchestra. Though I enjoyed the overall performance, my musical ear was immediately drawn to the mistakes.

When the whole church is singing with "one mouth" but not with "one heart," God hears the "sour notes" in relationships. When our songs of worship are flowing but there's bitterness and brokenness instead of unity, the Holy Spirit is grieved.

After thirty-five years in the church, I know that it takes a lot of endurance to hang in there with a bunch of other Christians. I've had to forgive a lot of people and confess my sin and receive forgiveness many times. I've had to swallow my words when they threatened the group's unity. I've had to let my vision die because other leaders haven't agreed with me.

The fruit of all of this is that I've become a little less selfish and a little more like Jesus. Isn't that what God is after in our lives? Isn't that what real worship should produce in us? This is my prayer: " … let God transform you into a new person by changing the way you think. Then you will learn to know God's will for you, which is good and pleasing and perfect" (Rom 12:2 NLT).

Chapter 13
Work, Rest, and Worship

*The opposite of a slave is not a free man. It's a worshipper.
The one who is most free is the one who turns the work
of his hands into sacrament, into offering.*[1]
— *Mark Buchanan*

In a recent article called "Americans Don't Like Their Jobs," Roy Rummler reports that fifty-five percent of American workers are dissatisfied with their work. In a survey supported by many other research projects, Rummler reports, " ... only 51 percent felt their jobs were interesting — falling from a high of 70 percent."[2]

I am not one of the ones who are dissatisfied. I count it a privilege to know what a gift it is to work hard and enjoy it. The writer of Ecclesiastes says, "I know that there is nothing better for men than to be happy and do good while they live. That everyone may eat and drink, and find satisfaction in all his toil — this is the gift of God" (Ec 3:12-13). The ability to enjoy what God has given us is in itself a gift.

Yet in a fallen world the work of humankind is tainted with frustration. Ever since the fall of man and the introduction of sin to the world, work became onerous and burdensome. God said to Adam:

> ... Since you listened to your wife and ate from the tree
> whose fruit I commanded you not to eat, the ground is

cursed because of you. *All your life you will struggle to scratch a living* from it ... By the sweat of your brow will you have food to eat until you return to the ground from which you were made... (Gen 3:17-19; NLT, emphasis added).

Without eternity in view, work is a bitter pill; for the minimum wage laborer who can't make ends meet, for the over qualified executive who has been laid off and can't find a job, and for the struggling artist who is tremendously talented but can't produce income through their art.

Work Is Good

Work was originally created, like everything else God made, to be *good*.

> In the beginning, God created. He created. He did something. He *made* something. He fashioned heaven and earth. The week of creation was a week of work ... The foundational truth is that work is good. If God does it, it must be all right. Work has dignity: there can be nothing degrading about work if God works. Work has purpose: there can be nothing futile about work if God works.[3]

After his work of creation, God set humans to the task of work: "The Lord God took the man and put him in the Garden of Eden *to work it and take care of it*" (Gen 2:15, emphasis added). God created work just as he created the earth and all that is in it; he created it as a good thing. God created Eve as a "helpmate" for Adam. They were *coworkers*.

The kingdom of God is here to restore our original relationship with God, and to transform all our endeavors, including our daily work. God has reclaimed and redeemed us to work unto him, not in frustration but with purpose and gladness. Let's take a look at work through God's eyes.

First, we have the example of Jesus. Most of his life he was a carpenter. Think of Jesus' long hours of working with his hands, sweating and serving and finding satisfaction in doing his job well. Fully man yet fully God, he enjoyed hanging out with his Father as he exerted himself in physical labor. I'm sure he sought to please his Father and his customers with every project and I'm sure he gave his clients a fair shake.

Then there was Paul, who worked hard both as tent maker and as an apostle, empowered by God's grace. " ... I worked harder than all of them [the other apostles] — yet not I, but the grace of God that was with me" (1 Cor 15:10). He was very productive — a tireless worker. He gives the Corinthians a list of his qualifications to legitimize his genuine apostleship, saying, "We work hard with our own hands ... " (1 Cor 4:12). He rouses the church in Thessalonica to labor diligently, urging them to: "Make it your ambition ... to work with your hands, just as we told you." "We gave you this rule: if a man will not work, he shall not eat" (1 Thess 4:12, 2 Thess 3:10).

In the first century, most people worked with their hands doing arduous and menial tasks. Millions of people were slaves in the Roman Empire and Paul challenged them to see work as sanctified, a holy act, an offering of worship. Paul instructed his friends to change their way of seeing their daily chores, to work not for men, but *as unto the Lord.*

Paul exhorts the church:

> Slaves, obey your earthly masters with deep respect and fear. Serve them sincerely as you would serve Christ. Work hard, but not just to please your masters when they are watching. As slaves of Christ, do the will of God with all your heart. Work with enthusiasm, as though you were working for the Lord rather than for people. Remember that the Lord will reward each one of us for the good we do, whether we are slaves or free (Eph 6:5-8 NLT).

Regardless of our station in life, the promise of reward for good work fills us with hope. Even if men don't notice our attention to detail, God will. As we do the will of God with all our heart, we see beyond the next paycheck to our heavenly reward. We find dignity in our high calling. Empowered by a deep connection with God's sovereign calling, we can find joy in our work, knowing the Lord will reward us.

Martin Luther affirms the sanctity of every occupation, every job done well:

> The maid who sweeps her kitchen is doing the will of God just as much as the monk who prays — not because she may sing a Christian hymn as she sweeps but because God loves clean floors. The Christian shoemaker does his Christian duty not by putting little crosses on shoes, but by making good shoes, because God is interested in good craftsmanship.[4]

Made in God's Image

God made us in his image. As his offspring, we reflect his glory. We are creative and productive because he is creative and productive. We like to make beautiful things because he endowed us with an imagination like his own. When we finish a job that requires skill and tenacity, we have great satisfaction.

I have friends in all fields of work who are successful and happy in their jobs. A part of them really comes alive when they talk about the way God is blessing their business. My friend Matthew, a successful lawyer, says, "When I think of my work as an offering to God, one of my touchstones is a quote from Eric Liddell: 'I believe God made me for a purpose, but he also made me fast. And when I run I feel His pleasure.' I love what I do. I recognize that God takes pleasure in my excelling at talents He has given me."

My friends who have successful careers see God's favor on their work and are delighted to generously share from their earnings to support God's work around the world. They humbly acknowledge that all they have is a gift from God and believe that "the money belongs to him." In Christ, they all have a sense of purpose and fulfillment in doing their work. They work not just for an earthly reward but an eternal one, too. No Christian who loves God first and foremost should apologize for aspiring to do well in their chosen field. The Bible doesn't teach the elimination of aspiration but the transformation of it.

We have a glorious identity as God's ambassadors on the earth. The psalmist expresses his astonishment to God over the glory he has bestowed on man: "You made him a little lower than the heavenly beings and crowned him with glory and honor. You made him ruler over the works of your hands; you put everything under his feet" (Ps 8:5-6). Saint Irenaeus, a second century early church father and apologist put it beautifully when he wrote, "The glory of God is man fully alive."

We reflect God's glory. John Eldredge encourages us not to "fear our glory" but to embrace it and live from it. "Living from your glory is the only loving thing you can do. To admit we do have a new heart and a glory from God, to let it be unveiled and to embrace it means we must come out of the boat, take the throne, be what he meant us to be. And that feels risky but it is also exciting. It is coming fully alive."[5]

God gives us talents that he wants us to invest, to use for his glory. He's not glorified when we hide our "glory" under a bushel; he doesn't want us to bury our talents in the ground. In the parable of the talents, Jesus essentially says, "Use what I've given you and watch it multiply!" (Matt. 25).

Writing, performing and recording worship music is part of the job God gave me. While there is always a danger of self-aggrandizement in the arts, God calls me not to "fear my glory" but to boldly use my gifts to their fullest potential. It's who he made me to be. So I've written hundreds of songs over the past thirty years; some have just been between God and me, some have touched a few lives, and some have gone far and wide. I'll probably keep writing songs until I die. At the end of my life, my songs will most likely be conversations between God and me alone.

Gregory The Great — The Contemplative and Active Life

Considered one of the greatest popes in the history of the church, Gregory the Great (540-604) gives us a very helpful model for dedicating our lives to God in the workplace. Born the son of a Roman senator and an aristocratic mother, Gregory received an excellent education and proved to be a very intelligent and skillful leader in both spiritual and administrative roles. As prefect of Rome, his responsibilities were to coordinate the business of the church with government officials. His accomplishments were far ranging, including negotiating treaties with occupying armies and sending missionaries throughout the world.

Earlier in his life, when carrying less responsibility, Gregory had more time for contemplation. It was easy to contemplate God, Gregory mused, when you are not "scurrying to meet the avalanche of human needs that confront you as bishop."[6] Many a modern day pastor and busy mother would agree.

Gregory's wholehearted embracing of a busy life is encouraging to the vast majority of us who struggle to live a devoted life while working in a secular context. He embraced a life "that simultaneously contemplates God and engages in purposeful activity."[7] He said, "The active life belongs to many, the contemplative to few."[8] In an era when monasticism flourished and was viewed as the holiest path a person could take, Gregory lifts up the active life of work as a high calling from God.

Gregory's approach to "contemplation" is very practical. He compares our interludes of prayer amidst a busy life to a grasshopper that leaps up towards heaven but inevitably falls back to the earth.[9] He viewed action and contemplation as complementary, not in conflict with each other. These lessons from a sixth century pope are timeless. Through Gregory the Great, God shows us the sacred value of our secular work.

My friend Paul, who worked as a pastor for several years before starting a business, describes the melding of the sacred and secular:

> When I started out on my working life as a residential flooring contractor, I looked at earning money at work as a means to an end. Christian ministry was what I felt 'called to,' and I worked in a job to pay for my family's needs. I saw the two roles as separate, as though one were 'sacred' and the other 'secular.' In recent years, my perspective has changed to view everything I do and everywhere I go as an opportunity to participate in building God's Kingdom.

Brother Lawrence: Dishwasher

I know of no other figure in church history who understood work as a holy offering to God like Brother Lawrence. In a modern world full of people who are either bored or irritated with their daily work, we desperately need to learn from the example of this man who approached every activity with prayer and gratitude. Brother Lawrence practiced the presence of God continually. Here is an excerpt from his well — known work, "Practicing the Presence of God:"

> The time of work," he wrote, "does not with me differ from the time of prayer. In the noise and clatter of my kitchen, while several persons are at the same time calling for different things, I possess God in as great a tranquility as if I were upon my knees at the Blessed Supper.

Brother Lawrence found a way to perform menial tasks with love: "We ought not weary of doing little things for the love of God, who regards not the greatness of the work, but the love with which it is performed."

Serving the Lord, not *chronos*

Psalm 127 is a well-known warning against over working.

> Unless the Lord builds the house, its builders labor in vain. Unless the Lord watches over the city, the watchmen stand guard in vain. In vain you rise early and stay up late, toiling for food to eat — for he grants sleep to those he loves (Ps 127:1-2).

If we forget that God is working even as we work, we'll frantically push too hard.

For many years I saw the next part of this psalm as unrelated to the first verses: "Sons are a heritage from the Lord, children a reward from him. Like arrows in the hands of a warrior are sons born in one's youth. Blessed is the man whose quiver is full of them …" (Psalm 127:4-5). I have six sons and two daughters. I *do* feel blessed. At times, I'm literally quivering because of so much blessing! But what does that have to do with work?

Eugene Petersen sees the gift of children as an example of God's work in and through us. In contrast to the anxious labor that builds cities and guards possessions, the psalm praises the effortless work of making children." Children are:

> … born not through human effort, but through the miraculous processes of reproduction which God has created among us … The entire miracle of procreation and reproduction requires our participation, but hardly in the form of what we call our work … We participated in an act of love which was provided for us in the structure of God's creation.[10]

God made each one of us to do certain things well. When we're functioning in our God given role, it's almost like the reproduction process — we're simply fitting into "the structure of God's creation." To some people he gives the gift of watch-making, to others the gift of teaching and to others the gift of cooking. He gave me the gift of worship leading. After over three decades of leading worship, I still marvel at the miracle that happens: when I simply play guitar and sing, heaven comes down and people connect with

God. When we do what God *made us* to do, it doesn't have to be anxious toil.

I know it's the same with many of my family and friends: when we find our niche as workers, there's an easy rhythm to our work. For Linda, caring for people's medical needs comes naturally because God wired her with a scientific mind and a compassionate heart. My friend Ron is an accountant. He is gifted in working with numbers, details and complex formulas. As I discuss my bookkeeping and taxes with him, it seems that for him, working with the complexities of the tax world are almost as easy as breathing.

In the workplace, we are surrounded by God's "sons and daughters." Regardless of their spiritual orientation, they are God's offspring. No matter what kind of job, career of profession we have, our work is about relationships with *people*. "As Christians do the jobs and tasks assigned to them in what the world calls work, we learn to pay attention to and practice what God is doing in love and justice, in helping and healing, in liberating and cheering."[11]

As working worshippers, we set ourselves and our time apart for God. But if we let it, time can be a harsh tyrant, sucking the life out of us. The Greeks understood that time could either be a vehicle for high purposes or destruction. In Greek culture there were two different words for time, *chronos* and *kairos*. These two words connote two distinctly different ways of looking at time.

Kairos is defined as an undetermined period of time in which something special happens. What the special something is depends on who is using the word. Viewing our lives through the lens of *kairos* gives us a sense of purpose and opportunity. Time is a gift to be used for good. Jesus, Paul and Brother Lawrence operated in the *kairos* view of time. They saw every moment as a chance to glorify God.

While *kairos* is qualitative, *chronos* has a quantitative nature.

The word *chronos* refers to chronological or sequential time and is taken from one of the gods in the Greek pantheon.

> *Chronos* was a nasty minor deity, a glutton and a cannibal who gorged himself on his own children ... Goya depicted him in his work *Devouring His Children.* In the painting, *Chronos* is gaunt and ravenous, wild-eyed with hunger. He crams a naked, bloody-stumped figure into his gaping mouth. He was always consuming, never consummated.[12]

This description of *Chronos* illustrates the way we can be devoured by an overly busy schedule. We can be enslaved to the tyranny of *chronos* time. James Bryan Smith has some very helpful things to say about our need to create "margin" in our lives.[13] He says:

> We add so much to our schedules that we have no "margin," no space for leisure and rest and family and God and health ... We live in a culture that rewards busyness and overextension as signs of importance .... The number one spiritual sickness of our day is "hurry sickness."

To create margin in his own life, James learned to *say no* to non-essential activities. He advises his readers to say "no" to "anything that is not absolutely necessary to the well-being of your soul or the welfare of others ... when we lack margin, it is our own doing and is a sure sign we have stepped outside the kingdom. So be honest and be ruthless with your schedule. Your spiritual, relational and physical health depend on it."

James notes that, "more than any other time in history, we have become obsessed with productivity, speed and efficiency."[14] He quotes economist Jeremy Rifkin who writes, "while other cultures might believe haste makes waste, we are convinced that speed reflects alertness, power, and success."[15] Smith says, "Our impatience has made life a dizzying blur. And as a result, our spiritual lives are diminished. As we try harder, we are becoming spiritually shallow and deeply disappointed — not exactly a recipe for a robust life."

Robert Barron writes: "the deepest part of the soul likes to *go slow*, since it seeks to savor rather than to accomplish; it wants to rest in and contemplate the good rather hurry off to another place."[16]

The Cost of Being Overly Busy

I'm a typical firstborn child; I'm very conscientious and I enjoy working hard in all areas — whether it's music, academics, or in my own backyard. I enjoy accomplishing things, whether it's writing a song or building a garden shed.

But my greatest strengths can also be my greatest weaknesses. I get so focused on my work that I forget about my other priorities. If I'm not careful, I get tunnel vision, and all I can think about is accomplishing the next task. I think this is a common problem for many men. If we're in control, working hard and seeing results, we're happy. But if we're not accomplishing something, we're not content. This is partly due to being influenced by a culture that views rest as laziness. We are falsely taught that our worth comes from what we produce or earn.

One area that can suffer is our family relationships. Because I'm in overdrive so much of the time, I default to working instead of paying attention to the people I love the most.

The payoff from our closest relationships is less dramatic than finishing a project or hitting that next goal at work. Relationships with our spouses and children involve hanging out, listening, and taking an interest in others instead of pushing our own agenda. It's more about *being* than *doing*. When I don't stop for recreation with my family, I'm robbed of the joy of a noon hour basketball game with my boys or a 5:00pm bike ride with my daughter Lizzie.

If I'm driven by the delusion that nothing is more important than work, I'll never take my kids for a day trip to the beach in White Rock.

When my work consumes me, I forget that I'm in the people business. I don't have the emotional resources to be kind and helpful; I become short-tempered and easily angered. My work day never ends; instead of calling it quits at 5:00 or 6:00, I keep plowing all through the evening, turning my back on my family. I never cross a line that says, "my work is finished."

On September 15, 2006, I was praying in the morning, asking the Lord for a word of encouragement. Immediately I felt God was saying "you're trying too hard" and then I saw in my mind's eye a picture of a foot letting up on the gas pedal of a car. God was saying, "slow down, don't drive so fast!" This was two days before the first Sunday morning meeting of a new church plant I was helping to lead. God knows that in my eagerness I sometimes put too much pressure on myself and on others; I expect too much progress too quickly (read: *impatience*). So he gave me a picture that communicated very clearly; relax, don't push so hard. Trust me.

Another sign that we're overextending is physical stress and pain. When I overwork, I often get headaches and backaches from too many hours at the computer. When I ignore God's guidelines for rest, I pay the price with physical pain. This is one way God gets my attention.

God designed us to *need* rest — body, soul and spirit. If I get exhausted from overwork, I lose perspective. I can't think as clearly. I feel overwhelmed because I've robbed myself of the rest God intends for me. It's harder to trust God and be cheerful when I'm emotionally and physically depleted.

The statistics show that many Americans are suffering from sleep deprivation. Dr. Siang-Yang Tan reports that in the 1850s the average American slept 9.5 hours a night. Today the average American sleeps under seven hours a night. "A poll done by the National Sleep Foundation showed that forty-nine percent of American adults have sleep related problems."[17] We endanger our own lives when we mess around with our God given limits: Bertrand Russell said, "One of the symptoms of an approaching nervous breakdown is the belief that one's work is terribly important ... ."[18]

I'm self-employed, so if the productivity bar is being set too high, I only have myself to blame. There are a few reasons I drive myself too hard. One is a lack of trust in God to provide. If you're a salesman or a small business owner, you know what I mean. I have to trust God to provide work for me. A lack of faith results in a lack of peace, and sometimes in working too hard. When I slip into a doubting attitude, I put my hope in the work instead of God who provides work and income. Simply put, that's idolatry.

My "to do" list is not my God. But sometimes it would seem that way. At the end of a day or the end of a week, I'm annoyed by having so many unfinished items on my list. As wisdom slowly takes control of me, I pry myself away from my desk and take the Lord's offer of an intermission. How silly it is to willingly choose servitude to overworking when the Lord himself has opened the door for us to go free.

Jesus calms down his followers who are worried about daily provision with these words:

> What I'm trying to do here is get you to relax, not be so preoccupied with getting so you can respond to God's giving. People who don't know God and the way he works fuss over these things, but you know both God and how he works. Steep yourself in God-reality, God-initiative, God-provisions. You'll find all your everyday human concerns will be met. Don't be afraid of missing out. You're my dearest friends! The Father wants to give you the very kingdom itself (Luke 12:29-32, *The Message*).

If we *really* believe in God, we will trust him to help us get enough work done within the hours of the day and days of the week that he has created. Then, we'll rest. Our simple trust is worship, and it's precious to God.

God's Gift of Sabbath

Work done in the context of eternity points us towards rest. When we realize that our days are numbered and that "we can't take it with us," we'll be more inclined to not work ourselves to death. Sabbath rest reminds us that God is infinite and we are finite. In stopping to rest, we agree with the way God chose to create us.

One of the main purposes of the Sabbath day is to *remember* that God delivered us from slavery. God gave Moses this commandment to pass along to us:

> Observe the Sabbath day by keeping it holy, as the Lord your God has commanded you ... . Remember that you were slaves in Egypt and that the Lord your God brought you out of there ... . Therefore ... observe the Sabbath day (Deut 5:12, 15).

As slaves to the Egyptian Pharaoh, the Hebrews had no option of resting. But we have the privilege of resting. Not to rest is to refuse to acknowledge God's design. Ironically, we place ourselves back in bondage to slavery when we choose work over the gift of rest.

Part of me reacts to the word *Sabbath* negatively, probably because I associate the idea with legalism. When I hear *Sabbath*, I think of Old Testament rules and regulations, and legalistic branches of the church that follow man made rules, taking the fun out of a day of rest, like no TV or games. But what did God have in mind when he designed Sabbath rest? Jesus said: "...The Sabbath was made for man, not man for the Sabbath" (Mark 2:27). Jesus wasn't a legalist. To show that Jesus wasn't bound to the strict Pharisaical interpretation of the law, Jesus healed people on the Sabbath and gave his approval to rescuing an animal in distress on that day. While he calls us to take a breather from our daily grind, he doesn't forbid us to help someone on our day off.

God's intention has always been to bless us in response to our obedience: "Oh, that their hearts would be inclined to fear me and keep all my commands always, *so that it might go well with them and their children forever*" (Deut 5:29, emphasis added). God's design in giving the law through Moses was: " … so that you may *live* and *prosper* and *prolong your days* in the land that you will possess" (Deut 5:33). God has never been a kill-joy.

If we go back to the roots of the Sabbath day, we see God calling his people to follow God's example of resting on the seventh day. In the New Testament, Jesus expands the scope of the commandments from observation of outward rituals to the writing of those laws on our hearts.

With the coming of Jesus, we see the idea of Sabbath rest extending far beyond a once per week ritual. Rest is an orientation, a way of being and seeing, and second, a set of outward habits. Rest isn't a feeling and isn't primarily to be found on vacation. It's not an emotion. The essence of a Sabbath heart is being conscious of God's presence at all times.

Richard Foster explains it well:

> We learn over time and experience how to bring the reality of resting in God into the confusion and busyness of daily life. We learn to work resting. We learn to live on two levels at once. On the one level we carry on the ordinary task of our day. But on a deeper level we live out of inward promptings and whispered words of wisdom.[19]

My wife has an interesting interpretation of the story of Martha and Mary. Mary was sitting at the feet of Jesus, just listening. Martha was bustling about getting the housework done. Linda says, "Martha forgot that she was loved. It wasn't an over-activity problem. I have to be a Martha — I have to get a lot of stuff done. But I can still find Jesus even when I'm busy."

Brother Lawrence encourages us to worship while we work: "Do not forget him but think of him often. Adore him continually. Live and die with Him. This is the glorious work of a Christian; in a word, this is our profession. If we do not know it, we must learn it … ." He prays:

> O my God, since Thou art with me, and I must now, in obedience to Thy commands, apply my mind to these outward things, grant me the grace to continue in Thy Presence; and prosper me with Thy assistance. Receive all my works, and possess all my affections.

Brother Lawrence made it his "profession" to adore the Lord continually. But he did so with freedom, not legalistic bondage. Staying focused on God wasn't easy and his mind often wandered. I find his determination to worship God at all times both inspiring and challenging: " … we must serve God in a holy freedom. We must work faithfully without trouble or disquiet, recalling our mind to God mildly and with tranquility as often as we find it wandering from him."[20]

Today many people feel enslaved, trapped in their daily work, especially in "lower" positions such as kitchen work. In contrast, Brother Lawrence shows us it's possible to be content as a slave of Christ in any job. This is so radical and so biblical. May we have the mind of Christ to understand that the greatness of the task isn't the point, but the love with which it is performed.

A. W. Tozer said, "Faith is the gaze of a soul upon a saving God."[21] As we think on him, we can find rest in the midst of turmoil. Jesus said, "Come to me, all who are weary and burdened, and I will give you rest. Take my yoke upon you and learn from me, for I am gentle and humble in heart, and you will find rest for your souls" (Matt 11:28-29).

Jesus takes the laws of the Old Testament and teaches us to write them on our hearts. The laws become part of the fabric of every waking moment. Instead of merely "don't commit adultery," Jesus said, "don't lust after a woman." Instead of "repay your neighbor an eye for an eye," Jesus said "love your enemies." Similarly, instead of one day of Sabbath, he calls us to abide in an ongoing peaceful place of Sabbath rest. Rest is both a way of thinking and an outward practice. It's more than a ritual, it's a relationship; it's the peace of God that penetrates and slows our frantic pace.

Rhythms of Rest

When it's time for a day off, I begin to slow down and sometimes feel out of sorts. There's no adrenaline rush from plowing through my "to do" list. Sometimes I feel depressed. It takes a while to turn off my work engine. Slowly I shift my orientation to non-productivity mode. Ironically, it takes a conscious effort to surrender myself to rest mode. In those awkward moments of shifting gears, it's almost as if I can hear the Lord saying with a twinkle in his eye, "Remember this feeling? You haven't felt it for a while — it's called *rest.*"

But taking one day off every week is only part of the picture. There's also the rhythm of daily rest. Bill Hybels' ritual of rest is a great example. Bill figured out that he needed some firm boundaries to have a chance at a long life of productive ministry. He came up with a practice of "crossing a daily finish line."

Bill's day of work begins early in the morning and ends at around 4:00 pm, and then he goes for a forty minute run with a few friends. His "ritual" is then to have a shower, put on casual clothes and hang out with family or friends in the evening. He has a sense of "emotional completion" as he goes through this routine. In contrast to Bill's routine of rest, three quarters of the pastors that he mentors and coaches have no idea when their day ends. Some of them are proud to say, "I'm never off the clock."

It took fifteen years for Bill to figure out that he had such a strong work ethic that he had to physically remove himself from the area to get a day and half off. So every Sunday afternoon he drives or flies to a tiny cottage on Lake Michigan. He says, "the ritual for me begins when I'm driving down our gravel driveway, toward our little cottage .... I exhale and I can feel it in my body ... the stress just goes out of my body. It's my payoff for a hard week of work and I can unplug."

Conclusion

The writer of the book of Ecclesiastes concludes that it is good to enjoy your daily work: "I know that there is nothing better for men than to be happy and do good while they live. That everyone may eat and drink, and find satisfaction in all his toil — this is the gift of God" (Ecc 3:12-13).

God has "placed his glory on us." His imprint is on us. He is pleased to see us fully coming alive as we use the gifts he has given us. In humble gratitude, we realize that every ability and skill and shred of knowledge is a gift from him. Everything we do, we do unto the Lord. Like Paul, we can be shining examples for God in the workplace — generous, kind and full of integrity.

Chapter 14
Worship and the Risk of Faith

*Risks are not to be evaluated in terms of the probability of success,
but in terms of the value of goal.*
— Ralph Winter, founder of the U.S. Center for World Mission

*The safest place for ships is in the harbor
but that's not why ships were built.*
— Anonymous

There's a popular term in Christian circles these days. We use it to describe wise decision-making and priority setting. The term is "balance." To have the right proportion of work, play, worship and ministry is to have balance. In our church services, if we are doing too much singing and not enough Bible study, we might be out of balance. If I am working too much and not taking time to rest or to gather with Christians for worship, I would be off balance. These are sensible ideas, and necessary for spiritual, physical and emotional health. It keeps us from being too extreme in any one segment of life.

But the idea of balance can be misunderstood and misapplied. In pursuit of balance, we can end up diluting our loyalty to God. We can give in to self-protection and self-preservation, our zeal for God can be easily compromised and our faith become sadly lukewarm.

What sort of scales should we use to check our balance? How can we avoid becoming so well adjusted that we look no different at all from the rest of secular society? What is God's idea of balance?

Worshipers Are Risk-Takers

When the white-hot revelation of the glory of God bursts in, worshipers do things that aren't normal. They march to the beat of a different drum. The Bible is full of people that were captured by a revelation from God and who became insanely devoted to God. By human standards, they would be considered crazy and imbalanced.

When the Lord said to Abram " ... leave your country, your people and your father's household and go to the land I will show you," (Gen 12:1) "Abram left, as the Lord had told him ..." (Gen 12:4). Hearing God's voice emboldened him to take a risk of faith. The author of Hebrews tells us "By faith Abraham ... obeyed and went, *even though he did not know where he was going*" (Heb 11:8, emphasis added). Without any guarantees, medical provision or police protection, he left behind all the security of his family and country of origin. How "balanced" was that?

As a worshipping teenager, David's zeal for the Lord energized him to risk his life to defend the Lord's honor. His heart of worship drove him to attempt the impossible, to reject the armor of Saul and plunge into battle, trusting in God's authority rather than the inventions of men, like "spear or sword or javelin." He challenges and slays the giant so that " ... the whole world will know that there is a God in Israel" (1 Sam 17:46). How balanced was that? This was a zealous worshipper whose actions perfectly expressed the zeal of his songs to Yahweh.

The apostle Paul is a shining example of a worshiper whose life is full of risk. It all begins with a light from heaven flashing around Paul as Jesus reveals himself. From this time on, for Paul, " ... to live is Christ and to die is gain" (Phil 1:21). Once he got his marching orders from Jesus, Paul began to preach. As he quickly became a powerful preacher, the Jews conspired to kill him, keeping a close watch on the walls of Jerusalem for a chance to ambush him.

How balanced was Paul, the apostle to the Gentiles, when he continued his ministry even though he was " ... hard pressed on every side ... perplexed ... persecuted ... struck down ... suffering beating, imprisonments, riots, sleepless nights and hunger?" (2 Cor 4:8-9; 6:4-5). There was no question for Paul whether he should live a risk filled life to be a light to the Gentiles. He was compelled by the pursuit of God's glory. His love for God made him other centered. He didn't mind whether he lived or died, as long as he could help people and finish his race of faith. Balance as a form of tame safety was never on the agenda.

Are We Too Civilized?

Erwin McManus has written a book called "The Barbarian Way" in which he calls the church to the raw, primal faith of the early Christians. McManus contrasts the radical lifestyle of the early followers of Jesus to the watered down version of modern Christianity. When Christianity becomes too civilized, there isn't much talk of sacrifice and risk. Everyone is promised comfort, security, safety and prosperity. If safety and security are our main goal, then *losing* that worldly security can become a fear that defines our life. Max Lucado says it well:

> When fear shapes our lives, safety becomes our god. When safety becomes our god, we worship the risk-free life. Can the safety lover do anything great? Can the risk-averse accomplish noble deeds? For God? For others? No. The fear-filled cannot love deeply. Love is risky. They cannot give to the poor. Benevolence has no guarantee of return ... . The worship of safety emasculates greatness.[1]

The positive version of Lucado's statement, "The worship of safety emasculates greatness" is "the worship of *God* leads to greatness." When *faith* shapes our lives, we become people who worship and do the bidding of a great God. Worshipers of God are free to take risks because they are safe in God's care.

Here are some of McManus' observations on faith and risk:

> We have lost the simplicity of that raw, untamed, and primal faith … . Jesus is being lost in a religion bearing His name. People are being lost because they cannot reconcile Jesus' association with Christianity. Christianity has become docile, domesticated, civilized.[2]

> The result and proof of faith are that you get to live a life without risk, which is ironic when you realize that for the early church, faith was a risky business.

> The more you trust him, the more you risk on his behalf. The more you love him, the more you will love others. If you genuinely embrace his sacrifice, you will joyfully embrace a sacrificial life.

The barbarian call McManus describes isn't about a faddish trend among young people, it's about the ancient call to love the Lord our God with all of our hearts and to love our neighbor as ourselves. As Erwin says, "A world without God cannot wait for us to choose the safe path."

What Do I Risk?

While I find the stories of Bible heroes inspiring, my lifestyle looks very different. I'm not fighting nine-foot tall giants or traversing across a dangerous military zone. I'm not a prophet in the wilderness eating locusts and wearing animal skins nor am I in danger of being thrown to the lions. What does a radical life of faith look like for the middle class North American?

The root issues of living a life on the edge of faith are the same, regardless of our station in life or the age we live in. We are called to listen to God and obey him. We are to follow the unique path that God has for each of us, even if it's radically different from what our culture, or our family of origin would have us do. We are impassioned by the pursuit of God's glory. We do what Jesus asks us, even when we feel weak and overwhelmed by the task ahead.

While I was still a teenager, God took me by surprise. For the first time in my life, I really got a glimpse of him and worshipped him. Soon after, he began showing me powerful but vague glimpses of a calling to ministry. I graduated from university, eager to move forward. For the next few years, I found myself in humble jobs that gave me just enough money to survive while I was doing in-service training in my church. I had seen enough of God to be launched into a faith journey. I didn't know where I was going, so I was forced to depend on God for guidance.

The sensible or "balanced" thing to do would be to pursue a normal career, or perhaps get a graduate degree to equip me for a profession. In fact, I was accepted to the Masters Degree program at UCLA for hospital administration, a field I found interesting. But somehow I knew deep inside that I wasn't meant to pursue a standard kind of job in the marketplace. I had to wait until God opened the right door of opportunity.

A few years after getting married to Linda, our first big leap was to relocate to Santa Barbara in 1983 to help out with a new church plant. This move was in response to a word from God I received while driving down the freeway one day — "move to Santa Barbara to help with the new church." We found jobs to meet our expenses while serving as intern pastors. We learned new ministry skills and traveled abroad to serve on a prayer ministry team. We were forging ahead into unknown territory, simply responding to the open doors before us.

In these early years, I made lots of mistakes in church leadership. I once heard someone say that church leaders learn and make mistakes just like everyone else, except they do it *in front of other people.* We learn to teach only by teaching; at first we may sound silly. My first attempts at leading worship were nerve-wracking experiences that left me drained. We learn to lead only by making lots of wrong decisions along the way. Then we have to admit that we were wrong. If embarrassment is one of the main costs of the faith journey, it's no big deal compared to the price paid by Christian martyrs.

After a year and a half of volunteer work in that church, we were invited to move to Canada, to help with another church plant. We left behind the familiarity and comfort of Southern California to go to a new country. As we prayed and waited on God, it seemed like the right thing to do. We launched out, sometimes wondering if we had made the right move. The cost of moving to beautiful British Columbia hasn't been great, except for the pain of leaving behind many friends and family members and a culture that was comfortable. Because we've helped plant several churches, we've left behind lots of dear friends along the way.

Go Everywhere

My personal path has involved lots of short-term travel to lead worship and teach on worship. In the last twenty-five years, I've visited twenty-nine countries on ministry trips of various kinds. One key moment for me in hearing God's call to the nations came when I was waiting for a dentist appointment. Next to the dentist's office was a travel agency. While waiting for my dentist appointment, I wandered over to this shop and stopped in front of a large rack of travel brochures. The brochures advertised destinations all over the world. God said to me *"that* is where I've called you to go." I realized he meant "everywhere." It made me weep.

On another occasion God told me "you are like seed in my hand; as a farmer scatters seed on his land I'm going to throw you out to the nations." I don't believe you get extra points with God by going overseas. There's plenty of need in our own backyard to keep us busy for a lifetime. International travel just happens to be part of my journey.

In 2002, our entire family of ten took a three-month trip to Hong Kong to share life with a community of full time Christian workers and new converts. We lived on a campus in the hills of Sha Tin that housed many new Christians, most of whom came out of drug addiction and other abusive situations.

In this brief mission experiment, our family shared meals, worship and community with lots of men who had never experienced a healthy family or a safe home. We were somewhat uncomfortable because of the hot climate, the language barrier and the unfamiliar routine, but it was nothing compared to the hardships a full time missionary faces. It was another great learning experience that was possible only because we took a big chunk of time, energy and money to do something out of the ordinary.

Raising and Teaching our Children

Another dimension of our lives is having a large family. Telling the long version of that story would require an entire book, but the relevant point for this chapter is that parenting is itself a risk of faith. When we dedicate ourselves to God, it means raising our children to follow him. It means teaching them everything we can, and including them in a lifestyle of serving others. It means praying that they will have a genuine life-changing faith. But ultimately, we depend on God to reveal himself to our children and to instill in them a vibrant knowledge of himself that guides them for their whole lives. Linda specifically felt called by God to raise our kids to be worshipers.

My wife Linda has been a mother for twenty-four years and home-schooling our kids for the last twelve years. She feels specifically called to the ministry of discipling our children in the context of home schooling. While we can see good results on every level — spiritual, relational and academic, sometimes she wonders if her efforts will really pay off. When one of the kids is resisting her leadership or when there's a personality clash, she struggles but perseveres.

In my travels, I often mention to my hosts and audiences that my wife has taught our eight kids at home. I get all kinds of stares of unbelief and oohs and aahs. "How can she possibly manage all of that work?!" they ask. The way she manages it is that her life isn't about her own comfort. She doesn't require much time to herself. Her life is other-centered. Her love for God overflows into a passion to serve and train her kids to follow Jesus. For her it's a privilege; it's simply the right thing to do. The cost to her in time and energy is huge, but she has no regrets.

Amidst the strain of mothering and teaching many children, she hangs onto God, remembering his clear instructions to her to teach her children. She says, "I take risks because I know I'm loved and I can trust the one who loves me. In the role of making disciples, what you're asking for can *only* be done by the Holy Spirit." Worshipers who've caught the heart of God attempt the impossible. Ongoing intimacy with God fuels her to lavish love on our kids and trust him for the results.

On the hard days, she used to wonder what it would have been like to be a career woman. She comes from a highly educated family who placed a supreme value on professional achievement. She graduated at the top of her class in a very high-ranking university and could have easily moved up the ladder of professional success. As she journeyed with Jesus, that wasn't the path that opened up before her. She was content in being "change in the pocket of God," willing to be spent however God might choose.

But she is about to begin a new adventure. Linda is training to embark on a new career as a midwife. This will be the fulfillment of a vision she has had for many years. It took a lot of perseverance and patience even to get started on this path. For many years she has been mentoring young mothers, teaching on childbirth and assisting at births.

When I first met Linda, her plan was to go to India as a single missionary. Marriage was the farthest thing from her mind. She's a very missions-minded person and so for the past twenty-four years, her primary mission has been to raise our kids, and to lead them to the Lord. While her parenting role will continue, the demands are decreasing because the kids are growing up. Four of our kids are attending universities and one has already graduated. Linda's new mission will be to serve families in our community as a midwife. And perhaps her original vision of serving in a third world country will also be realized in the coming years.

At the age of forty-nine, Linda will begin a three-year university program that will qualify her to be a midwife. For the past three years, while applying to midwifery schools, she has shared with me her doubts about undertaking a new career at this stage of life. When I remind her that she graduated from UCLA with honors in the nursing program, she says, "that was a long time ago."

But I've encouraged her to go for it again. We both know this is a risk. It will require a huge output of time, energy and money even to complete her degree. But this is who God has *made her to be*, so it's a risk worth taking. Her passion is to make a difference in people's lives, to somehow pass on a blessing from God. Serving through midwifery is the most strategic use of her gifts to demonstrate Jesus' compassion.

Staying on the Edge

Whether it is stories from church history or the Bible, one thing is clear: worshipers are risk-takers. When you see Jesus, and

I mean *really* see him, it prepares you to take leaps of faith; but more than that, to live a life of faith. You find yourself doing things that may not always be sensible from a worldly point of view.

Faith and worship are interdependent. The worshiping heart is a believing heart; by faith, we see God, which leads us to worship him. In worship, we see more of God's grandeur and love. Beholding God's glory builds our faith and compels us to do acts of faith. In doing acts of faith we are acutely aware of our dependence on God, which in turn compels us to pray. So, faith and worship go hand in hand.

Simon Guillebaud, a missionary to Burundi who has had many close calls with death while living in a country racked by violence, explains how "common sense" can displace the adventure of faith:

"Common sense will so often rationalize averageness and lukewarmness — I shouldn't think there was ever a man or woman of God who followed the path of common sense at key decision-making times." Simon further explains that common sense is indeed a gift, but can be overruled by God's ways:

> I'm not advocating an abandoning of our critical faculties, a spontaneous embarking on ill-conceived adventures, or a jeopardizing of the safety and well-being of others. Neither am I saying that common sense is wrong, or is to be jettisoned as conflicting at all times with the life of faith. Common sense is a God-given faculty, an endowment without which we couldn't survive. However, common sense wouldn't advocate sending Jesus to the cross ... Common sense rationalizes away most of the dynamics of faith, because it operates on a different plane.[3]

Oswald Chambers speaks of a "glorious uncertainty" we have in walking by faith:

> The nature of the spiritual life is that we are certain in our uncertainties ... Certainty is the mark of the common-sense life; gracious uncertainty is the mark of the spiritual life ... Leave the whole thing to him, it is gloriously uncertain how he'll come in, but he will come.[4]

Hudson Taylor, the great nineteenth century missionary to China, said: "Unless there's an element of risk in our exploits for God, there's no need for faith."

Through every chapter of my life I've been in challenging situations that require me to do things I've never done before. Not always a comfortable and predictable life, but it forces me to stay dependent on God, asking for help every day. Linda and I haven't stagnated in growing as disciples of Jesus. We have to keep learning from him because we can't do life without him.

Applying the faith-risk lifestyle of our worshiping heroes to our own daily lives can be done without crossing oceans, leaving behind family and friends. One big key in knowing how to live out your worship is what you're good at doing and what you're trained to do. If he made you to be an accountant or a schoolteacher or a truck driver, then a worship-faith-risk life will look unique for you in your occupation.

Worship music ministry was a no-brainer for me. I started writing worship songs as a seventeen-year old baby Christian and haven't stopped writing since. When someone asked Brian McLaren asked why he writes so many books, he said, "I can't stop writing." I can relate. I had to do what was "in me." That meant pouring my life and resources into music ministry, regardless of how I benefited from it.

I won't elaborate on the other steps we should all take in figuring out God's will for your life — things like evaluating your gifts and abilities and asking for input from others who have seen your strength and weaknesses — but I will say that another key in being true to the revelation you've received is continuing to ask God "what do you want me to do today?" Aside from the obvious tasks of life, how does he want you to invest your time? You can only take one faith step at a time. Most of those steps are small, simple choices.

If you keep asking God what he wants you to do each day maybe he'll give you an idea that takes you way out of your comfort zone, something completely out-of-the-box — something that your friends might think is "way out of balance." Showing kindness to a stranger or engaging a coworker in a conversation that's more than superficial may be the kind of uncomfortable adventures of faith God is inviting you into. You don't have to cross an ocean; maybe you need to just cross the street.

I'm learning to take the risk of caring for people who can't return the favor. I'm learning that " … caring for orphans and widows … " (Jas 1:27 NLT) doesn't necessarily mean they'll be converted. True religion is to give despite what you get back. It's a risk to pour out your love to severely broken people. Sometimes you feel like you're pouring your life into a black hole. But the risk of faith means giving to "the least of our brothers" as if we were giving to Jesus himself.

Ralph Winter, founder of the U.S. Center for World Mission, said that, "risks are not to be evaluated in terms of the probability of success, but in terms of the value of the goal." What are the chances that your family member will receive Christ after twenty years of your prayers and discussions? What are the chances that your children will really own their faith and get God's vision for their lives? I don't know what the chances are, but the *value of the goal* is matchless. It's without rival. What else is worth our devotion and time and tears except the things that will last forever?

We join the heroes of faith listed in Hebrews 11 as we adventure into spiritual tasks that can only bear fruit by God's miraculous intervention. While some of the heroes of faith did mighty exploits and saw their dreams come true, others died before God's promises were fulfilled. While many of them are celebrated heroes, some were tortured, some faced jeers and flogging, while still others were chained and put in prison, and some were put to death by stoning and by the sword. The writer of Hebrews says "the world was not worthy of them ..." (Heb. 11:38). Rather than taking the safe way out, and living a long life on earth, they chose lives that were really worth living.

The risk of faith means we might not see the fulfillment of all of God's promises. We might care for a young Christian who never overcomes his addictions. We might serve a non-Christian spouse who never believes in Jesus. We might pray for and befriend a non-Christian neighbor who never seems to change. Sometimes things don't work out the way we hope.

Todd Hunter tells the story of seeing the baseball star Mickey Mantle strike out during an All Star game at Anaheim Stadium. As he walked back to the dugout, 46,000 people rose and gave Mickey a resounding ovation. That made no sense to Todd. Later, he realized that they were applauding Mantle for his amazing career.[5] He hit over 500 home runs and led his team to seven World Series championships. But he also struck out hundreds of times. Only five players have struck out more times than Mantle.

This is a picture of going for it in the kingdom. Sometimes we strike out. It takes courage and tenacity to keep stepping up to the plate to "hit the ball" and you risk getting hit by a pitch as well as striking out. But the only way you'll get a hit is to step up to the plate.

In a recent message to Vineyard leaders in Canada, Gary Best shared this quote from an anonymous source: "The safest place for ships is in the harbor but that's not why ships were built." Gary hasn't lived a risk free life of "staying in the harbor." He loves to see God's kingdom come to people and he has paid a huge cost as a pastor and national director of the Canadian Vineyard churches. He is still "yearning for the open sea." He has seen a vision on the horizon that has defined his life and he's determined to press on into more adventures of faith.

I hope I never stop pushing the envelope. I hope that I never settle for a life that is dominated by TV and self-indulgence. It sounds pretty boring compared to the joy and fulfillment of seeing God reach out his hand as I follow his lead, always trying to do things that are beyond me.

I encourage you not to stay within the confines of your own strength. If you do, how will God have the chance to demonstrate that he is God in you and through you?

Chapter 15
Worship Overflows in Justice

Justice and mercy are intrinsic to God and therefore intrinsic to the worship of God.
— Mark Labberton

My first few years of knowing God were amazing. As I sang and prayed "reveal yourself to me," I started to see the heart of God. My view of self, God and the world changed. I started asking different questions about my future. Instead of "how can I make a lot of money and be happy in life?" I started asking "what do you want me to do, God?"

I was experiencing the overwhelming privilege of being loved by the King. It didn't take long before I started to catch his generous heart. What is he like? He's full of compassion for other people:

> *Who is like the Lord our God*, the One who sits enthroned on high, who stoops down to look on the heavens and the earth? *He raises the poor from the dust and lifts the needy from the ash heap*; he seats them with princes, with the princes of their people. *He settles the barren woman* in her home as a happy mother of children ... (Ps 113:5-9, emphasis added).

I was beginning to catch the connection between worship and mission. I sang and prayed, "Give me your heart." He began to do it.

What I was experiencing was nothing new, but it was revolutionary. In the worship life, there's a never-ending cycle of absorbing more of the love of God and a corresponding urge to spread that love around.

John Piper, in his book *Let the Nations Be Glad*, speaks of worship as both the *fuel* and the *goal* of missions. "When the flame of worship burns with the heat of God's true worth, the light of missions will shine to the most remote people on earth." Piper goes on to say, "the goal of missions is the gladness of the peoples in the greatness of God ... Worship is the goal of missions because in missions we simply aim to bring the nations into the white-hot enjoyment of God's glory."[1]

When we consider the worthiness of God it turns us into worshipers and, in turn, mercy givers. When we see the glory, power and love of God as revealed in Jesus Christ, the natural and necessary response is extraordinary worship and generous mercy. When we discover God, he calls us to follow in his footsteps. When we become wed to Christ, we are wed to his cause.

Mark Labberton has written a book called "The Dangerous Act of Worship." It's all about the life changing implications of worship for every Christian. Mark opens our eyes to a rich biblical look at what worship really is:

> Worship names what matters most: the way human beings are created to reflect God's glory by embodying God's character in lives that seek righteousness and do justice. Such comprehensive worship redefines all we call ordinary. Worship turns out to be the dangerous act of waking up to God and to the purposes of God in the world, and then living lives that actually show it.[2]

Throughout scripture we see a progression of revelation, worship, transformation and action. You want examples? Try these on for size:

God reveals himself to Abram and it propels him on a

harrowing journey of faith into a foreign land. Abram's sojourn arises out of worship and revelation, but has a purpose far greater than his own life and family. All along the way God promises to bless Abram and to make him a "blessing to all nations." Blessing others was integral to the experience of knowing God.

Isaiah was entranced by a vision of the Lord in the temple (Isa 6), complete with worshiping angels, an outpouring of smoke and the shaking of the building. He was cut to the heart by an overpowering vision of God's holiness. When he cries, "It's all over! I am doomed, for I am a sinful man," (Isa 6:5) an angel comes to touch his lips with a coal from God's altar, symbolizing cleansing. Immediately, Isaiah is recruited by God to go spread God's message. True worship turns us inside out. We get cleaned up on the inside, and we give out the mercy we've received.

Jeremiah delivered a prophecy to Shallum, who inherited the kingship of Judah from his father King Josiah. While Josiah was generous to the poor, Shallum oppressed the poor and worshipped other gods. Jeremiah confronts Shallum, who had built a beautiful home to live in:

> But a beautiful cedar palace does not make a great king! Your father, Josiah, also had plenty to eat and drink. But he was just and right in all his dealings. That is why God blessed him. He gave justice and help to the poor and needy, and everything went well for him. *Isn't that what it means to know me?* (Jer 22: 15,16, emphasis added).

It's not enough to have an interior, mystical knowledge of God. We often sing, "I want to know you." If we really *know* him, one thing we'll do is help the poor. Over and over again we see this theme being trumpeted by the prophets. It's not enough to have a great church service.

I've had some extraordinary experiences of hanging out with Jesus by hanging out with the poor. In a sense, you can't really *know* Jesus unless you *do* what He did. Here's a quote from the "prophet" Bono that sheds light on this reality:

> God is in the slums, in the cardboard boxes where the
> poor play house. God is in the silence of a mother who has
> infected her child with a virus that will end both their lives.
> God is in the cries heard under the rubble of war. God is in
> the debris of wasted opportunity and lives, and God is with
> us if we are with them.[3]

Doing Church Isn't Enough

God is not impressed with people who really know how to
"do church" but forget about securing justice for the poor. As
a worship songwriter, verses like these from the prophet Amos
really get my attention: "Away with the noise of your songs! I will
not listen to the music of your harps. But let justice roll on like
a river, righteousness like a never-failing stream!" (Amos 5:23-
24).

The songs I've written constantly point me towards action.
What am I *doing* to respond to the Lord's commandments? What
is the practical outworking of my worship? Mark Labberton
says, "we reflect the worthiness of God by how we love and serve
whomever and whatever God considers to be of worth."[4] It's easy
to sing, "Worthy are you, Lord." It's more challenging to actually
show mercy to the hurting and destitute.

The New Testament tells the same story. When the crowds
came to John the Baptist to be baptized, he could tell they weren't
sincere in their repentance. They were going through a religious
exercise by coming out into the desert to see this wild prophet. He
doesn't pull any punches when he asks them to "Prove by the way
you live that you have repented of your sins and turned to God.
Don't just say to each other, 'We're safe, for we are descendants
of Abraham.' That means nothing … "(Luke 3:8). John is saying,
"it's not about your family of origin, it's about what you *do.*"

The crowd asked, "what should we do?" John replied, "If you

have two shirts, give one to the poor. If you have food, share it with those who are hungry" (Luke 3:11 NLT). John is saying that feeding the hungry is one of the *most basic and fundamental* fruits of repentance. It's Christianity 101. It's very straightforward. As Bono says, "'love thy neighbor' isn't a piece of advice, it's a command."[5]

Kay Warren, wife of author and pastor Rick Warren makes the same point:

> The bottom-line "proof" of our love for Jesus is a surprising measurement. It's not found in the ways we have typically used to evaluate spiritual maturity. Proof of our love for Jesus is found not merely in attending church, reading the Bible, singing praise songs, or serving as an usher or an elder (although each of these activities is an important part of a growing spiritual life), but in loving and serving the sick, the poor, the weak, and the marginalized.[6]

Knowing the Bible Isn't Enough

"On one occasion an expert in the law stood up to test Jesus…" (Luke 10:25). This is the beginning of the story of the Good Samaritan. Someone who knew the Bible really well came to Jesus to ask about how to get to heaven. He knew the right answer; love God and love your neighbor. But his motives weren't right; he wanted to *justify himself*, so he asked Jesus, " … And who is my neighbor?" (Luke 10:29, emphasis added).

This "expert in the law" wanted to protect himself from a broad definition of "neighbor." He felt fine about helping the people who lived on his side of town, but the idea of helping a lowly Samaritan would have been repulsive to him. Jesus tells the story in which the Samaritan is the hero because he *does* something to help someone in dire need. Jesus is essentially saying to him "it's not just about knowing the Bible, it's about what you *do*." He says to the Bible expert: " … *Do this* and you will live" (Luke 10:28 NLT, emphasis added).

From this story, we learn to open our hearts wide to our neighbors, whether they live across the street or across an ocean.

John Wimber's New York Taxi Ride

Here is a story I heard John tell many times in conferences.

Years ago in New York City, I got into a taxi cab with an Iranian taxi driver who could hardly speak English. I tried to explain to him where I wanted to go, and as he was pulling his car out of the parking place, he almost got hit by a van that had a sign reading *The Pentecostal Church*. He got real upset and said, "That guy's drunk." I said, "No, he's a Pentecostal. Drunk in the spirit, maybe, but not with wine." He asked, "Do you know about church?" I said, "Well, I know a little bit about it; what do you know?" It was a long trip from one end of Manhattan to the other, and all the way down he told me one horror story after another that he'd heard about the church. He knew about the pastor that ran off with the choirmaster's wife, the couple that had burned the church down and collected the insurance — every horrible thing you could imagine. We finally get to where we were going, I paid him, and as we're standing there on the landing I gave him an extra large tip. He got a suspicious look in his eyes; he'd been around, you know. I said, "Answer me this one question." Now keep in mind, I'm planning on witnessing to him. "If there was a God and he had a church, what would it be like?" He sat there for a while making up his mind whether to "play" or not. Finally, he sighed and said, "Well, if there was a God and he had a church, they would care for the poor, heal the sick, and they wouldn't charge you money to teach you the Book." I turned around and it was like an explosion in my chest. "Oh, God." I just cried, I couldn't help it. I thought, "Oh Lord, *they know*. The world knows what it's supposed to be like. *The only ones that don't know are the Church.*

When you joined the kingdom, you expected to be used of God. I've talked to thousands of people, and almost everybody has said, "When I signed up, I knew that caring for the poor was part of it; I just kind of got weaned off it, because no one else was doing it." Folks, I'm not saying, "Do something heroic." I'm not saying, "Take on some high standard, sell everything you have and go." Now, if Jesus tells you that, that's different. But I'm not saying that. I'm just saying, participate. Give some portion of what you have — time, energy, money, on a regular basis — to this purpose, to redeeming people, to caring for people. Share your heart and life with somebody that's not easy to sit in the same car with. Are you hearing me? *That's where you'll really see the kingdom of God.*

Joyce Rees

Another person who has *really* seen the kingdom of God among the poor is a friend of mine named Joyce Rees. Joyce was raised in the church and knew the Lord as a child. But as a teenager she wandered from the faith and was turned off by hypocrisy in the church. Then she was the victim of a terrible accident in a pickup truck. Joyce says:

> I had three broken vertebrae, a broken pelvis, and a broken knee. I suffered a massive brain trauma. The brain injury was the worst of all — the doctors said I had 2 to 10 years to recover. They told my parents that my best hope would be to be a clerk in a gas station.[7]

Three months later, she was miraculously healed when she received prayer. While laying on the floor after the prayer, she had an encounter with God:

> It felt like I had a blanket laying over my whole body. I thought they had put a blanket over me for modesty. When I realized it wasn't actually a blanket, I got really scared in what I would describe as a "reverent fear." I said in my head "what is this?" and I heard a voice saying "this is me; this is my peace." I didn't have to ask who "me" was. I started repenting. That's when I told him "if you let me off the floor I won't be just like a church Christian. I'll really follow you."

Joyce describes her response to this incredible gift of restored health:

> If someone walked up to you and gave you the most valuable gem in the whole world, you wouldn't just walk off and say "thanks." You'd want to respond with radical generosity in return. The healing I received was excessive, lavish kindness and I knew I had to respond appropriately. To say, "Oh, thanks

for the miracle," wasn't going to cut it. So my life of worship began right there.

Joyce went on to become a pastor in the youth department of a mega church in Langley, B.C. and later a sought after speaker in many denominations across Canada. Then she had another life changing experience.

> Somewhere along the way, I got re-converted. Something happened to me. I started realizing God's heart for the poor — for the widow, foreigner and orphan — people who live in the margins. If I was going to disciple people to be God-worshippers, why had I never been taught that caring for the poor was central to following Jesus?

Joyce was invited to help out at a food bank in Langley that was run by Christians. When I started serving at the food bank, I kept encountering Jesus in crazy ways." One experience she had at the food bank was helping a Somalian refugee lady get food for herself and her little twin boys.

> It was the beginning of my realizing that this is where God resides. He inhabits these kinds of places. If you want to have intimacy with God you have to get around the poor. I kind of got addicted to that because I kept getting revelation of who God was. I wasn't spiritually apathetic anymore.

After her experience with the food bank in Langley, Joyce visited a ministry in the downtown eastside of Vancouver, and later became the executive director, a position she held for eight years. This is one of the most concentrated areas of homelessness, drug use and prostitution in North America and the world. About 20,000 poor people live in five square miles. There is a higher rate of AIDS and HIV infection here than in Botswana. The World Health Organization labels it as having a pandemic with the AIDS virus.

When she knew the Lord was leading her to quit her pastoring job, she felt kind of ripped off. She had "served many meals" of teaching people to seek the Lord and now that there was some deep renewal happening in the church, she felt she was "missing out on the dessert." Things were "getting good" at the church; people were becoming more spiritually fervent.

Then she realized that being in the downtown eastside was the real "dessert." Joyce says, "Here at Jacob's Well is the manifest presence of God in a "turbo" kind of way. When you are where Jesus is most present, you get the most of Jesus. It kind of makes sense. If you have a choice of watching a documentary of where Jesus once visited or actually being where Jesus is *right now*, you don't watch the documentary. You go where Jesus is now. So I began to wander around encountering Jesus among the poor."

Joyce explains her day-by-day practice of asking God for direction in a sea of need:

> The downtown eastside is a particular social construct that has very grave issues. This isn't everyone's context. But in that context, I could easily be overwhelmed by all the people asking for a hand out, all the decaying bodies, and the deep brokenness — lots of people with mental health issues. I had to ask God everyday, "give me eyes to see, ears to hear and a heart to obey." I just wanted to see the one person you want me to help today. To give someone the banana out of my lunch, to stop and pray for someone or to have coffee with someone.

In another social context, there might be thousands of healthy looking people. In that case, you have to ask God for eyes to see the one person who is broken. We had a guy around fifty years old come to our workshop about catching God's heart for the poor. He was from West Point Grey, a wealthy neighborhood. We did an exercise in which we told the people in the workshop to look for the image of God in our neighborhood — to look for what's missing and what's present and try to sense the Lord's presence. They did the exercise and came back to the classroom, had a nice discussion and then she said to them, "I dare you to do this same exercise in your own neighborhood."

The next day was Sunday. That afternoon the man from West Point Grey explained to his wife that Joyce encouraged us to go for a walk in our neighborhood and look for the image of God. He said, "I'm going to take the dog out for a walk but I don't think I'm going to hear anything from God." On his walk, all of a sudden he saw all the Filipino nannies in his neighborhood. He had never noticed them before.

This was the beginning of a journey of trying to find relationship with one nanny. Soon they met a nanny in the park, had a chat with her and felt like the Lord said, "that's the one." Then they found out that she had Thursday nights off. So they started having her over for dinner and found out that she was only earning $800 per month. Most of that money was going back to the Philippines to support an extended family network of about twenty people. That's a type of indentured servitude; she was never going to get out of that situation. So they sponsored her to become Canadian and bring her children and her husband and her mother to Canada. It radically changed her life and the lives of her family and village.

That family heard God for *one person*. It wasn't the downtown Eastside; it was one of the richest neighborhoods in Canada. Worship is about learning what's going to please Jesus' heart. We have to know what he's up to; we have to join him in his heart activity. Looking for the one person we can help is something we should be able to practice wherever we're live. It doesn't matter what neighborhood we live in. We've got to have eyes to see.

Worshiping in Action

In a church plant I helped lead for a few years, on the last Sunday of each month, we went out into the community to serve and attempt to *be Good News*. We did this instead of having a regular church service. We put together free barbeques in low-income neighborhoods, handed out groceries to the needy, and prayed for people's ailments and tough situations.

On one Sunday, five of us visited a lady named Kim. We had received a tip from her friend, Peter, that she had been out of work and could use some groceries. My son, Benjamin, was twelve years old. He and his friend James came along with two ladies and me. After hearing lots of stories about her beloved dogs who were playing at our feet in her little living room, we asked if there was anything in her life that we could pray for. She quickly responded that her left leg was numb below the knee, she had a bad back, and was suffering from depression. She had been unemployed and could barely find a reason to get out of bed some mornings. Her boyfriend had died a few years previously, and she was still grieving.

We prayed for several minutes and promised to keep in contact with her. She was very thankful for this visit from a group of strangers who simply came because they heard she was in need. We simply took the time to listen to her story and pray for her. She felt genuine compassion and concern. I don't know whether or not she received any physical healing.

About ten minutes after driving away from her house, my cell phone rang. It was Peter, the man who let us know about Kim's need. He said that Kim had called him in tears, overflowing with gratitude that we had come to help her. Peter said, "I almost started crying when she told me the story." Peter, the manager of a low-income trailer park, suggested that he could connect us with more people like Kim who needed help.

Our worship gatherings are deeper and have more integrity if they are followed up with visits to people like Kim. We are the church gathered, and the church scattered. We need to let people like Kim see that we actually care about them and want to help in a practical way. Isn't that what Jesus did?

Seeing the Big Picture

In Israel's history, there was a time when extravagant rituals of worship were detestable to God. Micah, Isaiah and Joel are some of the prophets who woke God's people up to the kind of worship God really wanted:

> With what shall I come before the Lord and bow down before the exalted God? Shall I come before him with burnt offerings, with calves a year old? Will the Lord be pleased with thousands of rams, with ten thousand rivers of oil? Shall I offer my firstborn for my transgression, the fruit of my body for the sin of my soul? He has showed you, O man, what is good. And what does the Lord require of you? To act justly and to love mercy and to walk humbly with your God (Mic 6:6-8).

Are we too preoccupied with creating the best "worship show" while all the world is full of suffering? There's not a simplistic answer to that question. Excellence in the arts doesn't necessarily preclude rivers of righteousness and justice flowing out from the church. But the church can make the mistake of catering to an entertainment-hungry society, labeling it as the worship that God desires, while forgetting about the foreigners, widows and orphans that are within a mile of the church's front doors.

Conclusion

When we see Jesus, we see the *great giver*. We see that it's truly more blessed to give than receive. We're so grateful when we ponder the mercy of God lavished on us. Our natural response is, "How can I show my gratitude?" In view of God's mercy, we give our bodies — not just our meditations, but our energy and time — to making a difference in our world. Through simple acts of kindness and joyful sacrifice, we proclaim the worthiness of Jesus by emulating his life.

Chapter 16
The Grace of Giving

... Give away your life; you'll find life given back, but not merely given back — given back with bonus and blessing.
— Jesus (Luke 6:38, The Message)

... When someone has been given much,
much will be required in return ... .
— Jesus (Luke 12:48)

I was really stingy when I was a kid. Penny pinching didn't even come close to defining me; I hoarded my money and refused to spend a single cent of it until there was something I *really* wanted. When I received God's grace for salvation, I slowly began to change my miserly ways. I *wanted* to start giving. My hard heart started to break open and I learned to share my time, energy and money to help others. I began to see that sharing my resources was just one way of responding to the lavish love of God. After a few decades of knowing times of want and times of plenty, I have learned that there is a direct connection between giving away money and living with integrity.

King David sheds light on this idea. After the collection of the offering for the construction of Solomon's temple, King David addressed the assembly and said:

> I know, my God, that you *test the heart and are pleased with integrity.* All these things have I given willingly and with

honest intent. And now I have seen with joy how willingly your people who are here have given to you. O Lord ... keep this desire in the hearts of your people forever, and *keep their hearts loyal to you* (1 Chr 29:17-18).

Giving our money to the work of God is an expression of our loyalty to him. He watches to see how we will use our money, the results being a test of our integrity. All our inner and invisible commitments, priorities and loyalties are manifest in our outer, concrete actions. As pastor of the Corinthian church, Paul brings up the subject of giving, " ... to test the sincerity ... " (2 Cor 8:8) of their love. This kind of integrity was what Jesus was getting at when he told the Samaritan woman about "worship in spirit and truth."

Giving is an act of worship, an expression of our confidence in him. In giving, we acknowledge that God is the source of every good thing. We surrender power as we surrender money. We cross over a line between the material and spiritual world, understanding that there is spiritual significance in our material gifts that will reap a spiritual reward for us.

So, yes, giving matters. Generosity is important. Materialism is probably the most powerful idol that threatens my authenticity as a Christian and I believe the same is also true for the church at large.

Part of the power of giving lies in the fact that it is a slap in the face to the god "mammon." As we give, we crush an altar of idolatry. In giving, we demonstrate in a practical way our belief that " ... Worthy is the Lamb, who was slain, to receive power and wealth and wisdom and strength and honor and glory and praise!" (Rev 5:12). When we give willingly and joyfully, we dethrone materialism and participate in the generous heart of God.

Billy Graham said, "If a person gets his attitude toward money straight, it will help straighten out almost every other area of his life."[1] Jesus knew what he was talking about; it really is true that we can't serve God and money. So if we get the love of money thing taken care of (which for me is a daily choice) it helps us put everything else in order. Giving helps me remember that God owns everything, including my body. It reminds me that "the earth is the Lord's, and everything in it, the world, and all who live in it …" (Ps 24:1). It puts back before my eyes the fact that I am like a flower, quickly fading in this world, here today and gone tomorrow to a better place. Giving helps me set my mind on heavenly things where Christ is seated.

Once Again, Grace Is at the Center

I've tried in this book to keep coming back around to the theme of grace. On the subject of giving, the bells of grace ring loud and clear throughout the New Testament. God's grace saves us, and it also empowers us. Paul continually emphasizes the fact that giving is made possible by God's grace, by his help. It isn't our heroic action. It's just an act of submission to God's enabling.

In Paul's second letter to the Corinthian church, we see him provoking the readers to generosity towards the poor church in Jerusalem. He points to the example of the generous Macedonian church to encourage the Corinthians to give. "Out of the most severe trial, their overflowing joy and their extreme poverty welled up in rich generosity" (2 Cor. 8:2). Many have taken the view that the Macedonians were a poor church, but their "severe trial" may have been temporary.[2] Whether they were always poor or not, they were very eager to give despite the severe trial they were undergoing. How can "overflowing joy" and "extreme poverty" co-exist except in the hearts of those who have been touched by the great Giver?

"They begged us again and again for the privilege of sharing in the gift for the believers in Jerusalem" (2 Cor. 8:4 NLT). The Macedonians saw giving as a "privilege." That's the heart of Christian giving. They weren't caving in to a heavy-handed preacher who was laying guilt trips on God's flock. They "begged" for the chance to give. They gave joyfully and freely. In the next chapter, Paul emphasizes this point again, "You must each decide in your heart how much to give. And don't give reluctantly or in response to pressure. 'For God loves a person who gives cheerfully'" (2 Cor 9:7 NLT).

This sense of privilege in giving echoes the heart of David, who prays: "But who am I, and who are my people, that we should be able to give as generously as this? Everything comes from you, and we have given you only what comes from your hand" (1 Chr 29:14). David felt humbled and privileged to be able to give. He really understood that *everything* — every possession — was a gift from God. He knew that God had entrusted him with possessions and it was his privilege and responsibility to give generously. David was acknowledging the great Giver by giving something back to him.

David's prayer: "Who am I to be able to give as generously as this?" indicates a posture of humility, a lack of pride. Worship and pride are opposites; if my attitude is "I deserve what I have because I've worked for every penny of it," I am ignoring my creator-God and exalting myself. This is selfish pride. If I take all the credit for my hard-earned money, I am boasting in my wisdom, power and riches. God warned the Hebrews to avoid this attitude: "You may say to yourself, 'My power and the strength of my hands have produced this wealth for me'" (Deut 8:17). This attitude prevails when we are blind to our source and sustainer.

Sharing

Paul was a tremendous example of a man from a well-to-do family who poured out his life for the benefit of the less fortunate. He was in "the top few percent in his society in terms of level of education."[3] The chances are that Paul was ... at home in more prosperous levels of society."[4] Despite his elite education and position in society, he worked hard as a tent-maker while simultaneously pastoring and planting churches. "In everything I did, I showed you that by *this kind of hard work* we must *help the weak,* remembering the words the Lord Jesus himself said: 'It is more blessed to give than to receive'" (Acts 20:35, emphasis added).

Here is a man who freely shared all of his gifts and resources — his loving concern for the churches he planted, the sweat of his brow to earn money for daily expenses, and his well-trained mind to teach his friends and co-workers.

We see Paul, a rare case of a Jew who was also a Roman citizen, laying down his privileged position in society to serve the needs of people in every socio-economic category. He followed the example of Jesus by taking a downward step to make others rich in faith, explaining his actions with the words "For you know the grace of our Lord Jesus Christ, that though he was rich, yet for your sakes he became poor, so that you through his poverty might become rich" (2 Cor 8:9).

The second chapter of Acts is one of my favorites in the Bible. We see what happens when real revival comes. The result is a riveting revelation of the Lord's goodness, a depiction of believers who experience a deep day-to-day community as they eat with one another and worship together, sharing not just their resources but a sense of awesome reverence of God that pervades the community.

All of these characteristics of revival flow out of the work of the Holy Spirit in their midst. Peter said " ... repent ... be baptized ... and you will receive the gift of the Holy Spirit" (Acts 2:38) and it is true that there is a direct connection between receiving the Holy Spirit and sharing material goods. "What we do or do not do with our material possessions is an indicator of the Spirit's presence or absence."[5]

Paul encourages the well off Corinthian church to share with the needy church in Jerusalem, " ... that there might be equality" (2 Cor 8:13). We see the same idea in Acts 2, where "All the believers were together and had everything in common" (Acts 2:44). Out of the overflow of love and community, the believers wanted to help one another by sharing their goods.

In this letter "Paul is not enunciating the ideal of some fully egalitarian communism. But he does recognize that there are extremes of wealth and poverty which are intolerable in the Christian community. If those who are better off will simply provide from their surplus, all of the most basic human needs of the more impoverished will be met."[6]

"The term used for "giving" in this New Testament context is not the typical Greek word for making a gift. Instead the New Testament adopts the Greek word *koinonia*, which means "sharing." As Christians shared life in Christ, their family relationship was expressed by a sharing of financial and material resources."[7]

Generosity is one of the keys to real *koinonia*. When we freely give, we're freed from the prison of isolation and we share the joy of friendship in Christ. I'm not financially needy, but when my friends support my ministry, I feel more deeply connected to them. Sharing our things and time with one another builds unity. The strata of socio-economic classes disappear. Generosity, and the unity it fosters, is a spiritual-social phenomenon.

Here is a wonderful story of the interplay between the spirit of generosity, the gathering of the community and conversion to Christ — a twentieth century Acts 2 episode:

> Dr. Truett of Texas was invited to a church that was raising $6,500 to dedicate a church building. After $3,500 had been promised, the offerings ceased. Then a plainly dressed woman arose and spoke to her husband who was taking the

names. "Charley, I wonder if you would be willing to give our little cottage, just out of debt. We were offered $3,500 for it yesterday. Would you be willing to give our little house for Christ that His house may be free?" The fine fellow responded in the same high spirit: "Jennie, dear, I was thinking of the same thing." Then looking up at Truett with his face covered with tears, he said, "We will give the $3,500."

Then there followed a scene beggaring all description. Men and women sobbed aloud, and almost in a moment the $3,500 was provided. Then without invitation there came down the aisle men and women, saying, "Sir, where is the Saviour, and how can we find him?"[8]

In this story, one couple's generous gift provoked others to give. This is yet another example of the great benefits of gathering together for worship. Gathering together for worship helps us "spur one another on toward love and good deeds" (Heb 10:24). Dr. Truett's story also shows us the evangelistic effect of radical giving in response to the Holy Spirit's urging. If an unbeliever sees such a thing, they sense something genuine and powerful is motivating the act, and they take another step closer to Jesus.

Erwin McManus gives a wonderful description of the spirit of generosity as compared to greed:

While the greedy see the world with limited resources, the generous always operate from an abundance mentality. The greedy take measures to ensure they will never be without; the generous give without fear ... The generous invest their lives in the prosperity of others ... They have discovered that life is most enjoyed when we give ourselves away ... The generous give more than their things; they genuinely give themselves.

Generosity is love in action, and love is measured in giving, not taking. The generous ... engage every dimension of human experience from a dramatically different vantage point. Their agenda is always to make a contribution. They are committed to leaving every encounter having given more than they have taken. They are investors rather than consumers.[9]

I especially like Erwin's description of the "emotionally generous people:"

You don't identify them as such; you just know you love to be around them. You enjoy their company and cannot spend too much time with them. They naturally invest through the economy of human emotion in you. You always feel as if you have received more than you have given. You're both indebted and made free by a generous giver.[10]

I think Jesus was "emotionally generous" and that's one reason people wanted to be around him. This is why everyone including tax collectors and prostitutes were attracted to him — he was emotionally generous; he freely offered friendship. He was critical mostly of the self-righteous religious people.

Eating Together

I'm so glad that eating is a regular practice of the church! Luke describes the scene after Pentecost where they " … met in homes for the Lord's Supper, and shared their meals with great joy and generosity" (Acts 2:46 NLT). Sharing the food of our table is love in action. This simple gift of our time and food conveys love and builds friendship. It's a way of honoring and serving our friends.

Many years ago, Bishop Hughes of the Congregational church in Boston described a certain deacon who said to himself:

> I cannot speak in prayer meeting, I cannot do many other things in Christian service, but I can put two extra plates on my dinner table every Sunday and invite two young men who are away from home to break bread with me.

He went along doing that for more than thirty years. He became acquainted with a great company of young men who were attending that church, and many of them became Christians through his personal influence.

When he died he was to be buried in Andover, thirty miles distant, and because he was a well-known merchant, a special train was chartered to convey the funeral party. It was made known that any of his friends among the young men who had become Christians through his influence would be welcomed in a special car set aside for them. One hundred and fifty of them came and packed that car from end to end in honor of the memory of the man who had preached to them the gospel of the extra dinner plate."[11]

God does not ask most of us to preach or speak eloquently among a large group of people. But this deacon steadily invited two guests to dinner each Sunday and eventually saw a great harvest. Most of us can share a meal with a friend or two, bringing a lasting impact of God's love.

Simplicity

In the stories and scriptures we've just looked at we see the *inward* attitude of simplicity expressed in an *outward* lifestyle of simplicity. In matters of worship, we always start from the inside and work outwards. Living with the discipline of simplicity creates the right orientation for a life of freedom and generosity, not just with our money but with our time and talents.

Richard Foster shares three basic attitudes of simplicity:

1. what we have we receive as a gift,

2. what we have is to be cared for by God, and

3. what we have is available to others.[12]

If we live out these attitudes, we'll be free from anxiety about our possessions.

"Simplicity is freedom. Duplicity is bondage. Simplicity brings joy and balance. Duplicity brings anxiety and fear."[13] These simple statements are loaded with profound meaning; they ring so true with my spirit but it's still a challenge for me to walk out these principles moment by moment. I haven't yet detached myself from my possessions enough to be totally free of anxiety. I haven't yet gotten rid of all of my stinginess and I sometimes find in myself a reluctance to let other people use my stuff, hanging on to it too tightly. When my behavior doesn't line up with what I believe, there is duplicity. Not letting people use my things is incongruous and inconsistent with my stated value of sharing. "Inwardly modern man is fractured and fragmented. He is trapped in a maze of competing attachments."[14]

It is true that "knowing your purpose simplifies your life. It defines what you do and what you don't do."[15] My purpose in life is to love God with all my heart and love my neighbor. I settled on that plan a long time ago. Giving money to help others isn't a strain because it naturally flows out of my life's purpose. It feels good when my actions are congruent with my beliefs, and likewise, I don't spend very much time thinking about the next recreational or house décor item I want to buy because that doesn't fit with my life's purpose. Sure, occasionally I buy a non-essential item, but the great majority of the time I'm focused on more important things. The peace of mind I get from living a life of purpose is worth a lot to me.

Singleness of mind and heart means we can love God, trust him for everything and he'll take care of the rest. Real life isn't found in a frantic race of hoarding and grabbing all we can get. Following Foster's second attitude of simplicity means we won't worry about our retirement accounts, our investments, the value of our house or even the stability of our job. We should certainly be wise in managing all of these things, but ultimately we're dependent on him. Recent economic upheaval has shown us that the stock market and value of real estate are no place to put our trust. In the end, God is sovereign and he cares for us. When we trust in God, we are free to give.

After losing everything, Job realized that he was trusting in riches instead of God:

> Have I put my trust in money or felt secure because of my gold? Have I gloated about my wealth and all that I own? Have I looked at the sun shining in the skies, or the moon walking down its silver pathway, and been secretly enticed in

my heart to throw kisses at them in worship? If so, I should be punished by the judges, for it would mean I had denied the God of heaven (Job 31:24-28 NLT).

Recently a friend of mine purchased an income generating property in a U.S. city that has suffered from severe real estate devaluation. It's a good investment for my friend. Many investors are capitalizing on "buying low" with the thought of eventually "selling high." That's a wise investment strategy. After hearing about my friend's investment, I started to think about the possibility of borrowing money to buy a townhouse to rent out.

A week or two after I started entertaining that idea, the Lord gave me a very brief but clear picture of myself stuffing food into my mouth. The message was clear: you don't need another investment; don't be like a person who has already had enough to eat but keeps gorging himself on more and more. I thank God for sending me those kinds of warning messages, whether they come in the form of a "picture" or a solid knowing in my heart that something is wrong. Simplicity is freedom. Simplicity brings joy and balance.

This story is also a good illustration of the error of making a legalistic system out of the use of our possessions. An investment that's right for one Christian isn't necessarily right for another. One factor here is the income level of two people. For one person, a certain investment would be a small outlay of cash in relation to their income while for another, it would create undue financial pressure, hinder their giving, and create anxiety. Foster says that living in simplicity isn't tied to your income level: "It [living in simplicity] has nothing to do with abundance of possessions or their lack. It is an inward spirit of trust. The sheer fact that a person is living without things is no guarantee that he or she is living in simplicity."[16]

The guiding principles here are not rules and regulations. If that were so I would have reason to boast about my generosity and I'd have reason to criticize others who aren't giving. That's not the heart of grace. The guiding principle is to follow Jesus, let his word form our behavior, and ask him to expand our hearts and acts of generosity more and more.

Money Is a Good Thing, The Love of Money Is a Bad Thing

This leads us to the topic of the nature of money. Money in itself isn't a bad thing: "no scripture ever declares *money* as the root of all kinds of evil, but rather the *love* of, allegiance to or attachment to money in the fashion that led Jesus to declare, "You cannot serve both God and money."'[17]

The Bible shows that God blesses his people with material provision and rewards the generous:

> Dishonest money dwindles away, but he who gathers money little by little makes it grow (Prov 13:11).

> Honor the Lord with your wealth, with the first fruits of all your crops then your barns will be filled to overflowing, and your vats will brim over with new wine (Prov 3:9-10).

> Remember this: Whoever sows sparingly will also reap sparingly, and whoever sows generously will also reap generously (2 Cor 9:6).

> … Give away your life; you'll find life given back, but not merely given back — given back with bonus and blessing. Giving, not getting, is the way. Generosity begets generosity (Luke 6:38 *The Message*).

The overwhelming message of the Bible concerning possessions and money is clear: don't be attached to money, and be very generous.

> … And if your wealth increases, don't make it the center of your life (Ps 62:10).

> An overseer should not be a … lover of money (1 Tim 3:3).

Don't love money; be satisfied with what you have. For God has said, "I will never fail you. I will never abandon you" (Heb 13:5 NLT).

But people who long to be rich fall into temptation and are trapped by many foolish and harmful desires that plunge them into ruin and destruction (1 Tim 6:9 NLT).

Religion that God our Father accepts as pure and faultless is this: to look after orphans and widows in their distress and to keep oneself from being polluted by the world (Jas 1:27).

How Much Should We Give?

We see a minimum of one tithe of ten percent being the standard in the Old Testament, with periodic second and even third tithes for the poor:

> As we move into the New Testament era, however, we note several important contrasts. The Epistles never call for a tithe. There is no single worship center and no priesthood to be supported by the old, annual temple tithe. While giving to support individuals who minister full time is mentioned in the New Testament, no letter suggests this be done through a local tithe. The New Testament emphasizes a deep concern for the poor and needy, especially within the family of faith. Paul and others did organize offerings to be taken for those in hunger-ridden foreign lands. But the guidelines for giving that Paul laid down nowhere mentions or implies that the tithe is to be used to measure a Christian's obligation.[18]

"It seems significant that no other New Testament [besides Luke 11:41-42] explicitly commands [tithing], while the principles of generosity and sacrifice … will suggest that different people should give varying percentages based on their varying circumstances."[19] The story of the widow's mite — a widow who gave everything she had — shows us that God values sacrifice. Rather than giving a minimum, our hearts should be inclined towards increasing in generosity, and making sacrifices for the benefit of others.

The statistics show that rich American Christians on the whole haven't caught the vision of generosity. Wealthy Christians give a much lower percentage of their money than low-income believers. In the following survey that is many years old, the salary amounts are much lower than today's levels, but the lesson is still relevant:

> The Russell Sage Foundation several years ago published the results of a survey. In the United States, families with a net income of less than $3,000 a year gave more than 60% of all the money donated to charity; families whose income was less than $5,000 donated 82% of the total; families with an income between $10,000 and $20,000 a year gave only 1.9% of their income! According to an Internal Revenue Service analysis, Americans who itemize their deductions give less than 3% of their adjusted gross incomes to church and charity.[20]

While there are many generous American Christians, on the whole we haven't learned that "you can't serve God *and* money, but you can serve God *with* money."[21]

We Find Our Life By Giving It Away

In the upside-down kingdom of God, we gain freedom by letting go of our stuff. It seems backwards to the natural human mind, but that's how God set up his universe. God really does take care of us if we hold loosely the things he has given us. Those who give the most get the most.

Paul says to the Corinthians: "and God is able to make all grace abound to you, so that in all things at all times, having all that you need, you will abound in every good work" (2 Cor 9:8). The word "all" is used four times for emphasis.

While there is the promise of reward in heaven for helping the poor and giving generously, stern warnings are given to those who hoard their wealth. James warns the wealthy not to amass wealth for self-indulgence: "You have spent your years on earth in luxury, satisfying your every desire. You have fattened yourselves for the day of slaughter" (Jas 5:5). Paul tells Timothy:

> Tell those rich in this world's wealth to quit being so full of themselves and so obsessed with money, which is here today and gone tomorrow. Tell them to go after God, who piles on all the riches we could ever manage — to do good, to be rich in helping others, to be extravagantly generous. If they do that, they'll build a treasury that will last, gaining life that is truly life (1 Tim. 6:17-19, *The Message*).

In the story of the "rich fool" in Luke 12:16-21, a man asked Jesus to tell his brother to divide the family inheritance with him. This "rich fool" wasn't a fool because he was rich, but because he was "not rich towards God." "The rich man demonstrates an unrelenting, self-centered focus and an unmitigated accumulation of surplus goods, with no thought for anyone else."[22]

When we read the word *rich* most of us quickly think of a friend who has more money than we do, but we don't think that word applies to us. But compared to global standards, and by first century standards, the great majority of us are rich. Living in a first world country tends to make us myopic on the subject of riches.

In her book *Hope Lives,* Amber Van Schooneveld shares:

> Did you drink clean water today without risk of death or disease? Are you wearing a pair of shoes? Do you have a dry, safe place to sleep tonight? Did you eat today? You are rich. You are richer than billions of others. The Gross National Income per capita in the United States in 2003 was $37,610. In India it was $530. In Ethiopia it was $90.[23]

These figures help us adjust our eyeglasses to see our lives through a global economic lens.

While we never want to lose sight of "the grace of giving," nor do we want to close our eyes to global realities or to the clear teaching of Scripture. The Bible cuts across the grain of materialism with a sharp and powerful sword. If the scripture's teaching on money causes us to blanch and recoil it means we need to ask Jesus for more of his heart and less of the world's ways in our lives. Remember: "Simplicity is freedom. Duplicity is bondage. Simplicity brings joy and balance. Duplicity brings anxiety and fear."[24]

On February 18, 2002, I recorded this entry in my journal:

> During worship, on the day of the annual offering for the poor, the Lord gave me a beautiful picture of myself taking a crown off my head and reaching up to put it on Jesus' head. My face was lit up with a huge smile. The Holy Spirit met me powerfully in worship. The words given to me that morning were of God's huge resource to provide everything I need.

One picture was of a magic carpetbag like Julie Andrews' character in *Mary Poppins*; you never know what's going to come out of it. Looking back over the past several years, there have indeed been a lot of surprises of provision and guidance in my life, many of them supernatural.

On another occasion he showed me a picture of a treasure chest with smoke rising up from it. The box symbolized my tithes and offerings; the smoke represented a pleasing aroma of incense, indicating that this gift of gold was pleasing to him.

" ...When someone has been given much, much will be required in return; and when someone has been entrusted with much, even more will be required" (Luke 12:48 NLT). I have been entrusted with a lot of knowledge, gifts and resources, and if you are reading this book in a room with glass in the windows, with food in your belly and shoes on your feet, you should know that you have too.

Will you join me in this prayer?

"Lord, Help me use what you've given me wisely. Help me to always keep heaven in view. Help me enjoy the freedom and joy that flows from simplicity. Help me grow in the attitude and action of generous giving."

Chapter 17
Finishing Well

Life is a test, life is a trust and life is a temporary assignment.[1]
— Rick Warren

If our worship can be seen as a journey, then it could be said that life is a marathon. After all, the idea of life being like a race is a biblical metaphor. We are told to " … Run in such a way as to get the prize" (1 Cor 9:24). We are encouraged to " … run with perseverance the race marked out for us" (Heb 12:1). Maybe racing's really not your thing and running doesn't appeal at all so the metaphor loses its power, but stick with us, will you?

In this long race I've seen some amazing sights, and it has been a mix of lush green valleys, panoramic mountain top sites and a lot of steep hills. I've been exhilarated and exhausted, both dazzled and dismayed by the route I've taken. I have a lot of friends who've "bitten the dust." They have lost their marriages, lost their desire for God, and lost their way. Like a marathon, the side of the road is littered with people who have quit because of injury, distraction or discouragement. But for me, as I look forward to the last thirty or so years of my life, I want to keep running the race until the end.

William Carey (1761-1834), missionary to India, is often called "the father of modern missions." Near the end of his life, when one of his supporters wanted to write his biography, Carey said this:

> If one should think it worth his while to write my life, I will give you a criterion by which you may judge of its correctness. If he gives me credit for being a plodder, he will describe me justly. Anything beyond this will be too much. *I can plod. I can persevere in any definite pursuit.* To this I owe everything[2] (emphasis added).

The race of faith is less about sprinting, and more about staying in the race, even if it's at a plodding pace. In a sermon series on endurance, John Piper shared with his congregation: "I pleaded with them to be "coronary Christians,"— the sort who keep going for the long haul because their heart is filled with life, hope and purpose — and not "adrenal Christians" — who wear out after a brief push of industrious serving … . Not that adrenaline is bad … it gets me through a lot of Sundays. But it lets you down on Mondays …"[3]

As I watch my parents enter the wintertime of their lives, the eventual end of my own earthly life becomes more real to me. The psalmist who complained of a grievous sickness said, "My times are in your hands" (Ps 31:15). God is sovereign over the length of our lives: "Man's days are determined; you have decreed the number of his months and have set limits he cannot exceed" (Job 14:5).

Wise Investors

Whether we are facing a seemingly endless stretch of track or aware of the finish line looming up, there is a question that we all must answer: what are we going to do with the time God gives us?'

I have some friends who faced that question well when they were in their fifties. While their peers were thinking about

232

retirement options, vacation homes and a lot of golf, these friends had a big God-vision that meant there was more than leisure pursuits on the horizon for the last decades of their lives.

Randy Butler has been a friend of mine for around twenty years. We are around the same age, and were both worship leader-songwriters in the Vineyard Church movement beginning in the late 1980's. Randy has planted and pastored churches and except for a three-year period of full-time pastoral ministry, he has worked as a building contractor to support his ministry. He now runs a small family-powered building company along with three of his kids.

In 2009 during the U.S. economic meltdown, their work slowed down to nothing. Randy explains that "there was no work and no check for three months. After the slowdown, there was zilch. We were depleted down to nothing." To make ends meet, they began to sell their possessions. They sold their tractor, his piano, his Martin D-18 guitar [ouch!], and other things. They couldn't make their property payments for a few months. After fifteen years of running a building business, "it felt horrible" to get so far behind. They were "squeezing the last little bit out of every toothpaste tube."

The situation looked very bleak. Finally, the work began to roll in. Just a few months after this period of recovery from near bankruptcy, Randy went to Haiti with "Mercy Response" for three weeks last summer. He led a team of thirty builders who helped construct living quarters for serving teams from North America. All of this was to support the long range rebuilding effort after the devastating earthquake in Haiti.

Randy's tenuous financial situation didn't keep him from investing his life in helping the poor. He didn't let fear of another economic slow-down keep him from generously giving his time and talents. He left his son, Ian, to run the family business in their busiest time of the year. It may not have been good "business sense" but it was good "kingdom sense."

Our family visited Randy's family on July 4th of this year and saw their rural property. It's five acres of northwest forested land that they cleared themselves. It's a peaceful place. They are living in a small camper-trailer while his mother and two youngest children live in a small home on the same property.

The trips to Haiti and other mission fields are only a small part of the overall picture of the Butlers' life. Several years ago, he and his wife Marlys heard a sermon series by Archibald Hart on "Finishing Well." These talks really stimulated them and immediately they started discussing what they were going to do together for the rest of their lives. Hearing those messages sparked a vision to use their rural acreage as a retreat center to care for all kinds of people — writers, pastors, and kids who have suffered from human trafficking. They've already started this ministry even though they really don't have the facilities for it. While living in the tiny little camper-trailer, they unselfishly invite people to stay in the more comfortable main house. It's the start of a working ranch where people can come to take a respite, connect with an agrarian lifestyle and get rejuvenated.

Paul wrote to Timothy, "Be sure to use the abilities God has given you … Put these abilities to work" (1 Tim 4:14-15 Living Bible). This is simply what the Butlers are doing. Randy acquired the skill of carpentry from his father and today he is simply using what God gave him to bless others. Randy and Marlys also have the gift of hospitality. It's their joy to take care of people; I've felt it when I'm around them. Nobody is pressuring them to invite people to stay; they're just doing what God created them to do and loving it. They're following the maxim from Romans: " … since we find ourselves fashioned into all these excellently formed and marvelously functioning parts in Christ's body, let's just go ahead and be what we were made to be …"(Rom 12:5 *The Message*).

Like Abraham, Randy and Marlys don't mind living in a tent or a trailer for a while. They are excited about the "second half" of their earthly sojourn. Their sights are set on a permanent heavenly dwelling and they're storing up for themselves treasure in heaven.

Mac and Louise Jardine

Mac and Louise Jardine are another couple who are investing wisely. We were on the same church pastoral staff in the early 1990s in Surrey, British Columbia and I've known few people who love to worship more than Mac and Louise. In 1992, the Jardines and I were in Hong Kong, for an equipping conference led by John Wimber. While Mac was sitting in the front row, he had an open-eyed vision of Jesus in the guise of Uncle Sam. "Uncle Sam" was pointing his finger at Mac and saying "I want you here" (in Hong Kong). It looked to Mac like a US army recruiting poster.

Louise wasn't the least bit interested in moving to Hong Kong but God has a way of getting his message across to people who truly want to obey him. Within a few years they were living in Hong Kong, ministering to street people and drug addicts. They moved with their two youngest children from a comfortable townhouse in Surrey to a tiny room at "Hang Fook Camp" in Hong Kong.

For a short time they oversaw a small discipleship school made up of teens and twenties from Canada, and then they joined the staff of St. Stephen's Society, a ministry with a focus on helping the poor. For the next ten years, they served the poor and experienced God like never before. Louise talks about "seeing Jesus in the face of the poor." As she would kneel down to give a rice box to a granny who was sleeping on the street, she would see Jesus. As she prayed for a former drug addict who was abused by his parents and thrown out on the street, she would see Jesus.

They stayed in this ministry role, both in Hong Kong and in the Philippines, for the next ten years. Because Mac and Louise were intimately connected to God as worshipers, they learned to love the things Jesus loves and do the things Jesus does. Now in their late sixties, they live in Canada most of the year, ministering to church leaders. The rest of the time they help with church plants Bangkok, Thailand and other locations in Asia.

When I talk to Mac and Louise about ministering in a Vineyard church in the slums of Bangkok, their faces light up as they tell stories of homeless people finding Jesus as well as a loving community. They tell stories of the abused receiving healing. At an age when most people are thinking about retirement, Mac and Louise are still pressing on. For Mac, the word 'retire' is 'the R-word'— it's like a swear word. Mac wants to die with his boots on. Mac and Louise may not be "sprinting" anymore, but they are definitely in the race, slowly moving towards the finish line.

Mac and Louise are great examples of people who are not engrossed in the things of this world. They know that our "stuff" isn't important; it's not going to last. They live in a small apartment that is loaned to them by a good friend. They see the shortness of this life and live by heaven's economy. They are a living embodiment of the scripture that says " ... the time is short. From now on ... those who buy something, [should live] as if it were *not theirs to keep*; those who use the things of the world, as if *not engrossed in them*. For this world in its present form is passing away. I would like you to be free from concern ... " (1 Cor 7:29-32, emphasis added).

Keys to Persevering to the End

In the long, hard marathon of life we need to persevere: "We want each of you to show this same diligence to the very end, in order to make your hope sure. We do not want you to become lazy, but to imitate those who through *faith and patience* inherit what has been promised ... You need to *persevere* so that when you have done the will of God, you will receive what he has promised" (Heb 6:11-12 and 10:36, emphasis added).

If there's one thing that helps me persevere, it's knowing that I'll be rewarded. I like to get paid for my efforts, whether in money or friendship or eternal currency. Jesus promised that *in this life* we will be well rewarded. "I tell you the truth," Jesus replied:

> ... no one who has left home or brothers or sisters or mother or father or children or fields for me and the gospel will fail to receive a hundred times as much in this present age (homes, brothers, sisters, mothers, children and fields — and with them, persecutions) and in the age to come, eternal life (Mark 10:29-30).

I haven't gone to deepest darkest Africa as a missionary but I've left a lot of friends and family behind in my many relocations. And God has rewarded me richly. I've made some sacrifices but they don't feel like sacrifices. That sentiment is echoed by many missionaries. I don't pick up a sense of regret or remorse when I talk to Jackie Pullinger about her choice to leave behind her life in England to be a missionary in Hong Kong. She is full of joy.

Another key to being diligent to the very end is joyfulness. Joyfulness in the midst of hardship energizes us. Reflect on the words of David Livingstone, Scottish missionary to Africa in the mid-nineteenth century:

"In response to people's extravagant praise and comments to him during his 'selfless' life, he wrote in his journal, 'People talk of the sacrifice I've made in spending so much of my life in Africa. Can that be called a sacrifice which is simply paying back a small part of the great debt owing to our God, which we can never repay? Is that a sacrifice which brings its own blessed reward in healthful activity, the consciousness of doing good, peace of mind and a bright hope of glorious destiny hereafter? Away with the word in such a view and with such a thought! It is emphatically no sacrifice. Say rather it is a privilege.'"4 There's not a shred of regret or self-pity here. Livingstone received a reward *in the doing* of his work.

For Livingstone missionary work brought "it's own blessed reward in healthful activity." His life had a purpose that gave him a good reason to get up every morning. He enjoyed "the consciousness of doing good" and "peace of mind." He didn't think of his work in Africa as a sacrifice, though there were tremendous hardships and dangers he faced. For him, it was a privilege. Joy flows from knowing we are in the center of God's will. Joy is central to endurance.

Motivated by the Promise of Eternal Reward

Jesus said: " ... store up for yourselves treasures in heaven ... " (Matt 6:20). His words suggest that we can actually invest our life in a way that creates heavenly treasure. It's true; I am motivated to invest wisely because *I will benefit in eternity.* Hasn't God has designed us to work for rewards? In employment, we work for the reward of money. In marriage and family life, we work for the reward of loving, being loved and seeing children mature. In *all* of life, we're working *for God*, who rewards us in eternity.

"For we must all appear before the judgment seat of Christ, that each one may receive what is due him for the things done while in the body, whether good or bad" (2 Cor 5:10). This is good news because the ball is in our court; *we* take the actions that store up heavenly treasure.

One of my favorite people in the Bible is Abraham. He left his home country when he was seventy-five years old to begin a journey of faith. He wandered around for twenty-five years before he received the promised child, Isaac. He had the guts to try something new at an advanced age. He went for years at a time without hearing anything from God about his promised inheritance, but he stayed in the race.

And he was motivated by the vision of a heavenly reward. "By faith he made his home in the promised land like a stranger in a foreign country; he lived in tents ... For he was looking forward to the city with foundations, whose architect and builder is God" (Heb 11:9,10). Abe was *looking forward to the reward of heaven*.

Abraham's pace must have felt tortoise-like for much of the time. He was a plodder. He had to deal with family conflict and a land-grabbing nephew named Lot. Though Abraham was the leader of the expedition out of Haran and the elder deserving of "first dibs" on new land, he graciously let young Lot take his pick of pasture-land. As a citizen of heaven who was looking forward to "a better city" and "a better country," Abe could hold loosely his worldly goods, securing peace in his earthly family and treasure above. Abe was a wise investor and a race-winning tortoise.

Climbing the Mountain

On Father's Day, June 20, 2010, during a Sunday morning family worship, discussion and prayer time, Linda had this word for me as our children were gathered around me in prayer:

> I saw you as a mountain climber, climbing up a very high mountain. You were dressed in heavy climbing gear (ropes, etc.), and there was snow on this beautiful high mountain peak. I had an impression of you as a strong man (the meaning of your name, Andrew is 'strong'). You were tired as you were nearing the top and the oxygen was thinning. The Lord is going to be your oxygen. The Lord was saying, 'you're almost to the top, and *the view is going to be really beautiful.*'

Linda continued, "As a 'mountain climber' in life, you see and value something that not everyone sees and you're willing to make a long climb to get there. When people climb Mount Everest, they pass dead bodies and take a big risk to go to the top."

The imagery of "the top of the mountain" in Linda's word, means two things to me. First, it means finishing this particular season of life with its unique challenges. Second, it means finishing my *entire* life. After the short term "climb," I'll be able to rest a bit and "enjoy the view." All the while, I'm energized by seeing a kingdom and Lord who are *invisible.* This is how Moses kept right on going: "It was by faith that Moses left the land of Egypt. He was not afraid of the king. Moses *kept right on going* because he kept his eyes on the one who is *invisible*" (Heb 11:27 NLT, emphasis added).

Life is a long, hard climb but the view at the top will be out of this world. It will be worth waiting for and working for. " … No eye has seen, no ear has heard, and no mind has imagined what God has prepared for those who love him" (1 Cor 2:9). Sometimes we feel like giving up, but we know there's only one right choice; to keep on marching. "So let's not get tired of doing what is good. At just the right time we will reap a harvest of blessing if we don't give up" (Gal 6:9 NLT).

As we climb, God will be our oxygen. He will be our source, our sustenance and our strength. Like any mountaineer who attempts Everest, we need to be constantly breathing in God's air. We must never try to shortcut his word or his love, and none of us win prizes for going it alone and pushing God aside.

Think of the thousands who have stood on top of the world's tallest mountain. Surely they must have felt like they had achieved something truly noteworthy, something that would be spoken about. But we only remember the names of a handful. Yet our reward is eternal. Athletes and mountain climbers pursue their goals " … for a gold medal that tarnishes and fades. You're after one that's gold eternally" (1 Cor 9:25 *The Message*).

Are you like Abraham? Do you see things that not everyone else can notice? Do you see a holy city waiting? Are you motivated by invisible things? That's the worshiper's heart. Are you like a mountain climber who gets a crazy notion to climb a treacherous mountain because you're filled with faith and vision? That's the worshiper's heart. Are you ready to risk when those around you are looking to relax? That's the worshipper's heart.

God's Instruments

In the 1600s Antonio Stradivari lived in the small Italian town of Cremona. His innovations in the design and building of stringed instruments resulted in a unique sound that is world famous to this day. His 300 year-old Stradivarius instruments are still played by some of the best musicians of our time. Ivry Gitlis is one of them. He says, "I have a violin that was born in 1713. It was alive long before …. I don't consider it as my violin. Rather, I am perhaps its violinist, I am passing through its life."[5]

We are like those instruments; created by a timeless master, from each of us comes a unique and beautiful song. We are like the musician too; we do not own what is in our hands, we are merely passing through. Whichever view you take, the Great Conductor calls us all together, drawing us in to play our part in God's symphony.

A Closing Prayer

"Lord, play your tunes through us. Breathe your breath through us. Fashion us, change us, and let the music of our lives bring hope and joy and healing. Don't let us be distracted by the beautiful earthly sounds all around us; help us enjoy them and see them as pointers to heaven. Help us not to devote our lives to things that will end when we die. Let the words of our mouths, the meditations of our hearts and the work of our hands be pleasing to you, that we will be able to say when we reach the top of the mountain, "I have fought the good fight, I have finished the race, I have kept the faith" (2 Tim 4:7).

"Therefore, since we are surrounded by such a huge crowd of witnesses to the life of faith, let us strip off every weight that slows us down, especially the sin that so easily trips us up. And let us run with endurance the race God has set before us" (Heb 12:1 NLT).

"By no means do I count myself an expert in all of this, but I've got my eye on the goal, where God is beckoning us onward — to Jesus. I'm off and running, and I'm not turning back. So let's keep focused on that goal, those of us who want everything God has for us ... " (Phil 3:14-15 *The Message*).

May you know what it is to feel the worshipper's heart beating within you. May you grow in confidence to take risks, to give freely and scan the horizon for the pillar of cloud that guides your steps. May you love the Lord with all your heart, soul and strength, displaying the results in a million different mosaic patterns. May you sweat, cry, rage, mourn, rejoice and march clearly ahead all because of what you sense the Lord is whispering to you. May you care less about self-promotion or self-advancement, but instead grow to love this adventure for what it is; a journey to the very heart of God.

Endnotes

Chapter 1: A New Life

1. Watchman Nee, *Christ, the Sum of All Spiritual Things* ((New York, NY: Christian Fellowship Publishers, 1973), 8.

2. Todd Hunter, *Giving Church Another Chance* (Downers Grove, IL: InterVarsity Books 2010), 110.

3. Richard Foster, *Celebration of Discipline* (New York, NY: Harper & Row, 1978), 138.

4. Leonard Sweet and Frank Viola, *Jesus Manifesto* (Nashville, TN: Thomas Nelson, 2010), 96-97.

5. Annie Dillard, *Pilgrim at Tinker Creek (Harper Perennial Modern Classics)* (Cutchogue, NY: Buccaneer Books, 2007), 34.

6. Timothy Keller, "Heavenly Worship," Redeemer Presbyterian Church. New York, NY.

7. Dallas Willard, *The Divine Conspiracy: Rediscovering Our Hidden Life in God* (New York, NY: HarperCollins Publishers, 1998), 21.

8. Marc Nelson, "I Have Found," Mercy/Vineyard Publishing (ASCAP).

9. F. F. Bruce, *Paul, Apostle of the Heart Set Free* (Grand Rapids, MI: Wm. B. Eerdmans Publishing Company, 2000), 38.

10. Ibid., 71.

11. Sweet and Viola, *Jesus Manifesto*, 1.

12. Keller, "Heavenly Worship."

13. Sweet and Viola, *Jesus Manifesto*, 15.

14. Ibid., 34.

15. Ibid., 26.

16. Ibid., 20.

17. Gary Kinnaman, *The Beginner's Guide to Praise and Worship* (Ann Arbor, MI: Servant Publications, 2003), 28. Kinnaman is quoting the *New International Dictionary of the New Testament*.

Chapter 2: It's All by Grace

1. Andy Park, "Precious Child," Mercy/ Vineyard Music, 1989.

2. Andy Park, *To Know You More, Cultivating the Heart of the Worship Leader* (Downers Grove, IL: InterVarsity Press, 2002), 44-45.

3. Ibid., 46-47.

4. Bruce, *Paul, Apostle of the Heart Set Free*, 21.

Chapter 3: Treasure Seekers

1. William Temple (15 October 1881 — 26 October 1944) was a priest in the Church of England. He served as Archbishop of Canterbury from 1942-44.

2. James Owen, "Lost Gold of the Dark Ages," National Geographic Society http://news.nationalgeographic.com/news/2009/09/photogalleries/ anglo-saxon-gold-hoard-pictures/ (accessed 2010 September 3). May 2010, Volume 217, No. 5.

3. "Daily News Update," http://newsup.net (accessed 2010 April 9).

4. Don Williams, "Worship," Coast Vineyard Church. La Jolla, CA.

5. Foster, *Celebration of Discipline*, 138.

6. John Eldredge, *Journey of Desire* (Nashvile, TN: Thomas Nelson, 2000), 177.

7. Foster, *Celebration of Discipline*, 1.

8. Keller, "Heavenly Worship."

9. Ibid.

10. William Sperry, *Reality in Worship*, ed. Thomas S. Kepler, The Fellowship of the Saints: An Anthology of Christian Devotional Literature (New York, NY: Abingdom-Cokesbury Press, 1963), 685.

11. Jack Moraine. Gilbert, Arizona. Jack is the Senior Pastor of Vineyard Community Church in Gilbert, AZ.

12. Donald W. Burdick, ed. *Zondervan Niv Study Bible* (Grand Rapids, MI: Zondervan Publishing House, 2002), 1830.

13. William Kennedy, "The Turtle on the Fence Post," *New York Times*, March 24 2002. A book review of *The Misunderstood Presidency of Bill Clinton*, by Joe Klein.

14. Dallas Willard, *Renovation of the Heart* (Colorado Springs, CO: Navpress, 2002), 101.

15. James Bryan Smith, *The Good and Beautiful God* (Downers Grove, IL: InterVarsity Press, 2009), 20.

16. Foster, *Celebration of Discipline*, 2.

17. James Houston, "The Haunting Challenge of Spiritual Formation," *Denver Seminary Magazine* (Summer 2006): 5.

18. Foster, *Celebration of Discipline*, 5.

Chapter 4: Prayer: Conversations with God

1. Mother Teresa, *Everything Starts from Prayer* (Ashland, OR: White Cloud Press, 1998), 39-40.

2. Willard, *The Divine Conspiracy*, 243.

3. David Winter, *Closer Than a Brother* (Wheaton, IL: Harold Shaw Pub., 1976), Introduction.

4. Thomas Merton, *Contemplative Prayer* (London: Darton, Longman & Todd, 2005), 37.

5. Leslie Weatherhead, *A Private House of Prayer* (Nashville, TN: Abingdon Press, 1958), 28.

6. Philip Yancey, *Prayer: Does It Make Any Difference?* (Grand Rapids, MI: Zondervan Publishing House, 2006), 15.

7. Willard, *The Divine Conspiracy*, 241.

8. Frederick Buechner, *Now & Then* (San Francisco, CA: Harper & Row, 1983), 32.

9. C. S. Lewis, *Mere Christianity* (New York, NY: Macmillan, 1967). From: Simon Guillebaud, *For What It's Worth* (Apex, NC: Monarch Books, 2007), 66.

10. Simon Tugwell, *Prayer: Living with God* (Springfield, IL: Templegate Publishers, 1975), 35.

11. C. S. Lewis, *Letters to Malcolm: Chiefly on Prayer* (London: Geoffrey Bles, 1964), 35.

12. David Peterson, *Engaging with God* (Grand Rapids, MI: Eerdmans Publishing Company, 1993), 98.

13. Lewis, *Letters to Malcolm*, 109.

14. Abraham Joshua Heschel, *I Asked for Wonder* (New York, NY: Crossroads, 2000), 18.

15. Yancey, *Prayer: Does It Make Any Difference?*, 108.

16. Eugene Petersen, *Working the Angles* (Grand Rapids, MI: Eerdmans Publishing Company, 1987), 30-31.

17. Yancey, *Prayer: Does It Make Any Difference?*, 107.

18. Eugene Petersen, *The Contemplative Pastor* (Grand Rapids, MI: Eerdmans Publishing Company, 1989), 103-104.

19. Ole Hallesby, *Prayer* (Minneapolis, MN: Augsburg Publishing, 1994), 155.

20. Joyce Huggett, *The Joy of Listening to God* (Downers Grove, IL: InterVarsity Press, 1987), 34.

21. Guillebaud, *For What It's Worth*, 76.

22. Eugene Petersen, *Christ Plays in Ten-Thousand Places* (Grand Rapids, MI: Eerdmans Publishing Company, 2005), 117-118.

Chapter 5: Partners with God

1   Linda Park, "Personal Communication."

2   Dallas Willard, *Hearing God: Developing a Conversational Relationship with God* (Downers Grove, IL: InterVarsity Press, 1983), 56.

Chapter 6: God Talks to His Friends

1. Teresa, *Everything Starts from Prayer*, 35.

2. Dallas Willard, *Hearing God: Developing a Conversational Relationship with God* (Downers Grove, IL: InterVarsity Press, 1983), 19.

3. Jackie Pullinger, "Personal Communication," Watershed Café in Langley, Canada.

4. Willard, *Hearing God*, 31.

5. Gary Beebe, *Longing for God, Seven Paths of Christian Devotion* (Downers Grove, IL: InterVarsity Press, 2009), 177.

6. Ibid., 185.

7. Ibid., 184.

Chapter 7: Be Like Little Children

1. Cindy Rethmeier, "An Interview with Todd Hunter."

2. Ibid.

3. Willard, *The Divine Conspiracy*, 61.

4. Ibid., 76.

Chapter 8: Living a Grateful Life

1. Mark Buchanan, *The Rest of God* (Nashville, TN: W Publishing Group, 2006), 67.

2. Brother Yun and Paul Hattaway, *The Heavenly Man* (London: Monarch Books, 2002), 84-85.

3. M. Scott Peck, *The Road Less Traveled* (New York, NY: Touchstone, 1978), 15.

4. Ibid., 67.

5. Brother Lawrence, *The Practice of the Presence of God* (Brewster, MA: Paraclete Press, 2010), 76.

6. Andy Comiskey, "Sermon," Anaheim Vineyard.

7. Andy Park, "An Interview with Linda Park." Surrey, B.C., Canada.

8. Eugene Peterson, *A Long Obedience in the Same Direction* (Downers Grove, IL: InterVarsity Press, 1980), 50.

9. Paul Scherer, *The Word of God Sent* (New York, NY: Harper & Row, 1965), 166.

10. Peterson, *A Long Obedience in the Same Direction*, 50.

11. Mike Mason, *Champagne for the Soul* (Colorado Springs, CO: Waterbrook Press, 2003), 12.

Chapter 9: Worship and Suffering

1. Philip Yancey, *The Bible Jesus Read* (Grand Rapids, MI: Zondervan Publishing Company, 1999), 112.

2. Andy Park, "An Interview with Glenn Hansen." Langley, B.C., Canada.

3. Brian Doerksen, "Will You Worship," Mercy/Vineyard Publishing (ASCAP) / Vineyard Songs (Canada) / ION Publishing.

4. James Bryan Smith, *The Good and Beautiful God* (Downers Grove, IL: InterVarsity Press, 2009), 40.

5. G.B. Caird, *Paul's Letters from Prison: Ephesians, Philippians, Colossians, Philemon, in the Revised Standard Version: The New Clarendon Bible* (New York, NY: Oxford University Press, 1976), 70.

6. Smith, *The Good and Beautiful God*, 48.

7. Yancey, *The Bible Jesus Read*, 30.

8. Smith, *The Good and Beautiful God*, 49.

9. Andy Park, "Yet I Will Praise," ION Publishing/Vineyard Songs Canada.

10. Sara Richardson, "The Story Behind the Music," http://www.sararichardsoninfo.com/sara (accessed September 10 2010).

11. Quoted by Joni Eareckson Tada in Rick Warren, *The Purpose Driven Life* (Grand Rapids, MI: Zondervan Publishing Company, 2002), 194.

Chapter 10: Contentment vs. Greed

1. Craig L. Blomberg, *Neither Poverty nor Riches* (Downers Grove, IL: Intervarsity Press, 1999), 132.

2. "Evny," Merriam-Webster Dictionary http://www.merriam-webster.com/dictionary/envy (accessed September 10 2010).

3. Foster, *Celebration of Discipline*, 71.

4. Willard, *Renovation of the Heart*, 107.

Chapter 11: Worship, Contentment, and Addiction

1. Beebe, *Longing for God, Seven Paths of Christian Devotion*, 118.

2. Peterson, *A Long Obedience in the Same Direction*, 146.

3. Don Williams, *12 Steps with Jesus* (Ventura, CA: Regal Publishing, 2004), 9-10.

4. Gerald May, *Addiction and Grace* (San Francisco, CA: Harper and Row, 1988), 4.

5. Williams, *12 Steps with Jesus*, 15-17.

6. Tom Wright, *Bringing the Church to the World* (Minneapolis, MN: Bethany House, 1992), 44-52.

7. Williams, *12 Steps with Jesus*, 26-27. Don quotes Wright, *Bringing the Church to the World*, 44-52.

8. Quoted by John Eldredge, *The Journey of Desire* (Nashville, TN: Thomas Nelson Publishers, 2000), 154. From Willard, *The Divine Conspiracy*.

9. Williams, *12 Steps with Jesus*, 26.

10. Ibid., 27.

11. Williams, "Worship." 2002.

12. Ibid.

13. Williams, *12 Steps with Jesus*, 26-27.

14. Peterson, *A Long Obedience in the Same Direction*, 149.

15. Ibid.

16. Andy Park, "Just Like a Child," Vineyard Songs Canada, Mercy / Vineyard Publishing. 1999.

Chapter 12: Worship and Unity: Humility vs. Pride

1. Quoted from: Foster, *Celebration of Discipline*, 96.

2. Quoted from: Matthew Woodley, *Holy Fools: Following Jesus with Reckless* (Carol Stream, IL: Tyndale House Publishers, 2008), 148.

3. Gary Kinnaman, "How Much Is Enough," Vineyard Community Church, Gilbert, Arizona.

4. Foster, *Celebration of Discipline*, 97.

5. Ibid., 148.

6. Francois Fenelon, *Christian Perfection* (Minneapolis, MN: Bethany House Publishing, 1975), 34.

7. Foster, *Celebration of Discipline*, 45.

8. Erwin McManus, *Uprising: A Revolution of the Soul* (Nashville, TN: Thomas Nelson, 2003), 144.

9. Beebe, *Longing for God, Seven Paths of Christian Devotion*, 58.

10. Anonymous, *The Cloud of Unknowing* (San Francisco, CA: HarperSanFrancisco, 2001), 21.

11. McManus, *Uprising: A Revolution of the Soul*, 120.

12. "Official Site of the Zinzendorf," http://www.zinzendorf.com/ (accessed September 10 2010).

13. "Moravian Revival," http://www.evanwiggs.com/revival/history/moravian.html (accessed September 10 2010).

Chapter 13: Work, Rest, and Worship

1. Buchanan, *The Rest of God* 24.

2. Roy Rummler "Americans Don't Like Their Jobs," Meridian Workplace Examiner http://www.examiner.com/workplace-in-meridian/americans-don-t-like-their-jobs (accessed September 10 2010).

3. Peterson, *A Long Obedience in the Same Direction*, 104-105.

4. Buchanan, *The Rest of God* 23.

5. John Eldredge, *The Journey of Desire, Searching for the Life We've Only Dreamed Of* (Nashville, TN: Thomas Nelson Publishers, 2000).

6. Beebe, *Longing for God, Seven Paths of Christian Devotion*, 227.

7. Ibid.

8. Richard J. Foster and Gayle D. Beebe, *Longing for God: Seven Paths of Christian Devotion* (Downers Grove, IL: InterVarsity Press, 2009), 233.

9. Ibid., 229.

10. Peterson, *A Long Obedience in the Same Direction*, 105-106.

11. Ibid., 107.

12. Buchanan, *The Rest of God* 36.

13. Smith, *The Good and Beautiful God*, 128-131.

14. Ibid., 174.

15. Jeremy Rifkin, *Time Wars* (New York, NY: Simon & Schuster, 1987), 71.

16. Robert Barron, *Heaven in Stone and Glass* (New York, NY: Crossroad, 2000), 40.

17. Smith, *The Good and Beautiful God*, 33. A quote from Siang-Yang Tan.

18. Bertrand Russell, *The Conquest of Happiness* (New York, NY: Liveright Publishing, 1996), 61. Russell was a British author, mathematician, and philosopher. The above reference is a reprint of the book he authored the above book in 1930.

19. Foster and Beebe, *Longing for God*, 235.

20. Lawrence, *The Practice of the Presence of God*.

21. A.W. Tozer, *The Pursuit of God* (Camp Hill, PA: WingSpread Publishers, 1992), 181.

Chapter 14: Worship and the Risk of Faith

1. Max Lucado, *Fearless* (Nashville, TN: Thomas Nelson Publishers, 2009), 10.

2. Erwin McManus, *The Barbarian Way, Unleash the Untamed Faith Within* (Nashville, TN: Nelson Books, 2005), 12, 30, 37, 53.

3. Guillebaud, *For What It's Worth*, 33-34.

4. Oswald Chambers, *So Send I You/Workmen of God: Recognizing and Answering God's Call to Service* (Uhrichsville, OH: Discovery House, 1987).

5. Todd Hunter, "Risk Taking," *Vineyard Newsletter*1987.

Chapter 15: Worship Overflows in Justice

1. John Piper, *Let the Nations Be Glad* (Grand Rapids, MI: Baker Books, 1993), 11-12.

2. Mark Labberton, *The Dangerous Act of Worship, Living God's Call to Justice* (Downers Grove, IL: InterVarsity Press, 2007), 13.

3. Paul (Bono) Hewson, "Acceptance Speech at Naacp Awards," Los Angeles, 2007.

4. Labberton, *The Dangerous Act of Worship, Living God's Call to Justice*, 27.

5. Hewson, "Acceptance Speech at Naacp Awards."

6. Kay Warren, "Serving Jesus by Serving Others," Purpose Driven Connection http://www.purposedriven.com/article.html?c=115102&l=1 (accessed September 10 2010).

7. Joyce Heron, "An Interview with Andy Park," Surrey, British Columbia, Canada.

Chapter 16: The Grace of Giving

1. Hunter, *Giving Church Another Chance*, 125. A quote by Billy Graham.

2. Blomberg, *Neither Poverty nor Riches*, 191. "Although some have argued for an inherent poverty in the Macedonian churches, what we know of that province in the mid-50's in general suggests that they were relatively prosperous …" (2nd Corinthians was written around AD 55).

3. Ibid., 177.

4. Nils A. Dahl, *Studies in Paul: Theology for the Early Christian Mission* (Minneapolis, MN: Augsburg Publishing House, 1977), 35.

5. Gerhard Krodel, *Acts* (Minneapolis, MN: Augsburg Publishing House, 1986), 95.

6. Blomberg, *Neither Poverty nor Riches*, 194.

7. Lawrence O. Richards, *The Teacher's Commentary* (Wheaton, IL: Victor Books, 1987), 870.

8. Paul Tan, "They Dared Lose Home," Bible Communications http://www.tanbible.com/tol_ill/tol_ill_giving.htm (accessed September 10 2010).

9. McManus, *Uprising: A Revolution of the Soul*, 157.

10. Ibid., 158.

11. "Dinner Plate Gospel," F. M. Barton Publisher http://books.google.com/books?id=mxopAAAAYAAJ&lpg=PA494&ots=LPHnTr_Qr3&dq=%22the%20gospel%20of%20the%20extra%20dinner%20plate%22&pg=PA494#v=onepage&q=%22the%20gospel%20of%20the%20extra%20dinner%20plate%22&f=false (accessed October 26 2010).

12. Foster, *Celebration of Discipline*, 77.

13. Ibid., 69.

14. Ibid., 70.

15. Warren, *The Purpose Driven Life*, 31.

16. Foster, *Celebration of Discipline*, 76.

17. Blomberg, *Neither Poverty nor Riches*, 211.

18. Richards, *The Teacher's Commentary*.

19. Blomberg, *Neither Poverty nor Riches*, 136.

20. Paul Lee Tan, *Encyclopedia of 7,700 Illustrations* (Garland, TX: Bible Communications, Inc., 1996).

21. Hunter, *Giving Church Another Chance*, 125. A quote by Selwyn Hughes.

22. Blomberg, *Neither Poverty nor Riches*, 119.

23. Amber Van Schooneveld, *Hope Lives* (Loveland, CO: Group Publishing, 2008), 19.

24. Foster, *Celebration of Discipline*, 69.

Chapter 17: Finishing Well

1. Warren, *The Purpose Driven Life*, 42.

2. George Smith, *Life of William Carey* (London: John Murray, 1909 (Public Domain)), vi.

3. John Piper, *The Roots of Endurance* (Wheaton, IL: Crossway Books, 2002), 11.

4. Guillebaud, *For What It's Worth*, 204. A quote from David Livingstone.

5. Ivry Gitlis, "The Art of Violin (DVD)," Quoted by Ivry Gitlis.

Bibliography

"Evny," Merriam-Webster Dictionary http://www.merriam-webster.com/dictionary/envy (accessed September 10 2010).

"Moravian Revival," http://www.evanwiggs.com/revival/history/moravian.html (accessed September 10 2010).

"Official Site of the Zinzendorf," http://www.zinzendorf.com/ (accessed September 10 2010).

"Dinner Plate Gospel," F. M. Barton Publisher http://books.google.com/books?id=mxopAAAAYAAJ&lpg=PA494&ots=LPHnTr_Qr3&dq=%22the%20gospel%20of%20the%20extra%20dinner%20plate%22&pg=PA494#v=onepage&q=%22the%20gospel%20of%20the%20extra%20dinner%20plate%22&f=false (accessed October 26 2010).

"Daily News Update," http://newsup.net (accessed 2010 April 9).

Anonymous. *The Cloud of Unknowing*. San Francisco, CA: HarperSanFrancisco, 2001.

Barron, Robert. *Heaven in Stone and Glass*. New York, NY: Crossroad, 2000.

Beebe, Gary. *Longing for God, Seven Paths of Christian Devotion*. Downers Grove, IL: InterVarsity Press, 2009.

Blomberg, Craig L. *Neither Poverty nor Riches*. Downers Grove, IL: Intervarsity Press, 1999.

Bruce, F. F. *Paul, Apostle of the Heart Set Free*. Grand Rapids, MI: Wm. B. Eerdmans Publishing Company, 2000.

Buchanan, Mark. *The Rest of God* Nashville, TN: W Publishing Group, 2006.

Buechner, Frederick. *Now & Then*. San Francisco, CA: Harper & Row, 1983.

Burdick, Donald W., ed. *Zondervan Niv Study Bible*. Grand Rapids, MI: Zondervan Publishing House, 2002.

Caird, G.B. *Paul's Letters from Prison: Ephesians, Philippians, Colossians, Philemon, in the Revised Standard Version: The New Clarendon Bible*. New York, NY: Oxford University Press, 1976.

Chambers, Oswald. *So Send I You/Workmen of God: Recognizing and Answering God's Call to Service*. Uhrichsville, OH: Discovery House, 1987.

Clayton, Adam, Larry Mullen, Dave Evans, and Paul Hewson, "Crumbs from Your Table," Universal Music Publishing Group

Comiskey, Andy, "Sermon," Anaheim Vineyard,

Dahl, Nils A. *Studies in Paul: Theology for the Early Christian Mission*. Minneapolis, MN: Augsburg Publishing House, 1977.

Dillard, Annie. *Pilgrim at Tinker Creek (Harper Perennial Modern Classics)*. Cutchogue, NY: Buccaneer Books, 2007.

Doerksen, Brian, "Will You Worship," Mercy/Vineyard Publishing (ASCAP) / Vineyard Songs (Canada) / ION Publishing,

Eldredge, John. *Journey of Desire*. Nashvile, TN: Thomas Nelson, 2000.

_____. *The Journey of Desire*. Nashville, TN: Thomas Nelson Publishers, 2000.

_____. *The Journey of Desire, Searching for the Life We've Only Dreamed Of.* Nashville, TN: Thomas Nelson Publishers, 2000.

Fenelon, Francois. *Christian Perfection.* Minneapolis, MN: Bethany House Publishing, 1975.

Foster, Richard. *Celebration of Discipline.* New York, NY: Harper & Row, 1978.

Foster, Richard J., and Gayle D. Beebe. *Longing for God: Seven Paths of Christian Devotion.* Downers Grove, IL: InterVarsity Press, 2009.

Gitlis, Ivry, "The Art of Violin (DVD)," Quoted by Ivry Gitlis,

Guillebaud, Simon. *For What It's Worth.* Apex, NC: Monarch Books, 2007.

Hallesby, Ole. *Prayer.* Minneapolis, MN: Augsburg Publishing, 1994.

Hattaway, Brother Yun and Paul. *The Heavenly Man.* London: Monarch Books, 2002.

Heron, Joyce, "An Interview with Andy Park," Surrey, British Columbia, Canada,

Heschel, Abraham Joshua. *I Asked for Wonder.* New York, NY: Crossroads, 2000.

Hewson, Paul (Bono), "Acceptance Speech at Naacp Awards," Los Angeles, 2007,

Houston, James. "The Haunting Challenge of Spiritual Formation." Denver Seminary Magazine (Summer 2006): 5.

Huggett, Joyce. *The Joy of Listening to God.* Downers Grove, IL: InterVarsity Press, 1987.

Hunter, Todd. "Risk Taking." *Vineyard Newsletter* 1987.

_____. *Giving Church Another Chance.* Downers Grove, IL: InterVarsity Books, 2010.

Keller, Timothy, "Heavenly Worship," Redeemer Presbyterian Church,

Kennedy, William. "The Turtle on the Fence Post." *New York Times*, March 24 2002.

Kinnaman, Gary. *The Beginner's Guide to Praise and Worship*. Ann Arbor, MI: Servant Publications, 2003.

_____, "How Much Is Enough," Vineyard Community Church, Gilbert, Arizona,

Krodel, Gerhard. *Acts* Minneapolis, MN: Augsburg Publishing House, 1986.

Labberton, Mark. *The Dangerous Act of Worship, Living God's Call to Justice*. Downers Grove, IL: InterVarsity Press, 2007.

Lawrence, Brother. *The Practice of the Presence of God*. Brewster, MA: Paraclete Press, 2010.

Lewis, C. S. *Letters to Malcolm: Chiefly on Prayer* London: Geoffrey Bles, 1964.

_____. *Mere Christianity*. New York, NY: Macmillan, 1967.

Lucado, Max. *Fearless*. Nashville, TN: Thomas Nelson Publishers, 2009.

Mason, Mike. *Champagne for the Soul*. Colorado Springs, CO: Waterbrook Press, 2003.

May, Gerald. *Addiction and Grace*. San Francisco, CA: Harper and Row, 1988.

McManus, Erwin. *Uprising: A Revolution of the Soul*. Nashville, TN: Thomas Nelson, 2003.

_____. *The Barbarian Way, Unleash the Untamed Faith Within*. Nashville, TN: Nelson Books, 2005.

Merton, Thomas. *Contemplative Prayer*. London: Darton, Longman & Todd, 2005.

Nee, Watchman. *Christ, the Sum of All Spiritual Things*. (New York, NY: Christian Fellowship Publishers, 1973.

Nelson, Marc, "I Have Found," Mercy/Vineyard Publishing (ASCAP),

Owen, James, "Lost Gold of the Dark Ages," National Geographic Society http://news.nationalgeographic.com/news/2009/09/photogalleries/anglo-saxon-gold-hoard-pictures/ (accessed 2010 September 3).

Park, Andy. "Precious Child." Mercy/Vineyard Music (1989).

_____, "Precious Child," Mercy/ Vineyard Music, 1989.

_____, "Just Like a Child," Vineyard Songs Canada, Mercy / Vineyard Publishing,

_____, "Yet I Will Praise," ION Publishing/Vineyard Songs Canada,

_____. *To Know You More, Cultivating the Heart of the Worship Leader.* Downers Grove, IL: InterVarsity Press, 2002.

_____, "An Interview with Glenn Hansen," June 18, 2010.

_____, "An Interview with Linda Park," Surrey, B.C., Canada.

Park, Linda, "Personal Communication,"

Peck, M. Scott. *The Road Less Traveled* New York, NY: Touchstone, 1978.

Petersen, Eugene. *Working the Angles.* Grand Rapids, MI: Eerdmans Publishing Company, 1987.

_____. *The Contemplative Pastor.* Grand Rapids, MI: Eerdmans Publishing Company, 1989.

Peterson, David. *Engaging with God.* Grand Rapids, MI: Eerdmans Publishing Company, 1993.

Peterson, Eugene. *A Long Obedience in the Same Direction.* Downers Grove, IL: InterVarsity Press, 1980.

_____. *Christ Plays in Ten-Thousand Places.* Grand Rapids, MI: Eerdmans Publishing Company, 2005.

Piper, John. *Let the Nations Be Glad.* Grand Rapids, MI: Baker Books, 1993.

_____. *The Roots of Endurance*. Wheaton, IL: Crossway Books, 2002.

Pullinger, Jackie, "Personal Communication," Watershed Café in Langley, Canada.

Rethmeier, Cindy, "An Interview with Todd Hunter,"

Richards, Lawrence O. *The Teacher's Commentary*. Wheaton, IL: Victor Books, 1987.

Richardson, Sara, "The Story Behind the Music," http://www.sararichardsoninfo.com/sara (accessed September 10 2010).

Rifkin, Jeremy. *Time Wars*. New York, NY: Simon & Schuster, 1987.

Rummler, Roy, "Americans Don't Like Their Jobs," Meridian Workplace Examiner http://www.examiner.com/workplace-in-meridian/americans-don-t-like-their-jobs (accessed September 10 2010).

Russell, Bertrand. *The Conquest of Happiness*. New York, NY: Liveright Publishing, 1996.

Scherer, Paul. *The Word of God Sent*. New York, NY: Harper & Row, 1965.

Schooneveld, Amber Van. *Hope Lives*. Loveland, CO: Group Publishing, 2008.

Scott, Kathryn. "At the Foot of the Cross." Vertical Worship Songs, Integrity Media (2003).

Smith, George. *Life of William Carey*. London: John Murray, 1909 (Public Domain).

Smith, James Bryan. *The Good and Beautiful God*. Downers Grove, IL: InterVarsity Press, 2009.

_____. *The Good and Beautiful God* Downers Grove, IL: InterVarsity Press, 2009.

Sperry, William. *Reality in Worship* The Fellowship of the Saints: An Anthology of Christian Devotional Literature, Edited by Thomas S. Kepler. New York, NY: Abingdom-Cokesbury Press, 1963.

Sweet, Leonard, and Frank Viola. *Jesus Manifesto*. Nashville, TN: Thomas Nelson, 2010.

Tan, Paul, "They Dared Lose Home," Bible Communications http://www.tanbible.com/tol_ill/tol_ill_giving.htm (accessed September 10 2010).

Tan, Paul Lee. *Encyclopedia of 7,700 Illustrations*. Garland, TX: Bible Communications, Inc., 1996

Teresa, Mother. *Everything Starts from Prayer*. Ashland, OR: White Cloud Press, 1998.

Tozer, A.W. *The Pursuit of God*. Camp Hill, PA: WingSpread Publishers, 1992.

Tugwell, Simon. *Prayer: Living with God*. Springfield, IL: Templegate Publishers, 1975.

Warren, Kay, "Serving Jesus by Serving Others," Purpose Driven Connection http://www.purposedriven.com/article.html?c=115102&l=1 (accessed September 10 2010).

Warren, Rick. *The Purpose Driven Life*. Grand Rapids, MI: Zondervan Publishing Company, 2002.

Weatherhead, Leslie. *A Private House of Prayer*. Nashville, TN: Abingdon Press, 1958.

Willard, Dallas. *Hearing God: Developing a Conversational Relationship with God*. Downers Grove, IL: InterVarsity Press, 1983.

_____. *The Divine Conspiracy: Rediscovering Our Hidden Life in God*. New York, NY: HarperCollins Publishers, 1998.

_____. *Renovation of the Heart*. Colorado Springs, CO: Navpress, 2002.

Williams, Don, "Worship," Coast Vineyard Church,

_____, "Worship," La Jolla,

_____. *12 Steps with Jesus*. Ventura, CA: Regal Publishing, 2004.

Winter, David. *Closer Than a Brother*. Wheaton, IL: Harold Shaw Pub., 1976.

Woodley, Matthew. *Holy Fools: Following Jesus with Reckless*. Carol Stream, IL: Tyndale House Publishers, 2008.

Wright, Tom. *Bringing the Church to the World*. Minneapolis, MN: Bethany House, 1992.

Yancey, Philip. *The Bible Jesus Read*. Grand Rapids, MI: Zondervan Publishing Company, 1999.

_____. *Prayer: Does It Make Any Difference?* Grand Rapids, MI: Zondervan Publishing House, 2006.

The Worship Journey Retreat

A Quest of Heart, Mind, and Strength

For local churches or leadership groups
A weekend retreat led by Andy Park

Worship and Prayer, Interaction, and Engaging with God's Word

▶ Themes for teaching and group discussion:
  - Encountering God's Kingdom in Worship
  - Knowing Jesus our Traveling Companion
  - Hearing from Jesus our Guide
  - Making Love Our Highest Goal
  - Work, Rest and Worship
  - Steering Clear of Obstacles in the Worship Journey
  - Finishing Well in the Walk of Faith
▶ Choice of subject material will be based on the needs of each group
▶ An emphasis on **interaction** with one another and God; not just listening to lectures

Goals

  - Renewal of passion for Jesus as the path, the guide, the fuel for the journey and the ultimate goal.
  - Re-kindled vision for a life of worship
  - Soaking in God's presence and Word

For more information on the *The Worship Journey Retreat* and all other booking inquiries, please contact Andy Park at info@andypark.ca

Lightning Source UK Ltd.
Milton Keynes UK

172872UK00002B/1/P